INTIMATE CRIMES

## CLARENDON STUDIES IN CRIMINOLOGY

Published under the auspices of the Institute of Criminology, University of Cambridge; the Mannheim Centre, London School of Economics; and the Centre for Criminology, University of Oxford.



RECENT TITLES IN THIS SERIES:

Respectable Citizens – Shady Practices: The Economic Morality of the Middle Classes
*Farrall and Karstedt*

Police Community Support Officers: Cultures and Identities within Pluralized Policing
*O'Neill*

Last Chance for Life: Clemency in Southeast Asian Death Penalty Cases
*Pascoe*

Policing Unlimited: Policing, Migrants and the Values of Bureaucracy
*Mutsaers*

Personalizing the State: The Anthropology of Law, Politics and Welfare at the UK's Margins
*Koch*

Common Enemies: Crime, Policy, and Politics in Australia–Indonesia Relations
*McKenzie*

Embodying Punishment: Emotions, Identities, and Lived Experiences in Women's Prisons
*Chamberlen*

# Intimate Crimes

Kidnapping, Gangs and
Trust in Mexico City

BY
ROLANDO OCHOA

OXFORD
UNIVERSITY PRESS

OXFORD
UNIVERSITY PRESS

Great Clarendon Street, Oxford, OX2 6DP,
United Kingdom

Oxford University Press is a department of the University of Oxford. It furthers the University's objective of excellence in research, scholarship, and education by publishing worldwide. Oxford is a registered trade mark of Oxford University Press in the UK and in certain other countries



First Edition published in 2019



Published in the United States of America by Oxford University Press
198 Madison Avenue, New York, NY 10016, United States of America

British Library Cataloguing in Publication Data
Data available

Library of Congress Control Number: 2019946252

ISBN 978–0–19–879846–0

*To Tracy, Félix, and Samuel*

# General Editors' Preface: Intimate crimes: Kidnapping, Gangs and Trust in Mexico City

By Rolando Ochoa

The *Clarendon Studies in Criminology series* aims to provide a forum for outstanding theoretical and empirical work in all aspects of criminology and criminal justice, broadly understood. The Editors welcome submissions from established scholars, as well as excellent PhD work. The Series was inaugurated in 1994, with Roger Hood as its first General Editor, following discussions between Oxford University Press and Oxford's Centre for Criminological Research. It is edited under the auspices of three centres: the Institute of Criminology at the University of Cambridge, the Mannheim Centre for Criminology at the London School of Economics, and the Centre for Criminological Research at the University of Oxford. Each supplies members of the Editorial Board and, in turn, the Series Editor or Editors.

There can be few who would dispute the fact that Mexico is faced with a series of crises in relation to security and crime which impact on social and political life, whether this be to do with drugs-related crime or politically-motivated criminal activity. The country has witnessed unprecedented kidnappings as part of this, including the abduction and murder of 43 students from a teachers' training college in 2014, which prompted national agonizing over the future of policing and ways to achieve social order and security. This book outlines the history of kidnapping in Mexico, from kidnapping as a politically motivated activity in the 1970s, to a crime which targeted the wealthy in the 1990s, and then to a widespread focus on middle and low-income victims in the 21st Century. But the book also goes well beyond this, to give sociological attention to a topic is that it is rife with rational agents faced with strategic interactions. The author recognizes this problem, and brings a thoughtful and appropriate theoretical framework to bear.

The methodology used in the study – analysis of an original database of kidnappings, mapping of the location of kidnapping by neighbourhoods, interviews and participant observation – provides the basis for new and original insights into the historical evolution of kidnapping, the process behind it and efforts taken by social groups to protect themselves from it. It is clear that it was the author's intention to find out how people in Mexico City deal with the risk of kidnapping when they have a limited recourse to the state or other conflict resolution possibilities. He discusses how this is reflected in the process of hiring an employee or, alternatively, how it is reflected in the experience of being hired as one. But once in the field, Rolando Ochoa quickly realised that this was just one part of a very complex story. In order to understand the dynamics of kidnapping and the trusting relationships that people foster to protect themselves, he realised that it was essential to look at the role of the state, and its interactions with society. Thus while the author centred his field research on the elite's survival strategies, he has also given attention to other factors in order to have a more complete view of the issues. This led him to carry out interviews with law enforcement officials such as prosecutors, police investigators, and district attorneys. The author also carried out interviews with employers and employees and tried to include the view of kidnapped victims to assess the effects of having been a victim. In the final area of research, the author draws on sociological analysis of trust-building in the context of violence, particularly signalling theory.

This work will undoubtedly appeal to academic researchers with an interest in policing, corruption, social order, and the relationship between law and society. Indeed, the book offers a 'thick description' and analysis which exemplifies the very best in qualitative research. We also think that the book will appeal to police practitioners, politicians, and policy-makers. As Editors, we commend the author for making significant contribution to the field of criminology and to our understanding of the complexities of kidnapping. We are very pleased to welcome *Intimate Crimes: Kidnapping, Gangs and Trust in Mexico City* to the *Clarendon Studies in Criminology* series.

Loraine Gelsthorpe and Kyle Treiber
Institute of Criminology, University of Cambridge
July, 2019

# Acknowledgements

My academic history begins in my country, Mexico. At the Centro de Investigación y Docencia Económicas (CIDE) I was lucky to have worked with brilliant Mexican academics, many of which continue to provide support and inspiration. Guillermo Trejo set me on the academic path and I always remember our work on indigenous social movements fondly, his support and encouragement in the initial phase of my path is very appreciated. Ana Laura Magaloni and Layda Negrete have always been super supportive, and provided much needed encouragement before, during and after my graduate studies. I am very fortunate to be a part of a wonderful, creative and committed generation of Mexican academics. I am grateful to Rodrigo Velasquez, Catalina Perez-Correa, Lorena Buzón and Claudio López-Guerra for their encouragement and support since the early days of our studies, through our PhDs and academic careers. I look forward to continued friendships and collaborations.

This project, ten years in the making, was not thought of overnight, it is the product of many people and organisations which supported it in many different ways. At the University of Oxford my DPhil supervisor Heather Hamill provided me not only with an intellectually enriching and supportive environment but also with a great example of what positive, constructive supervision is all about, and inspires me as I become a supervisor myself. This work would not have happened without her trust and ongoing support. Valeria Pizzini-Gambetta also provided excellent feedback, support and ideas as a part-time co-supervisor. Gabriella Elgenius was especially encouraging, particularly with regards to designing excellent qualitative methodology. As my examiners throughout – or through parts of - the PhD process I owe a lot to Federico Varese, Leigh Payne and Diego Gambetta (at Oxford) and Carlo Morselli (at the University of Montreal). Their intellectual influence will be clear throughout this book, and I hope to have contributed something, however small, to their monumental work. Oxford's Department of Sociology was the best place possible to undertake the bulk of this project and I am grateful for all their support and for the good fortune of spending time with such bright people. At the Latin American Centre at Oxford I want to thank Alan Knight for his support and encouragement as I transited from an MPhil to a DPhil, his work on Mexico will always be a source of inspiration. At St. Antony's College, Nuffield College and QEH I owe my gratitude to the lifelong friends I made there, you know who you are, and to the wonderfully diverse and intellectually challenging environment at the college, especially at the infamous Late Bar where a lot of amazing research was dissected, encouraged, and killed. The College's staff provided incredible support and encouragement as well. During my period at Oxford, Anne and Gil Loescher were not only perfect landlords but also academic/gardening role models and friends and I thank them for their support.

I wrote the thesis version of this material at the International Centre for Comparative Criminology (ICCC) at the University of Montreal, where I was a guest researcher of Carlo Morselli. Carlo has been a constant source of support since our first encounter at Oxford over a decade ago and I am very grateful for this. Also in Montreal, I spent two years at the International Centre for the Prevention of Crime, where I immersed myself in the world of policy and development. My experience there has proven extremely useful as an academic; at that organization, I am especially grateful to Paula Miraglia, Chantal Bernier and Kassa Bourne.

In Australia I have been lucky to find an amazing community of academics and friends who have been very supportive of this effort. Peter Homel at Griffith University gave me my first Australian job and made my landing a lot easier. Afterwards, I undertook a post-doctoral fellowship at the Department of Sociology at the Australian National University. I am especially grateful to Adam Graycar and Tony Makkai for the opportunity. The Department provided an ideal setting for doing the bulk of the work on this manuscript. There, I was fortunate to be a part of a group of passionate criminologists/sociologists. Special thanks go to Gavin Smith, Emmeline Taylor, and Jason Payne for their friendship and encouragement. I am also grateful to Rod Broadhurst for providing academic advice, and a place to work. Thanks go also to Helen Keane and Darren Halpin for their support and to the entire academic and administrative staff at the Department of Sociology. Macquarie University has provided me with an academic base at the Department of Security Studies and Criminology. I want to thank Ben Schreer and James Martin for the vote of confidence and for the patience in what was a long publishing process. I am happy to call many of my colleagues there friends. Special thanks go to Yves-Heng Lim for his support and friendship.

This research was made possible through funding from the Consejo Naciónál de Ciencia y Tecnología in Mexico (CONACYT). I cannot stress enough the importance CONACYT funds have for Mexican graduate students. At a time when funding for higher education in Mexico (including CIDE) is under attack, I would like to join my voice to those who are defending it.

I would also like to thank my editors at Oxford University Press, Lucy Alexander and Amy Baker for their patience and help navigating the publishing process. Two anonymous reviewers were instrumental in improving the manuscript and I appreciate their professionalism and positive feedback. I would also like to thank one anonymous member of the board of the Clarendon Studies in Criminology series for their thorough and constructive reviews and for helping the manuscript reach its full potential. I would also like to thank Ian Loader for suggesting I try OUP-CSC.

My friends in Mexico are very special to me, I am very lucky to have an amazingly supportive, fun and accepting group of lifelong friends and I want to thank you all for being in my life all these years and for all the years to come. Edronitas and honorary edronitas, I salute you. Huge thanks also go to Julieanne Lamond and Mark Reid in Canberra for their invaluable support and friendship, we were so lucky to have moved across the street from you. A very special thank you goes to the Ochoas: Carmen, Rolando and Mariana, I am very lucky to have you in my life and your support will always be appreciated, thank you for putting up with me, no matter what you are always in my heart. I would also like to thank the Fenwicks: Iris, Geoff, Joanne and Dean, Sadie and Holden for holding the fort in the northern lands. My family, Tracy, thank you for your patience and love; you have gone beyond the call of duty, especially during the times when I was not functioning very well. Two DPhils, two weddings, two children, two books, two academic careers are easier said than done, thank you. To my sons Samuel and Félix, I love you infinitely and I hope the world you grow up in is more peaceful, and greener than it is today, and that you may walk the streets of your city safe, happy and secure.

Lastly, but certainly not least, to all the people who put their trust in me during my research by sharing their stories, especially kidnapping victims, I admire your courage and determination to not let a horrible event define you. I would not be here without you and I hope this work helps, even in the most minute way possible, to make Mexico understandable, and perhaps, safer.

Peace.

# Contents

**Introduction** 1
A Modern-Day Avenger 1
Youth, Interrupted 3
Why Household Employees? 9
Theoretical Approach 11
Methodology and Field Research 13
Sensitive Research 15
The Kidnapping News Report Database, 1999–2010 19

**1 Crime, Trust, and Signaling** **21**
The Value of Mechanisms in Understanding the Social World 23
Signaling, Trust, and Risk 25
Vertical Integration 33
Kidnapping in Mexico: Context and Class 37

**2 Crime, Kidnapping, and Liberalization in Mexico in the Late Twentieth and Early Twenty-First Centuries (1994–2015)** **41**
The Transition to a Market Economy 42
Crime in an Open Market 46
The War on Drugs 50
Mexico Today: A State in Crisis 55
The New PRI 57
The New Role of the Military 66

**3 Kidnapping: A History of Gangs, Police, and Policy** **69**
In the Beginning: Left-Wing Radical Groups, Planes to Cuba, and Kidnapping as a Political Statement 73
The Heyday of the Black One: Police as Criminals and the Formation of the Perfect Kidnapping Gang 78

1995 Onwards: From the Ear Chopper and the Colonel to the Inexperienced Gang 82
Kidnapping in Mexico City 84
A Shift in Kidnapping 86
Not Just the Rich: Kidnapping at the District Level 86
Actors in Kidnapping 89
The Role of the States 98

**4 Survival Strategies: Wealthy Communities React 101**
The Elite Learn to Protect Themselves 102
Privatizing Security and Self 103
Capturing/Shaping the State 108
Family-Based Protection 112

**5 Avoiding an Intimate Crime 121**
What Is Trust Anyway? 121
Drivers, Trust, and Signaling 122
The Small World of Mexico City's Social Networks 126
Hiring 130

**6 The Employee's Perspective 145**
All in the Family: Networks and Vertical Integration 147
Signaling Trustworthiness 154
When the Relationship Breaks Down 164

**Conclusion 167**
The Centrality of Trust 172
Future Directions, New Questions 173

Methodological Appendix 181
News Reports Database 187

*References* 189
*Index* 201

# Introduction

## A Modern-Day Avenger

In July 2000, Sofia, a 25-year-old graduate and daughter of a Mexico City businessman was spending a weekend with friends in her family's summer house in the town of Cupantla, a small historic village outside of Mexico City. The town is a famous tourism spot and is known for its relaxed hippie-ish atmosphere, warm weather all year round, and a truly magnificent geographical setting among tropical flora and lush mountains. Many people from the City have second homes there and during the weekends the town becomes a vibrant, rich, and colourful market that surrounds the centuries-old church that serves as the town centre. Sofia came from an affluent family and had recently graduated.

After spending a day with good friends in town, Sofia and her guests went to bed for the night. As she slept that night, a group of armed men broke into the house, violently tied and gagged her friends, and took her hostage. Her father, Lucas X, then in Mexico City, soon received a dreadful phone call demanding a large ransom for her freedom. His daughter had been kidnapped and her captors threatened to kill her should the ransom not be paid. Terrified, Mr X, a very driven, strong person, sprung into action. He contacted the Federal Police and demanded they help with the rescue and delivery of the ransom. The police agreed to provide support. Mr X gathered the money, a deal was made with the kidnappers, and a drop-off was scheduled for a few days later. He spoke to his daughter one last time, only being able to repeat to her over and over 'te amo hija' (I love you my child). After the money was delivered, Mr X received a call saying his daughter would be freed soon. Time passed and no news arrived. Some time after, he received a call from the police. Sofia's lifeless body had been found in a field, shot in the back. Nearby, the bodies of three of the kidnappers were also found alongside the untouched

Intimate Crimes: Kidnapping, Gangs and Trust in Mexico City. First Edition. Rolando Ochoa © Rolando Ochoa 2019. Published in 2019 by Oxford University Press

ransom money. They had been killed in what appeared to be a fight among gangs. His daughter had been executed in apparent retaliation.

Devastated and immensely angry, Mr X demanded the authorities investigate his daughter's murder with all the resources of the law. Two people were soon arrested; the police claimed they were the culprits and practically closed the case. Mr X refused to believe it. As he grew increasingly impatient, the authorities grew weary and began ignoring him. Doors were closed, appointments were cancelled, and he was being thoroughly shut out by his own justice system. Driven by the love for his daughter, as he tells it, he closed his office in Mexico City, hired two bodyguards, legally bought arms, and dedicated the next twelve months of his life to investigating, on his own, the kidnapping and death of his daughter. He carried out interviews all over Cupantla and most other states in Mexico, drove over 75,000 kilometres all over the country, talking to anyone who had a story. He made connections in the police forces to gather inside information, got access to the files of his daughter's case, and slowly began mapping out a story of crime, corruption, incompetence, and murder that spanned two states and many more victims. His investigation centred on a criminal known as 'Ivanhoe I', who had been mentioned in an interview with one of those arrested for the kidnapping of his daughter. As the months progressed, Mr X identified every single member of the gang that kidnapped and killed his daughter. In all, seven people—six men and a woman—were involved. It also transpired that the kidnapping had been quite possibly set up by one of his household employees, who provided information to the kidnappers. He believed it could be the gardener.

He also uncovered the fact that many people in the Cupantla community knew of this gang and their activities, some even knew the names of the criminals themselves, and yet, in a perverse version of Lope de Vega's *Fuenteovejuna*, fuelled by fear, refused to do anything about it. Lope de Vega's play takes place in sixteenth-century Spain. In it, a landlord terrorizes the town of Fuente Ovejuna. Eventually, the landlord is killed, but the investigators are unable to carry out their job, as whenever they ask who killed the landlord, people answer 'it was Fuente Ovejuna'. In a sense, by protecting the culprits, Cupantla kidnapped and killed Sofia. In the end, Mr X detained, transported, and delivered to the authorities all the members of the gang that kidnapped and murdered his daughter Sofia. In short, he did the work his government refused to do. It took nine years for the last one of them to be sentenced. He could not serve time for the kidnapping/murder as at the time of the trial he was serving another sentence in another state for organized crime and thus could not be judged for the kidnapping.

Mr X repeatedly denounced the corruption and incompetence with which Sofia's case was investigated. No forensic analyses were carried out at the scene 'because it was raining', clothes belonging to one of the gang leaders were found splattered with Sofia's blood and were subsequently 'lost', goods stolen from his Cupantla home and then found at the kidnappers' houses were not retrieved as evidence. The list goes on and on. Lucas X is now one of Mexico's foremost activists in matters of justice reform and crime/corruption fighting.[1] Through the most terrible experience a father can imagine, he has become committed to justice reform.

## Youth, Interrupted

Mexico City's nightlife is legendary. If one knows where to look, there are opportunities for nightlife experiences and fun twenty-four hours a day, seven days a week. A staple of the City's nightlife is the *afters*, or clubs which open (or remain open) after everything else has closed. These clubs are known to close in the late morning and are popular with the City's twenty-four-hour party people.[2] In the early hours of the morning of 26 May 2013, the *Heaven* bar was pumping. Dozens of revellers drank and danced as dawn approached. This was not a rare occurrence, but rather another normal weekend in the City for the young people in the bar.

The bodies of some of these young people were found 50 kilometres out of the City, in a mass grave covered in concrete, asbestos, and lime. Their bodies were found three months after that night at *Heaven* after their parents protested, blocked roads, spoke to the media, and demanded, time and time again, that the disappearance of their children be investigated. DNA tests identified them all among the bodies found in that mass grave.

[1] I interviewed Mr X in Mexico City. Names have been changed throughout this book to protect anonymity.

[2] The reader can refer to Michael Winterbottom's 2002 cult movie of that name, which chronicles the legendary Manchester music and party scene in the 1980s and 1990s.

Thirteen youths were taken from the *Heaven* bar that night. Initially, no one raised the alarm. After all, it was not uncommon for these young men and women to not come home at the weekend. When they were finally reported missing by their parents, authorities were slow to respond. Mexico City had fought hard to gain a reputation as an 'armoured' city—a place where these kinds of things did not happen, a place where organized crime dared not go. Authorities were very reluctant to admit that this could happen under their watch. The City's mayor kept referring to the disappeared youths as 'absent' in an effort to avoid the dreaded K-word.

Eventually, they had to admit that the youths had been kidnapped when CCTV footage from the bar's security cameras showed a group of men taking thirteen men and women. The youngest was a 16-year-old boy, the oldest a 34-year-old woman. That grainy footage is the last time they were seen alive. It transpired that the youths were from the famous *barrio* of Tepito, one of the oldest and most well recognized neighbourhoods in the City. It is located in the old city centre and its history goes back to colonial times. Historically, Tepito has been a working-class neighbourhood, which in recent times has fallen prey to groups of organized criminal gangs who control drug flows and contraband in the City. Tepito and its inhabitants have a very strong identity and a deep-seated pride in their origins and their neighbourhood, which they have defended for decades against efforts to change or develop it by successive governments. Tepito is not known as *barrio bravo* for nothing. Unfortunately, insecurity and class prejudices have meant that it is now perhaps known more for crime than for its historical significance. This is relevant because once it was known that the kidnapped youths were from Tepito, and that their kidnapping may have been related to a feud between drug gangs in the *barrio*, public opinion seemed to change from alarm and dismay at the disappearance of the youths to an attitude which said 'they probably had it coming'. In fact, parents of the victims accused the government of discriminating against them because of the fact that they came from that neighbourhood. They consistently argued that, even though some of the youths were related to local criminals, they were not involved in any gang activity.

Eventually, the owner of the bar was arrested (his brother and co-owner was found murdered with his girlfriend) for his involvement. Not surprisingly, a number of local police officers were also detained, accused of being involved in the kidnapping and murder of the victims and of selling protection to the gangs involved. As the reader will discover in later chapters, the police are often involved in kidnappings, not as investigators or rescuers, but as perpetrators. The result of the investigation showed that the mass kidnapping and execution was in revenge for the killing of a drug dealer who competed with a gang from Tepito.

These are two very different stories which revolve around a single topic: kidnapping. While at first the two cases illustrated above seem very different—one victim is wealthy, the others are working class, one is drug-related, the other is not—there are a number of similarities that bind them together. At the end of the day, both were motivated by money, be it access to a wealthy person's fortune or competition for drug markets. The latter crime could be construed as a murder as well, since there is no evidence of a ransom being demanded. However, in the vernacular of crime in Mexico, this was also a *levantón*, a revenge kidnapping among drug-trafficking gangs. If one looks beyond the images of needless suffering and death, there are a number of other threads which tie these events together. In both cases, the victims were young, in both cases they died, in both cases the government's response was far from ideal, in both cases the parents of the victims had to pressure the government into acting and, in the case of Mr X, he had to act himself. Together, they paint a very concerning and disturbing picture and they illustrate the pain and suffering that kidnapping can bring to its victims, their families, and their communities. These stories are, sadly, repeated often in Mexico with different victims, different families, and different outcomes.

The cases mentioned above are terribly illustrative of the kind of situations that, on both a personal and an academic level, inspire this book. The fear, outright horror, and feeling of powerlessness in relation to this particular experience are felt all over Mexico. This situation has led me to ask how people can deal with this fear and how can they protect themselves from this kind of crime when the state is incapable, or unwilling, to provide this protection. I hope this work offers some justice to the suffering of kidnapping victims, even if it is only a tiny fragment.

In the early years of the twenty-first century, Mexico was experiencing a series of important changes. Democratization was ongoing after the electoral defeat of the party which had ruled the country for over seventy years. This was a time of deep optimism and hope. At the same time, the groundwork was almost finished for what was to become a wave of violence the likes of which the country had not seen since its revolution almost 100 before. During the same period, I was embarking on what was to become a career as a researcher. Through the study of ethnic mobilization and state repression, I arrived at the study of crime. Kidnapping had by then acquired a larger-than-life image as the pinnacle of evil and a sign of all that was wrong with the country. I became interested not only in crime(s), but in the way in which people, and communities, react to crime, how it affects their lives and decisions, how they build resilience so that, in the midst of high kidnapping rates, increasing homicide rates, and a weak rule of law, they still manage to live their lives.

Over the last decade, crime has become one of the most salient social phenomena in Mexico (Chambre Franco-Mexicaine de Commerce et d'Industrie 2004; Jiménez Ornelas 2000; Encuesta Mitofski 2005). The presence of powerful drug cartels, high poverty, inequality, and a weak rule of law have all been shown by previous research to have contributed to a significant increase in the country's crime rates (Bergman et. al. 2005a; Davis 2006a: 61; Magaloni and Zepeda 2004). Among the many crimes that affect Mexicans, one stands out as the most talked about and feared[3] kidnapping. Studies show that Mexico is in the top three countries worldwide where kidnapping is most common (Briggs 2002). In 2007, there were 112 kidnappings reported to the authorities in Mexico City alone (KNRD 2009). In 2016, there were 66,842 countrywide (Instituto Nacional de Estadistica, Geografia e Informatica 2017). Moreover, once the sole scourge of the wealthy, evidence from the City's Prosecutor indicates that kidnapping could be in the process of becoming more widespread and is beginning to affect sectors of the middle and working classes (PGJDF 2007). In this context, wealthy people—the ideal kidnapping victims—have been able to design and implement

[3] Fieldwork in Mexico City over the last ten years indicates that this particular crime is especially feared. It is almost always mentioned when people are asked about the crimes they fear the most; it goes without saying that homicide is the first. Its prevalence, 56 per 100,000 people in 2016 (Instituto Nacional de Estadistica, Geografia e Informatica 2017), is also high enough to keep it in both the media cycle and informal conversations.

strategies to avoid being victimized. They are now in fact more successful than other social classes at avoiding kidnapping. The question that arises, then, is how do potential victims design and negotiate survival strategies that protect them from this kind of crime? This question provides the central source of inquiry for this book. Thus, this book aims to present an analysis that will shed light on: (1) the dynamics and history of kidnapping in Mexico City; (2) the mechanisms by which some—wealthy—communities have reacted to this, which has had the unintended consequence of increasing kidnapping rates; and (3) how potential victims deal with the risk of being kidnapped by someone close to them in what has been called the 'treason phenomenon'. To achieve this, I focus on household employees.

At first sight, it would seem that the relationship between employers and employees in the household is quite banal; after all, anyone who hires a person to work in their home must be careful when selecting him or her regardless of crime rates. Most people everywhere take good care when hiring an employee, be it a nanny in London or a driver in Mexico City. This apparently unexceptional work relationship becomes important because we know that around 70 per cent of kidnappings in Mexico are, according to the National Prosecutor, planned or facilitated by either a member of the victim's family or a close employee (KNRD 2008). This means that a very high percentage of kidnappings are facilitated in some way by people in the victim's inner circle. Mexico's weak rule of law also means that employment contracts such as those that govern household employees have to be enforced informally, outside of the courts. These facts give added importance to the hiring process. The costs of hiring the 'wrong' kind of driver—one that will cooperate with kidnappers or is a kidnapper himself—is extremely high and certainly higher than it would be under conditions of a stronger rule of law and lower crime rates, as can be the case in more developed countries. A strong rule of law provides legal certainty and is itself a deterrent for criminals. A weak rule of law provides more opportunities for offending, as it decreases the likelihood of punishment. This is why I will focus on household employees.

Here, however, a caveat is necessary: this is not to say that the success of wealthy people in avoiding kidnapping is due *only* to improved hiring strategies, as hiring is one of a series of strategies implemented by this group. As I have mentioned, the state also has a role to play in this dynamic. Other strategies include, for example, cooperation and confrontation with the state at different times. In later chapters, I will describe how, for example, wealthy people provided water for an adjacent poor neighbourhood in exchange for more patrols from police, as well as how threats of divestment and loss of political support can make the government provide extra protection to the wealthy. More radical measures include the hiring of professional bodyguards. In the empirical chapters of the book, I will refer to these mechanisms in more detail. To achieve the goals set out herein, I focused most of the qualitative research undertaken for this book on one of the City's sixteen districts that, due to its historical crime rates and socioeconomic composition, makes for an ideal ground for the deciphering of this puzzle.

It is hoped that this research will contribute to existing literature on crime in Mexico and Latin America, and the literature on empirical work on trust and signaling theory, as well as broader criminological debates. First, the empirical study of kidnapping in Mexico City will shed light on the nuts and bolts of this particular crime, as well as the environmental, social, and institutional factors that make it so prevalent. While much has been written on the topic of kidnapping in the media and other outlets, a detailed, nuanced narrative of this crime has not yet been produced. Second, it will uncover the specific mechanisms that people use to protect themselves from criminals in a situation where the government does not fully provide protection, a situation that can be described as one of lawlessness (Dixit 2004). This point is of fundamental importance, as it helps us understand what happens in a context where the general protection of its citizens' physical integrity and property, one of the government's most important tasks, is left unattended. Third, it seeks to explore how wealthy people within Mexican society make their decisions at the individual level when their security is at stake. This will be illustrated by analysing how decisions of household employment between the employer and the employee are made, specifically how employers screen their employees for the properties of trustworthiness and loyalty and how prospective employees signal that they possess these properties. In short, this book will deal with the survival strategies implemented by potential kidnapping victims, how they go about operationalizing them, and how potential employees attempt to access work by giving out the correct signals.

## Why Household Employees?

The relationships between employers and household employees in Mexico City allow us to have a microscopic view of relationships based on trust. These relationships also give us an insight into how people make decisions in a context where access to the state as an enforcer of contracts is limited. This lack of institutional support provides a rich environment where we can observe human interaction with less interference by third parties, thus making our potential for analysis greater. There are other reasons for focusing on these interactions. First, while security, policing, and rule of law have been a central point of analysis for local and international researchers, the ways in which individuals react to a context of high crime have been somewhat neglected in Mexico (important exceptions to this are found in the work of Buffington 2001; Davis 1994; Guerrien 2006; and Ruiz Harrell 1998 and 1996). Second, logistical constraints do not allow me to research all above-mentioned reactions to crime, making it necessary to focus on a specific set of relationships that illustrate the theoretical efforts of this book.

Many households in Mexico (and most of Latin America) employ a considerable number of people in diverse duties such as drivers, cleaning staff, cooks, and nannies, some of whom reside in the household. According to De Vos (1987: 515), around 8 per cent of households in Mexico City 'contained a household member who was not related to the household head', and most of these are employees. These types of employees are given very high responsibilities. They feed, transport, and care for families and are often responsible for the well-being of children when their parents are working. Hiring someone to do these jobs is clearly, at the best of times, an important decision.

Mexico can very well be described as a 'relation-based economy' (Dixit 2004). In this environment, many activities, both social and economic, are carried out away from the government's sight. Many labour relationships are based on informal, sometimes spoken, contracts, which are very difficult to enforce by any government agency. Brambila and Cazzavillan (2008: 1) define the informal sector as 'all the income generating activities that are unregulated by institutions'. Employer–employee relationships in households are a very good example of this. None of my respondents had a written contract with their employers/employees, or any desire to have one. All agreements are verbal and negotiations regarding wages, responsibilities, and the like are carried out verbally between those involved. Most payments are given in cash and no taxes are paid on them. This kind of relationship is clearly very difficult to control for any government; the lack of tax records makes it almost impossible to even know the exact number of people that are involved in this kind of work, save for some estimates, as mentioned above. In this environment of informality and low government control, these relationships acquire a very important weight. When we know, as mentioned earlier, that a substantial number of kidnappings today are facilitated in some form by either family or close employees, we begin to understand the importance of choosing correctly.

The most common form of household employee in Mexico City is the cook/cleaner; this is supported by field research findings, where I observed that a significant number of households employed one, even if only for a day or two per week. This is always a female (in no case during fieldwork did I observe a male cook/cleaner, nor have I ever met one in thirty-five years of living and working in Mexico City) who is hired by the household to carry out tasks such as cooking for the family and the upkeep of the home, cleaning, washing, etc. Until recently, drivers were only used by people belonging to higher social classes. The need for more security has made it more common. The practice of hiring a driver has now become quite prevalent for a larger sector of the population. Some lower-middle-class families, for example, will even develop a long-term relationship with a specific taxi driver who will effectively become their personal driver. Some less affluent households hire staff that only work for one or two days a week. It is possible that the fact that wealthy families manage to vertically integrate their employees (Williamson 2005b), thereby locking them within the family milieu, while middle- and working-class people cannot afford to do this, has an impact on how safe those families become. The exact income levels of households that use drivers are not known, but observation suggests that most middle-class families and above who are able to afford at least one employee may at some point hire a driver. These employees are mostly from a working-class background and are commonly accessed through the employer's social network; they are then tested on a number of factors that establish whether or not they are to be trusted.

Intuitively, this relationship would seem to pose a further kidnapping risk as employees have access to sensitive information about their employers (their everyday whereabouts and wealth, for instance) for which potential kidnappers might pay handsomely, or be willing to use violence to learn.

## Theoretical Approach

The act of hiring a driver in Mexico City is a very rich example of a problem of trust. A high crime environment with limited state protection makes the risk of running into a criminal more present than in other situations where the rule of law is stronger. A potential driver in this situation not only needs to prove his proficiency at the wheel and knowledge of the City's streets, but, more importantly, he must also prove that he will not betray his employer by facilitating a kidnapping or other crime to be committed against said employer or their family. He must prove somehow that he is willing to protect the family's private information regarding their wealth, plans, schedules, and whereabouts, information to which he will certainly have access upon being hired. Once he is hired, a driver has almost instant access to this information and the family is exposed. This is why a clear assessment must be made before the decision is finalized. In a sense, he is hired not just to drive, but also to protect information. Faced with the decision to hire someone, the potential employer must decide whether or not he can establish that the potential employee is who he says he is and has the intentions he claims to have. In other words, he must establish his employee's trustworthiness before he hires him. This must be done in an environment where there is incomplete information—the employer does not know for sure what the employee's motivations are—and where there is a risk that a criminal may pass themselves off as a prospective driver or provide information to actual kidnappers. Therefore, the potential employer must make a series of trust decisions to determine if he is to hire the person in front of him. Since, in most cases, the employer will never have met the employee before, this decision must be made in a limited amount of time lest the hiring process be drawn out and too costly. What appears to be a menial decision turns out to be a sophisticated process.

The literature on trust (Cook 2001; Cook and Gerbasi 2009; Gambetta 1988; Gambetta and Hamill 2005; Hardin 2006; Sztompka 1999) and signaling game theory (Bacharach and Gambetta 1997; Gambetta 2009; also see Spence 1974) will provide theoretical tools for this book. Employers face both primary and secondary problems of trust (Bacharach and Gambetta 1997) as, throughout the hiring process, they must establish if the prospective employee has the properties they ascribe to a 'real' driver and also if the signs that tell them this are actually true or if they are facing someone passing themselves off as the real deal. How they solve these problems is the central focus of this book. Bacharach and Gambetta's (1997) outline of the trust game allows us to dissect the hiring process and look at it as a trust decision. In order to establish the potential employee's trustworthiness, the employer will look for certain qualities that he believes mean the other can be trusted. These qualities can be based on rationality, but can also be determined by cultural, religious, or other structural factors.

The mechanisms through which this relationship is played out can be deciphered using signaling theory. A branch of game theory (Gambetta 2009), signaling theory has become in the past decades more salient as a potentially important tool for sociological analysis. The theory develops a framework within which to understand how people make decisions regarding the truthfulness of the information they are receiving in an exchange when the other person involved in said exchange may wish to misrepresent information. This is based on the premise that many of the things we need or would like to know about other people with whom we engage are not observable. For example, an employer would like to know that the driver he is hiring is honest; however, honesty is not really observable to the naked eye. It has to be established through time and repeated interactions. Many times, however, people do not have the luxury of repeated interactions before they make a decision. How can individuals solve this problem? This is the dilemma that signaling theory helps us address. We can solve the problem of how to interact with someone else by 'establishing a connection between their perceivable features and their unobservable properties' (Gambetta 2009: 170). These perceivable features can be any observable trait, such as gender and race, to more personal factors, such as dress, body language, hairstyle, and even one's weight. They come presented in two forms: (1) as *signals* understood to mean purposive displays of features meant to convey a message or ownership of a certain trait (such as honesty); and (2) as *signs*, which can be anything in the environment capable of changing our beliefs or affecting our decisions (Gambetta 2009: 170). The decision to hire, I will argue, is based on the use of these tools.

To further support my work, I will also refer to parts of transaction-cost economics, specifically Williamson's work on vertical integration (Williamson 2005b). Vertical integration, understood as the decision to make or buy, can allow us to understand some of the hiring strategies of Mexico's elite with regard to their hiring of numerous members of the same family, thereby locking in what could be called their *employee production*. I will also refer to the literature on protection and extra-legal governance (Dixit 2004; Gambetta 1996; Skaperdas 2001; Skaperdas and Konrad 2004; Varese 2001) to illustrate and explain the informal context in which the relationships I study are carried out, started, and enforced. Moreover, I will also refer to work on kidnapping (e.g. Fajnzylber et al. 1998; Levitt and Rubio 2005; Rubio 2003) to illustrate the wider context of this crime.

While the quantity and quality of the literature on crime and kidnapping has been increasing in Mexico, especially in the last two years, a piece of research such as this one fills a void in the study of the micro consequences of macro processes such as changes in crime trends, a weak rule of law, and the state's struggles to impose a unified set of rules within a society. Large developing urban centres such as Mexico City have very specific socioeconomic, institutional, and geographical characteristics and thus also provide a unique testing ground for theories of the formation of relationships based on trust and protection. It also allows for the application of signaling theories in what can be described as an environment of relative lawlessness (Williamson 2005a).

## Methodology and Field Research

The district that is the main focus of this research, Miguel Hidalgo, is located at the north-western edge of the City. It covers an area of 42.99 square kilometres and comprises ninety-five *colonias* or neighbourhoods (INEGI 2005), with a population of 353,534 (INEGI 2008). This district is one of the richest in the country and houses a large proportion of the City's economic elite. It is virtually (although not formally) divided into a wealthy southern side and a working-class northern end. Both sides have pockets of middle-class neighbourhoods. Within this district, I focused my research on the neighbourhood of Polanco, located at the southern end.

There are a number of reasons why I chose this neighbourhood. First, it is home to a large number of wealthy individuals. It probably houses the second largest number of wealthy people in any neighbourhood in the City, exceeded only by the neighbourhood of Las Lomas, which, due to its very large geographical size and the fact that it straddles both Mexico City and the neighbouring State of Mexico, was not chosen for this study. Real-estate prices can be used as a proxy for estimating a neighbourhood's wealth. Analysis of real-estate prices by estate agents Propiedades.com (2017) show that the average house price in the neighbourhood in 2017 was of MEX $21 million pesos, or around US $1.1 million. Historically, wealthy communities, such as those of the Jewish, Lebanese, and Spanish, have settled and lived in this part of the City for generations. Polanco is a high-class residential and business area that began developing in the late 1930s and has since been home to very wealthy people. Most old houses, once the majority of the buildings there, have been or are now being replaced with very expensive, super-safe condos. Security is such a salient issue in this neighbourhood that, in a survey of thirty-three buildings in this area during fieldwork, it was found that all but five boasted private security as a matter of course in their sales pitch and adverts. Most news adverts for the sale of flats and houses there also mention the security arrangements for the building in question. Polanco is also a commercial hub known for its world-class restaurants, bars, and designer shops that line the wide, clean, tree-lined streets of its south-west side. Second, due to its economic composition, this neighbourhood was especially targeted by kidnappers in the 1990s and early 2000s, when, as I will show in upcoming chapters, an economic crisis triggered an important rise in all types of crime. It is known through police reports that both the Jewish community and the Spanish community in Polanco were until recently targeted by highly organized kidnapping gangs (KNRD 2009). However, as of 2007, there was only one kidnapping reported in this district, and we do not know for sure if it actually happened in Polanco. This fall in kidnapping rates fuels the enquiry presented herein. Third, the neighbourhood size and self-contained characteristics make it ripe for analysis of community-based protection mechanisms and also allow for observation of ecological issues, such as community cohesion, due to high-density urban living. In sum, it presents an ideal laboratory for the purposes of this book.

It was my desire to find out how people in Mexico City deal with the risk of being kidnapped when they have a limited or deficient recourse to the state or other legal conflict resolution mechanisms, and how this is reflected in the process of hiring an employee or, on the other side, of being hired as one. Once in the field, I quickly realized that this was just one part of a very complex story. This made me reflect that, in order to understand the dynamics of kidnapping and the trusting relationships that people foster to protect themselves, one must, at some point, look at what role the state, and its interactions with society, plays in the development and pervasiveness of these factors. While I centred my field research on the elite's survival strategies discussed above, I also tried to take into account other factors in order to have a more complete view of the issue at hand. This led me to carry out interviews with law-enforcement officials such as prosecutors, police investigators, and district attorneys. The elite do not live in a vacuum. They interact with the state and its agents regularly, they shape each other as much as crime shapes them, in a web of social relations. This is why it was important to have access to these actors and better inform the field research. I also carried out interviews with employers and employees. I also tried to include the view of kidnapping victims to assess what kind of effects having been a victim could have.

## Sensitive Research

One of the first issues that deserves discussion is the sensitive nature of this research. The topic of crime, personal security, and especially kidnapping (much more so for victims of kidnapping and the wealthy) can be classified as sensitive, as it fulfils the methodological definitions of such topics. Lee and Renzetti (1990: 512) argue that:

> A sensitive topic is one which potentially poses for those involved a substantial threat, the emergence of which renders problematic for the researcher and/or the researched, the collection, holding and/or dissemination of research data.

Dealing with areas of a person's life which may be 'private, stressful or sacred' (Lee 1993) is difficult and requires a certain level of trust between the researcher and the respondents. Thus, a long period of qualitative fieldwork became necessary. Five groups were sampled:

- middle- and upper-class individuals in the district of Miguel Hidalgo who have been victims of kidnapping;
- middle- and upper-class individuals in the district who have not been victims;
- household employees working with victims;
- household employees working with non-victims; and
- authorities that deal with this particular crime and others, as well as academic experts.

These populations require the previous establishment of some form of trust with the interviewer. It is because of this that network-based recommendations have a positive influence both on the access and the quality of the information released by the respondent. It must be said, however, that snowballing methods have limitations. On the one hand, they sometimes offer a certain bias. Lee (1993: 66) argues that, when using this method, 'one is still sampling with reference to the social structure, though this time in an implicit manner'. The type of respondents is heavily dependent on the social ties between members of the study population. This has a tendency to produce homogenous samples. In the case of this research, most kidnapping victims (by far the most difficult group to access). I used a snowball method for accessing respondents. I began asking within my social circle, then asking respondents for recommendations, and so forth. Many of the people I was able to interview are, for example, members of the middle and upper class. I had a difficult time gaining access to working-class victims, which resulted in the sample of kidnapping victims being somewhat—although not substantially—biased towards the former groups. This is a reflection of my position, as a

**Table I.1 Interviews by Group**

| Group | Interviews (N) | % female | % working class |
|---|---|---|---|
| Employers (kidnapped: 21%) | 29 | 62 | 0 |
| Employees | 14 | 40 | 100 |
| Law enforcement | 27 | 22 | 90 |
| Other | 8 | 50 | 25 |

Mexican and a native of Mexico City, in the social structure and the networks to which I have more access. In the end, the importance of this bias is reduced by the fact that this particular group did not offer substantially different information from the other groups concerned. Table I.1 shows details of my respondents, as well as the particular network to which they belong.

Table I.1 represents only the interviews I was able to record at the time (2008–09). Since I began researching this topic in 2007, I have carried out hundreds of conversations and informal interviews on the topic, and these also inform my knowledge on the subject.

The fieldwork for this project began with a two-month trip in early 2007. The longest single fieldwork stay took place over sixteen months in 2008–09. Since then, I have travelled to Mexico at least once a year, for up to three weeks at a time, and while sometimes it is other projects which take me there, this research has been ongoing. I was able to conduct seventy-eight interviews with the groups mentioned above. About 5 per cent of contacts refused an interview. Interviews were usually organized through a third party known to both respondent and myself. The interview would then be organized over the phone and finally done in person. Interviews generally took place in people's homes or in cafes/restaurants all over the City. The length of interviews varied, from thirty minutes to around two hours. I attempted to audio record most of the interviews, but this was not possible all of the time. In the informal environment in which many of the interviews took place, the presence of a voice recorder would have been, if anything, a distraction. In the case of law-enforcement agents, I was never able to record. I found that this particular group, more than any other, was reluctant to have a conversation recorded. This may be due to the fact that, these days, the police in Mexico are under constant scrutiny by society and the media, creating a certain fear within the institution of being named and shamed. Another explanation for this would be based on Hinton's work on the Argentine and Brazilian police (2006: 4), as she argues that, 'even in developed countries, the police are hierarchically organized, have a secretive *esprit de corps*, [and] resist external interference'; this could help to explain their reluctance to have their interviews recorded. Although most law enforcers spoke very freely (even, as we shall see, of their 'negative' activities), they were never comfortable with recording of any kind.

Over the years, I have also had hundreds, if not thousands, of conversations that I would try to steer towards my research questions. These happened in taxis, social gatherings, coffee shops, bars, shops, and newsstands, with acquaintances and their families and friends, academics, journalists, and many other actors. Most of these were set in an informal, impromptu environment. While I am not tallying many of these conversations in the final count of official interviews, they most certainly helped shape my vision of the narrative I will attempt to unfold here and the knowledge I acquired from them also informs this book.

Consent is always an important issue when undertaking the kind of fieldwork required by this book. It is very difficult to get a kidnapping victim to sign a consent form. It is even more difficult to get the same form signed by a member of the police force or a district attorney. The presentation of such paperwork would only put a distance between the researcher and the respondent, which would hamper any positive outcome of the interview or conversation. For these conversations to work, it is important to build a certain rapport and trust with the interviewee, something that 'demands a measure of intimacy that goes beyond the normal relationship between interviewer and informant' (Booth and Booth 1994: 417). In this sense, I will argue along the lines of Lee (1993) and contend that in cases such as the work presented here, consent is a 'developmental process' (103) that takes time and, on occasion, repeated interaction. As he argues:

> Discussion of sensitive or confidential information is usually only possible in these situations once trust has been established between the

fieldworker and the person being studied. Where this has been done consent becomes implicit. (1993: 103)

## The Kidnapping News Report Database, 1999–2010

Given the difficulty of gathering data on kidnapping in Mexico, I also built a news report database. The media have made a habit in the last years of reporting intensely on crime and kidnapping and therefore there is a wealth of information being printed every day. As crime rates rose in the mid-1990s, so did the media's attention to the topic. This has resulted in a large amount of news reports on these topics. Two national newspapers, *El Universal* and *La Jornada*, were used to build the database. They are two of the most important newspapers in the country (Mexico City being the capital of the country has not really developed a local newspaper industry) and as such were important sources of information. Both newspapers were accessed through their internet archives and at the newspaper depository of the National University (UNAM). All news reports containing the word *kidnapping* were selected and included in the database in the format of Rich Text Word documents and stored in a computer, subdivided by year. The database includes reports on press conferences made by authorities, reporting on kidnapping cases, statistics released by police, investigative journalism articles on kidnapping, opinion pieces on the same subject, and other articles where kidnapping is mentioned, such as criminal law reforms etc. The database consists of a total of 1,774 individual news reports.

I will use the information taken from this database throughout the book to illustrate the history of kidnapping in Mexico. I will also use it to help me reconstruct many of the informal strategies used by individuals in Mexico City. With it, for example, I was able to map and reconstruct rich information on kidnapping gangs and their development. Many instances of community protection strategies are also found there. Many of the 'hard' data actually available were also triangulated with the database to provide more trustworthy information. I will refer to this database using the acronym KNRD when citing information emanating from it.

This book is organized as follows. Chapter 1 provides the theoretical framework for the book. It introduces the concept of trust, as well as how signaling theory can help us to understand how trust is established, as well as how this can be linked to the issue of kidnapping. Chapter 2 discusses the Mexican political economy in the period 1994 to 2015. It provides the context in which kidnapping became a salient crime. It also serves to link important economic processes (such as liberalization and democratization) to the rise in crime and corruption, which opened the door for kidnapping to increase. Chapter 3 tells the story of kidnapping in Mexico from the 1960s and 1970s to the present. It maps out the evolution of the crime from a politically motivated one to an economic one. It presents the main actors in the story, the gangs which perpetrated it, their links to the police, and how policy had an impact on the development of kidnapping over time. Chapter 4 explores the reactions communities have had to kidnapping. Specifically, it looks at the strategies which, mostly wealthy, communities and families have implemented to avoid being victimized. Chapter 5 explores how trust can be used to understand how potential kidnapping victims can protect themselves in the process of hiring household employees. It explores how signaling can be used to establish trustworthiness in this context. Chapter 6 analyses the perspective of the employee; it explores what mechanisms they use to secure employment and how these relate to the employer's perspective. Lastly, a concluding chapter presents the contributions of the book to our understanding of kidnapping in Mexico, as well as possible areas for further work on the topic.

# 1

# Crime, Trust, and Signaling

In August 2015, a video surfaced online which showed a phone recording of a convoy made up of at least fifteen late model trucks and SUVs. They were stopped, blocking a lane of a federal highway in the northern state of Chihuahua, in broad daylight. The trucks were full of men wearing bulletproof vests; some wore ski masks and most were heavily armed with assault rifles (AK-47 and AR-15 assault weapons are preferred by Mexico's *sicários* (cartel hitmen)). The video shows about sixty men. In the background, a radio crackles with a voice asking for someone by name over and over again. The men look relaxed as they pose for the video, raising their hands and weapons as the cameraman repeats *vámos sicários* ('come on, killers!'). The video lasts for just over a minute.

Among the barrage of violent images and news to which Mexicans are subjected every day, this video was particularly intriguing. This was due not only to the fact that it was a very large convoy of trucks and the men were armed. What made this video special was the normalcy with which the men in it seemed to behave. There was no secrecy, no attempt at hiding, which would usually be expected of criminals—in this case, cartel killers. The purpose of the video is unknown; it was uploaded to YouTube, ostensibly by the person who filmed it. The men looked relaxed, happy, laughing, as if they were 'regular' people driving on their way to work (which in many ways they are, and they were). Indeed, the video could have been of a convoy of school buses. It gave a glimpse of the human side of these characters—people who are usually (and for good reason) shrouded in secrecy and fear. The image of the ruthless killer was suddenly replaced with an image of bonhomie and smiling faces, almost reminiscent of a Martin Parr photograph. It is evidence of how normalized these scenes have become—how unsurprising. It is through those

Intimate Crimes: Kidnapping, Gangs and Trust in Mexico City. First Edition. Rolando Ochoa © Rolando Ochoa 2019. Published in 2019 by Oxford University Press

visual experiences, and transmitting stories of crime, that security becomes an integral part of life in Mexico. Security seeps into many everyday conversations, and feelings of insecurity—real or imagined—are routinely experienced by Mexicans and, in many cases, they have their lives shaped by these events.

This situation has been exacerbated by the ever-increasing violence which has been thrust upon the population since 2006, when the Mexican chapter of the War on Drugs was launched. Chapter 2 will illustrate this in depth, but as an example, in 2006, there were 732 homicides linked to organized crime. In 2011, this same figure was 16,968 (INEGI 2015. Organized crime has become a fact of life for millions of Mexicans who live their lives alongside this deadly trade and the individuals involved in it. *Narcos* (drug traffickers/dealers) and other criminals do not exist in a parallel universe, far from the society they inhabit. They are embedded within society. They drive cars, eat at restaurants, own businesses, and have regular contact with both civilian populations and the State. It is not uncommon for citizens to be able to identify them—especially in smaller towns—as they go about their business. Kidnapping itself is, as the research in this book will reveal, another ingredient in the narrative of insecurity. Recent research reveals that kidnapping (among many other crimes) is once again on the increase in Mexico City (Morfin et al. 2016), as well as in other parts of the country.

This fear is very real. Risk of victimization is a factor taken into consideration in everyday decisions such as when to go out of the house, what school to send children to, where to spend (or not) holidays, etc. During the field research undertaken for this book, most interviewees in the City freely admitted to changing their schedules and activities as a result of crime concerns. This has affected the fabric of everyday relationships, as people consider the risk of being victimized when they are approached by a person on the street, when they spot a conspicuous SUV at night or when they go about their work lives. Interpersonal trust has, in many cases, suffered as a result of this. Erosion in the City's social capital (understood broadly as interpersonal and intercommunity trust, community engagement, etc.) is also evident, with many interviewees stating they had become less trusting in recent times. By necessity, this has affected the way in which many people form personal and professional relationships. The way in which people experience and make decisions involving trust has changed dramatically. One of the goals of this book is to understand and analyse exactly how this has happened.

## The Value of Mechanisms in Understanding the Social World

Understanding the 'social world' (Hedström and Bearman 2009: 4) requires a specific approach that allows us to understand people's actions and decisions, such as the decision to trust another person. Analytical sociology offers such an approach. This particular understanding focuses on explaining 'important social facts such as network structures, patterns of segregation, typical beliefs, cultural tastes, common ways of acting and so forth' (Hedström and Bearman 2009: 1). It is based on identifying the particular *mechanisms* by which these facts occur or are produced. This particular approach seeks to explain how certain events came about and how they sustain themselves over time, and it does so by looking at the specific mechanisms operating in each relationship.

In this sense, analytical sociology (and its mechanisms-based approach) is 'firmly anchored in the Mertonian tradition' (Hedström and Bearman 2009: 6) and focuses much of its attention on the generation of 'semi general middle-range theories' (Hedström and Bearman 2009: 6). The usefulness of this theoretical approach lies in its flexibility and reality-based empirical foundations. It provides the researcher with the tools to be able to explain the facts she observes without the rigidity and constraints of a large general theory. It allows for reality, rather than theory by itself, to guide the researcher and her enquiries. This is based on what is referred to as structural individualism: 'a methodological doctrine according to which all social facts, their structure and change are, in principle explicable in terms of individuals, their properties, actions and relations to one another ... that emphasises action-based explanations' (Hedström and Bearman 2009: 8). The motivation behind these action-based explanations is to reach the minimum unit of analysis of a social fact, that is, human action. Human action is ultimately the basis for all change we observe in society. Whether it is fuelled by beliefs, preferences, emotions, opportunities, or even signals, all 'relational structures are explained as intended or unintended consequences of individuals' actions' (Hedström and Bearman 2009: 4).

Another key factor within analytical sociology and the mechanisms-based approach is that they are based on the existence of micro–macro links. A macro property is defined as a property of a collectivity or a set of micro-level entities that are 'not defined by a single micro level entity' (Hedström and Bearman 2009: 10). This is not to say that macro properties are explained or caused by the micro-level entities. These micro-level entities *make up or constitute* the macro-level property. Thus, they do not have a causal relationship. Changes at the macro level are thus composed by changes at the micro level. This influence may be recognized and consciously taken into account by individuals or may also sway them in a non-conscious way. The mechanisms-based approach seeks to explain complex dynamics at the macro level through unearthing the most basic traits of their micro-level components. In the case of kidnapping, we see this crime as a macro-level event, and we attempt to explain changes in its behaviour by analysing the actions of those involved (directly or otherwise) in it.

A mechanisms-based approach seeks to explain an outcome by referring to the 'types of entities and activities through which the outcome to be explained is believed to have been brought about' (Hedström and Bearman 2009: 4)—in this case, how kidnapping affects trust. There exists a debate about the definition of a mechanism and many authors have explored this dilemma (see, inter alia, Elster 1989; Hedström and Swedberg 1998; Stinchcombe 1991), presenting their own definitions of what a mechanism actually is. I will, in line with Hedström and Bearman (2009), adopt Machamer, Darden, and Craver's definition (2000: 3). They state that 'mechanisms are entities and activities organised such that they are productive of regular changes from start or set-up to finish or termination conditions'. This particular definition is, I believe, clear enough, in that it allows us to understand exactly what a mechanism is and also opens up the possibility to analyse actions by individuals and explain them. Thus, a mechanism is composed of entities (for example, an individual with certain properties) and the activities and relations that such entities are involved in. This is compounded with its relations to other entities and their own activities, which will produce an outcome (change) of certain characteristics and regularity.

It is this approach I keep in mind when addressing the issue of kidnapping in Mexico City. Within the larger body of work on analytical sociology, we find the literature on trust and signaling. This body of research has been used to explain how trusting relationships are created and maintained. I set out in this book to explain how trust can be established in risky, weak rule-of-law situations and particularly how (wealthy) individuals solve problems of trust when taking into account the risk of kidnapping.

## Signaling, Trust, and Risk

Signaling theory is used to explain a series of problems of trust (Bacharach and Gambetta 1997; Cook and Gerbasi 2009; Gambetta 1996, 2009; Gambetta and Hamill 2005; Hardin 2006; Sztompka 1999). With origins in evolutionary biology (see Zahavi 1975), signaling has been used to explore decision-making processes such as recruitment into gangs (Densley 2012) and, more importantly for our case, in the seminal work of Michael Spence (1974), who uses signaling as a means to understand employment in the labour market from an economic perspective. Indeed, one could also situate this within the broader literature on governance (see, inter alia, Dixit 2004; Greif 1997; Macaulay 1963; Schelling 1958), which seeks to explore how humans govern their decision-making processes. This book can also be classified as a potential contribution to this body of literature, broadly understood.

Spence argues that during the hiring process two actors are involved, namely the employer and the employee. These two actors under many circumstances have never met and have limited information about each other. In his own words, 'the employer, in most hiring situations, is uncertain about the productive capabilities of the job applicant prior to hiring him, and usually for some period of time after hiring' (Spence 1974: 2). In this context, where information is imperfect and much information is not public, the actors in the relationship engage in a signaling game.

Every time the employer hires someone, according to Spence, he is entering a lottery 'whose outcome is the actual labour he receives' (1974: 6). The recruitment can be into a gang, a football club, a corporate job, or a drug cartel. What the employer is not certain about is whether or not he will in fact receive such labour and, if he does, what quality it will be. The employer will try to minimize his risk in hiring by looking for certain observable and non-observable signals from the employee that transmit to him his capabilities and credentials. These can be in the form of university diplomas, membership of a guild or professional organization, or more easily observable traits such as gender, age, and race. The employer will use his past experience in the market to make sure, as much as possible, that his new employee will be of the best kind possible or, in Spence's words (1974: 8), 'to estimate the conditional probability of competence of the employee'. The employee will try to generate the best impression possible by manipulating to the greatest extent possible the image he conveys to the employer. After all this, there will always be an element of uncertainty that may be minimized over time as the employee proves that he does indeed possess the qualities he has signalled. Thus, signaling solves the communication problems that exist between employer and employee.

Signaling theory (Bacharach and Gambetta 1997; Gambetta 2009; see also Spence 1974) helps us to understand how people make decisions regarding the truthfulness of the information they are receiving in an exchange when the other person involved may wish to misrepresent information. This is based on the premise that many of the things we need or would like to know about other people we engage with are not observable. For example, an employer would like to know that the driver he is hiring is honest; however, honesty is not really visible to the naked eye. It has to be established through time and repeated interactions. Many times, however, people do not have the luxury of repeated interactions before they make a decision. How can individuals solve this problem? This is the dilemma that signaling theory helps us to address. We can solve the problem of how to interact with someone else by 'establishing a connection between their perceivable features and their unobservable properties' (Gambetta 2009: 170). These perceivable features can range from any observable trait, such as gender, to more personal factors, such as dress, body language, hairstyle, and even one's weight. They are presented as: (1) signals understood to mean purposive displays of features intended to convey a message or ownership of a certain trait (such as honesty); and (2) signs, which can be anything in the environment capable of changing our beliefs or affecting our decisions (Gambetta 2009: 170). The decision to hire, I will argue, is based on the use of these tools to ascertain an employee's trustworthiness. This process is vital in a context of high insecurity.

As Seligman points out, 'the existence of trust is an essential component of all enduring social relationships' (1997: 13). Mexico is a good illustration of this. Most of the relationships I analyse in this chapter are part of an informal *relation-based economic system* (Dixit 2004), are under no written contract, and are governed by a limited rule of law (Magaloni and Zepeda 2004). Dixit (2004) establishes a distinction between a rules-based economic system and a relation-based one. In the former, all actors in society assume a certain number of rules that govern their actions; these rules are controlled and established a priori and provide certainty of outcome for most actors. In most cases, these relationships are arbitrated by a third party or are at least enforced by one, namely the State. In the latter, there is no such governance structure. Relationships are informal and, to an extent, sui generis in that they do not all operate under the same rules and are not all enforced by the same parties. Formal enforceable contracts are rare in this case, and many relationships in Mexico are based on different informal mechanisms.

The establishment of cooperative relationships in this environment requires a particular approach from those involved in the relationship. In this situation, actors must use diverse mechanisms in order to establish, maintain, and enforce cooperative relationships, since they know that the State or another party will not help in enforcing the deals they enter into. This is a problematic state of affairs, since it does not allow for a high level of certainty for anyone entering into a relationship. While on paper labour law protects individuals who enter into informal relationships, Mexico's lax enforcement and weak rule of law means this mechanism is rarely used. Thus, both employers and employees find themselves at a disadvantage. However, employers' higher economic status means they may be able to acquire protection from the State or other actors, which may reduce this disadvantage, while employees are often left wholly unprotected. The establishment of trust among actors before entering into, and during, such a relationship is one such vital mechanism that individuals can use to solve the issues of uncertainty. In line with Gambetta (2000: 4), I understand trust to mean:

> A particular level of the subjective probability with which an agent assesses that another agent ... will perform a particular action, both before he can monitor such action (or independently of his capacity ever to be able to monitor it) and in a context in which it affects his own action.

A key component of trust is uncertainty about other people's behaviour: 'It is related to the limits of our capacity ever to achieve a full knowledge of others, their motives, their responses to endogenous as well exogenous changes' (Gambetta 2000: 4). In the words of Seligman (1997: 21), 'trust involves a vulnerability occasioned by some form of ignorance or basic uncertainty of the other's motives'. If actors could achieve full knowledge of the true intentions of other agents and could base their decisions on this knowledge, trust would be rendered mostly useless. Cook and Gerbasi (2009: 222) dissect trust into four dimensions, namely 'competence and reliability', integrity, and honesty. This point is of paramount importance when we analyse the hiring process.

While technical capacity is important (drivers need to know how to drive), it is very cheap to acquire such an ability and therefore not too important for an employer. However, honesty and integrity are vital properties in this relationship. The employer needs to know that his employee will not betray his trust by harming him or his family through an information leak to criminals, or indeed by being a criminal himself. The very high cost of a betrayal of this sort gives us an idea of how important establishing this dimension is for the employer. However, our understanding of competence changes when we know that the work of the driver is not just as someone who (only) drives people around, but also as an actor who has a stake in protecting the family of his employer and their information. Here, both dimensions acquire nearly equal importance, and the employer needs to answer two questions: (1) can this driver protect my family and our private information? and (2) will this driver betray me and hurt me in the future? Indeed, it seems now that both questions require the same answer and can be posed as one: will this driver betray me and facilitate a crime against me? In this case, both dimensions of trust are intimately related and must both be fulfilled if the relationship is to be successful. How can potential employees answer this question?

Ideally, an agent would have full information about the other agent's intentions and preferences in order to make his decision. In reality, this condition is rarely (if ever) achieved and agents find themselves in an asymmetrical information situation in which the decision-maker (i.e. the truster) does not know what pay-offs govern the trustee. They do know, however, what options in terms of strategies each other has (in the case of a driver to hire or not and in the case of the driver to cooperate with the employer or share information with kidnappers). In line with Bacharach and Gambetta (1997: 149), I assume that actors will have different 'raw' and 'all-in pay-offs'. Raw pay-offs are purely rational. These are pay-offs motivated solely by profit maximization. All-in pay-offs, on the other hand, may differ from purely rational ones and are motivated by different mechanisms. They can be determined, for example, as a moral inclination to behave within the law, or a norm-based aversion to damaging the family name. In this sense, all-in pay-offs may limit the individual's desire to act based solely on rational motivations.

This is where an important asymmetry in information lies. The truster must find a mechanism to fill the void created by this asymmetry. In other words, he must define whether the trustee is governed by his all-in or raw pay-offs. Bacharach and Gambetta (1997: 150) call this a basic trust game. This applies to a type of game in which it is in an agent's best interest to cooperate, but he would be better off if he did not cooperate if the other agent decided not to cooperate and it is also in his best interest not to. When the trustee has proven to the truster that she is worthy of trust and therefore will do as expected by the truster, and the truster has done likewise, an equilibrium appears in which both actors are fulfilling each other's expectations (Bacharach and Gambetta 1997: 154). Establishing which set of pay-offs (raw or all-in) will prevail for the trustee in an interaction is what Bacharach and Gambetta (1997) call the primary problem of trust'.

Thus, the primary problem of trust involves the truster establishing whether the trustee has at least some of the requisite characteristics to mean they are trustworthy. First, the actors must establish which 'trust-warranting properties' are valid for this particular interaction. These properties are 'any property (or combination of properties) of a trustee in a basic trust game which suffices for him to be trustworthy' (Bacharach and Gambetta 1997: 7). We must assume that the actors in the relationship know what properties signal trustworthiness for that particular interaction. Good communication between actors is a very important part of this exchange, but it is difficult to pinpoint exactly how good communication is between actors in all interactions (Good 2000). Thus, problems of communication may also have to be overcome for the game to function.

Most trust-warranting properties are unique to each interaction or situation; one may work in one context, but may be useless or even set off a red light in another. A trustee is made trustworthy through many possible combinations of these properties. Rarely does only one property mean full trust is warranted. The more trust-warranting properties a person has, the more trustworthy he may be appraised to be. All of these properties transform the trustee's pay-offs from raw to all-in by overriding simple rational impulses. Punishment for defection itself may not be a straightforward property, but rather a propensity to respond to punishment, for example, may serve to make the trustee more trustworthy (Bacharach and Gambetta 1997). Thus, Bacharach and Gambetta (1997: 151) call any property (or combination of properties) in a basic trust game that suffices for the trustee to be trustworthy a 'trust-warranting property for that game'.

Once trustworthy properties have been observed, the secondary problem of trust arises. The truster must establish whether those properties on display by the trustee are to be trusted as real, or are a front for someone passing themselves off as something they are not. As these properties can be observable or not (Bacharach and Gambetta 1997), it is possible for an actor to copy or 'mimic' those properties to pass themselves off as the real thing in order to obtain instant, raw pay-offs. Bacharach and Gambetta call this person an 'opportunist' (1997: 10; see also Gambetta and Hamill 2005). In order to discern mimics from non-mimics, trusters must carefully analyse and weigh up the special properties, as seen through the signs displayed by trustees (Gambetta and Hamill 2005). Normally, the truster will know that there are signs that are very costly to mimic, such as gender or race, and others that are 'cheap', such as dress or certain documents. Costly signs will be hard to mimic and will therefore have a higher value for the truster in this interaction. Before making the decision to trust, the truster will therefore look for those signs that are costlier to copy for this interaction or a combination of them. Frank (1988) calls this the 'costly-to-fake principle'. The secondary problem of trust is solved when the truster can say, with good certainty, that the person in front of him is indeed who he says he is.

The costly-to-fake principle (Frank 1988) is also elaborated on as the cost condition in signaling theory (Gambetta 2009; Gambetta and Hamill 2005). It is defined as:

> ... a solution in which at least some truth is transmitted, provided that among the possible signals is one, s, which is cheap enough to emit,

> relative to the benefit, for signallers who have K, but costly enough to emit, relative to the benefit, for those who do not. If it is too costly to fake for all or most non-K signallers then observing s is good evidence that the signaler has K. (Gambetta 2009)

When the cost condition is fully accomplished, a sorting equilibrium arises—that is, an equilibrium in which there is no ambiguity that the signaller has the properties he claims to have. In reality, fully sorting equilibria are rare. Thus, there are signals that may be emitted by almost all individuals, whether or not they do indeed have the property being screened for. In this case, the equilibrium is called pooling (Gambetta 2009). Gender is such a sign.

The third kind of equilibrium that may result from a signaling game is called a semi-sorting equilibrium. In this special equilibrium, signs are emitted by all possessors of the property under analysis, but may also be emitted by non-possessors. In this case, the information transmitted is incomplete, but it is firm enough that the person making the evaluation may decide that it is likely that the property on display is actually possessed by the signaller. In the best of cases, very few non-possessors will be able to signal this property because 'the higher the proportion of non-Ksignallers who use this signal, the less conclusive is the evidence' (Gambetta 2009: 173). Many real-life situations end in this kind of equilibrium. In the case of hiring a driver, the most employers can hope for is a semi-sorting equilibrium (see, for example, the work of Gambetta and Hamill 2005).

Thus, I will argue throughout the book the following:

- The risk of kidnapping has pushed employers to perfect a hiring process that seeks to minimize the risk of victimization.
- The risk of kidnapping has meant that protection of the family's private information is a key component in the hiring process and a main concern for the employer.
- Potential drivers will try to ensure the best employment possible by signaling their possession of certain characteristics which they know are trust-warranting properties. By the same token, employers will look for certain hard-to-fake signals of properties they deem to be trust-warranting.

I will use an example to illustrate this. In the specific case that concerns us, a verbal recommendation about an employee from a close friend or family member is impossible to mimic, but a written letter of recommendation from a stranger is not, and the latter is therefore less valuable. A worthy letter will only be presented when the writer knows the prospective employee personally and knows for a fact that he is reliable, punctual, and discreet. In this sense, mimics will find it very hard to display this particular signal. However, there is no guarantee that even someone with a recommendation will be honest, as there are always black sheep, but the recommendation does reduce the chance of this happening, thus producing a semi-sorting equilibrium (Gambetta 2009; Gambetta and Hamill 2005). This will be a preferred outcome for the employer as he seeks to maximize the odds that he is hiring an honest driver. An example of this would be the following. When a wealthy person (W1) is in need of a driver, he will contact someone in his close social network (W2) to enquire about it. W2 will then ask his trustworthy employee (E1), who might recommend a family member or acquaintance (E2). It is the sum of the good reputation of W2 and E1 that counts in this transaction. E1 would hardly recommend a traitor since he knows he will be punished if his recommended person betrays W1, and W2 trusts his employee's recommendation enough to pass it on as he has already established, a priori, his employee's trustworthiness, proven by the fact that he is already hired. While there is always a risk that the recommended person might be a mimic or a weak link—a person who can be coerced to cooperate with criminals—this strategy seeks to assure that this risk is minimized. As we shall see in the following chapters, this strategy is very common when hiring.

This initial stage can be called a filtering stage. Using social networks to acquire information on and recommendations for prospective employees, trusters will save resources that would otherwise be spent probing deeper into a potential employee's identity when he is a complete unknown. Filtering through social networks allows the truster to begin on the right foot and reduce his selection pool to a manageable (and somewhat more certain) size. After this stage, the hiring process described above begins proper with the employer probing for the qualities he wants and the employee presenting such qualities. Enforcing this kind of relationship is an important issue and one that usually falls within the realm of coercion or a credible threat thereof, although 'it falls short of being an adequate alternative to trust' (Gambetta

1998: 220). The threat of coercion solves the dilemma not by bringing trust in, but rather by making it unnecessary. Trust becomes necessary when other mechanisms to ensure cooperation are not available. In the specific case of the relationships described in this chapter, the employer must know what properties to look for when deciding to hire a prospective employee. Some of these properties might be, for example, a clean driver's licence, no criminal record, good health, and freedom from addictions, as well as other less tangible ones, such as punctuality, discretion, and efficiency. A recommendation from a close acquaintance can be an example of a guarantee of these properties. It is important to mention that some of these qualities are not easily observable and sometimes can only be established after the person has been hired.

It is important to understand exactly what qualities an employer looks for in an employee and how exactly he can screen for them. It is also key to know how potential employees can present the qualities the employer wants. In Table 1.1, I present some ideal qualities that an employer might look for in a driver, as well as what might signal these qualities, followed by the screening process for each.

This list is by no means exhaustive, but it gives an idea of what actors will be screening for during the hiring process. The signs and attitudes listed might also be subject to mimicry, some to a greater extent than others. It is very difficult to pass oneself off as a 35-year-old person if you are 60, but it may be possible to obtain a clean police file in Mexico with the right connections. These strategies and their possibility to be copied and faked will also be the focus of further analysis.

## Vertical Integration

Transaction cost economics presents us with a concept which can be a useful complement to understand the phenomena analysed in this book. Specifically, the concept of vertical integration (Williamson 2005b) may help us understand how elites negotiate the risk involved in hiring employees. Vertical integration means that firms must make the decision whether to produce their own input resources or buy them in the open market. Simply put, they must decide whether to make or buy their inputs. Following Coase's (1937) lead, transaction cost economics attempted to deal

**Table 1.1 Qualities, Signs, and Screening Strategies**

| Quality (from hardest to easiest to mimic) | Sign | Screening for it |
|---|---|---|
| Discretion | Keeping information secure by not divulging it | Very hard to establish, relies heavily on recommendations and repeated interaction |
| Efficiency | Completing tasks quickly, without involving many people, and at low cost | Can be screened for only during test period |
| Helpfulness | Offering to do things in the household; volunteering for tasks | Only by observation |
| Age | Must be of a certain age, not too young and not too old (both are unreliable) | Proof by observation and papers |
| Presence | Certain physical appearance: not too short, strong-looking, muscular, clean-cut, wearing a suit (formal) | On observation |
| Family man | By communication and official proof | Asking for children's birth certificates, proof of marriage |
| Knowledge of the City | Getting to places without asking, knowing good routes in the City | Can be screened for during test period through tasks, sending him off to make collections, etc. |
| No criminal record | Police files | Checking police files |
| Driver's licence | A valid licence | Checking licence |

with the flaws in connection with the then-generalized idea in economics that transaction costs were zero.

This assumption posed a number of problems with our understanding of phenomena such as externalities (Williamson 2005b). Externalities are defined as 'effects on persons not directly privy to the decision leading to an activity' (Lin 2014: 1). For example, the opening of a factory may have indirect effects on the people who live nearby in terms of pollution or noise. These are not costs directly related to whatever the factory is making. Arrow (1969: 48) links the existence of vertical integration—borne out of the need to 'replace the costs of buying and selling on the market by the cost of intra-firm transfer'—to the need to understand that 'the costs of operating competitive markets are not zero'. In an environment of lawlessness (Dixit 2004), vertical integration becomes a potential solution to problems of uncertainty and lax contract enforcement, since it provides an arrangement that is less risky and easier to control. In fact, Williamson (2005) argues that even in an environment of strong rule of law, there is a need for a certain level of informal ordering, and that most firms enter into such arrangements, leaving the courts (and formal contracts) as a costly and last-resort option. In this context, whether to vertically integrate production is a decision all firms must make. Applied to the case of kidnapping, employers can vertically integrate all their labour and reduce externalities. Simply put, they can choose to hire their employees not only on a full-time basis, but also to select them from the same families. This, as the reader will see in upcoming chapters, saves time and resources not only for the employer, who will not need to enter the open market every time they hire, but also for the employees, who may benefit from easier access to jobs through their family or close networks.

Mexico City can easily fit into the context described by Dixit (2004) as one of 'lawlessness'. In this context, the government cannot, or will not, uphold the law (in terms of contract enforcement, etc.) all the time. This generates a need for some form of ordering outside of the State. It also creates the need for other 'workable arrangements' (Williamson 2005a) for cooperation. Continued cooperation, or the need thereof, is a vital component of this approach. Indeed, governance demands that, in contractual relationships, 'the continuity of the relationship is a source of value' (Williamson 2005a). We can also draw parallels between this and the relationships I am analysing. With time, continuity of the employer–employee relationship gains value in itself. Non-continuity may not only be costly, but it also presents a risk, since it exposes the employer to unknowns on a regular basis. This presents an extra incentive to seek stable contracts with employees.

Wealthy elites in Mexico City can (and indeed do) vertically integrate their household employees. They may do so by hiring members of the same family in full-time employment. In this way, the direct costs and other externalities of hiring are reduced. On the one hand, employees are locked in employment and so the risks of default from them are reduced. On the other hand, employing many members of the same family will enhance the benefits of vertical integration by adding a further dimension to it. The process of finding new employees when necessary is simplified as they can be easily referred by members of the family already employed in the household. This also assures a certain form of control, since the family employed has incentives only to recommend 'good' members of their family, since a default by one of their members may mean punishment for all. There can also be mechanisms in place for employed families to punish and deal with possible defaulters within their ranks.

This is reminiscent of Fearon and Laitin's work on inter-ethnic cooperation (1996). In their paper, they suggest that cooperation among ethnic groups may ensue when in-group informal policing leads to defusing of potential escalating conflict with another group. Fear of conflict will lead members of a group to deal rapidly with their own problematic members. Fearon and Laitin call this *spiral equilibrium.* On the other hand, members of the other group (in our case employers) will ignore some minor transgression as they know that these will be dealt with by the employee group—something the authors call *in-group policing equilibria.* For this to work, the second group (employers) must know that transgressions against them will be dealt with internally. In the case of the types of employment that concern us, an employer may want to vertically integrate a family into their employment if he knows that any default (or possibility of it) will be effectively dealt with by the employee group/family. In practice, this means that, following Fearon and Laitin's logic (1996), members of a family would at the very least try to police and control misbehaviour by other members, as the cost of said misbehaviour may affect the whole family unit. This last mechanism works in favour of the employer, who has a further incentive to vertically integrate employment.

Vertical integration, however, requires resources that may not be available to all. Wealthy families with high disposable incomes may be able to retain the services of a number of people (of the same family or not), full-time for an indefinite period of time. In this context, cooperation and continuity are important and may have a higher value. Middle-class families and below, on the other hand, may not have the necessary resources to achieve vertical integration. They may only be able to hire one part-time person, for example. This increases the risk of their employees coming into contact with criminals or leaking information. It also means that the relationship may not be as continuous as it should be, as the rewards for cooperation are less attractive, which puts these families at further risk. This may partly explain (along with other factors such as crime-fighting policy) why there seems to be a trend in wealthy people ceasing to be the main victims of kidnapping and middle- and working-class individuals taking their place.

## Kidnapping in Mexico: Context and Class

Mexico today has very high crime rates. Even before the current War on Drugs, crime was a central issue on the political and social agendas. Mexico's weak rule of law and very unequal access to justice and redress has been extensively documented (Bailey 2014; Davis 2006; Magaloni and Zepeda 2004, to name but a few). This means that legal premises such as contract enforcement, prosecution, and other such public services are not fully offered by the State. Indeed, research has shown that only money and political power grant people access to these goods (Ochoa 2012). This is not an overstatement: recently, the issue of Mexico's weak rule of law has been a constant presence in the media, as many politicians—among them many State governors—have been implicated in large-scale corruption, with little or no consequence. The political and economic elites in Mexico enjoy the fruits of massive wealth and impunity, while most the population struggle with poverty, lack of services, and a legal system that does not support them. It is in this context, which can be described as an institutional vacuum, that the relationships described in this book take place.

This vacuum has resulted in a significant growth in informality; indeed, many economic activities take place outside the legal framework. Informality takes up a significant part of all economic activity in Mexico. Many contracts are verbal and transactions are paid in cash to avoid taxation. Mexico can fit into the context described by Dixit (2004) as one of 'lawlessness'. In this context, the government cannot, or will not, uphold the law (in terms of contract enforcement etc.) all the time. As described above, this seems to work to the detriment of the poor and disadvantaged, who lack government protection in many areas of their life.

While informal-sector employment has increased considerably in recent times, particularly in developing nations (Dibben and

Williams 2012; Jutting and Laiglesia 2009; Trebilcock 2005), it is important to point out that household work in Mexico has always been of an informal nature and has existed for a considerably long period of time, capable of being traced back to colonial times (Kellog 2005). Thus, it may not necessarily be linked to the more recent explosion in service sector informality, which began its enormous growth as developing economies developed in the post-Second World War era. Having said this, the growth in informality adds importance to the sets of mechanisms through which people seek to govern their relationships in an environment where the State does not provide this service in an egalitarian manner.

This context of lawlessness is especially favourable to kidnapping, and this crime has been the focus of research in the past: it has been analysed from the prevention perspective (Pires et al. 2014), and the effects of deterrence policies have also been explored. Other analyses explore kidnapping from historical (Ochoa 2012) and economic perspectives (DeTotto et al. 2015). There are a number of types of kidnapping, with variations in length of time, strategy used by the criminals, and other factors. In this book, I will only refer to extortive kidnapping (DeTotto et al. 2015; Jimenez Ornelas and Islas de Gonzales 2002): this refers to those cases in which the demand for the release of the victim is conditioned on a monetary payment, usually from the family of the victim. As exemplified in the second vignette in the Introduction, titled 'youth, interrupted', other forms of kidnapping do occur in Mexico, such as revenge kidnappings among drug cartels (most of which end in homicide). However, most of the kidnappings in Mexico City are of the economic/extortive kind. I will not refer to what is known as *express* kidnapping. This kind of crime is becoming increasingly popular, as petty criminals see a potentially secure source of income from this. The victim is selected seemingly at random and with no prior research into her or his wealth. Victims are normally taken as they enter their cars or get into taxis. They are then driven around the City for a few hours or more and are forced to withdraw as much money as possible from their bank cards or credit cards. They are also relieved of their jewels and any other goods they may have on them, such as mobile phones. Eventually, if all goes well, they are released when their captors are satisfied that they have taken as much as possible. The key differences between this and extortive kidnapping are that: (1) little research is carried out on the victim; and (2) the victim's family are not contacted for ransom.

Chapter 3 will explore in detail the genesis of the gangs which perpetrate extortive kidnappings in the city. They began as sophisticated, hierarchical gangs in the 1990s (made up many times of former law-enforcement agents), which were then dismantled by the government's policing efforts and the ability of wealthy individuals to protect themselves effectively. This opened the door to smaller, less sophisticated gangs who entered the kidnapping market, but whose technical shortcomings made them focus their efforts on the poor and middle-class sectors—people who have less opportunity to protect themselves effectively from kidnapping.

The War on Drugs has produced over 150,000 deaths and over 25,000 disappeared among increases in all types of crimes (Prado Veiras 2016). Over 250,000 people have been internally displaced. It is possible that some of the disappeared have been initially kidnapped as part of the hostilities among the government, drug cartels, and, more recently, self-defence groups. Kidnappings as part of the drug war are not discussed in this book because they operate under different dynamics and mechanisms (i.e. they are not carried out for ransom, but rather as a form of retaliation). There is even a word for these types of kidnappings: *levantón* (literally, 'pick-up'), which differentiates them from the kidnappings to which I refer in this book.

When I write about wealthy people in Mexico City, I refer to upper-middle- and upper-class individuals. In this sense, I refer to Goldthorpe and colleagues' characterization of social classes (1980), which can be relatively easily transposed to the Mexican case. A small elite class stands at the very top of the schema, consisting of the top earners and business owners. In this category, one finds Carlos Slim, the world's third wealthiest person who, in 2009, after the economic downturn, commanded a fortune of around US$35 billion according to *Forbes* magazine (2010). Goldthorpe's service class constitutes the top of the class structure (upper class). People in this group are usually in the service or tertiary industry as owners or higher paid employees in administrative or strategic positions. The income within this class varies greatly in Mexico from a minimum of around US $5,000 per month for, say, an entry-level executive, to many times that for the top earners. It is perhaps more telling that this sector of the population, the top 10 per cent of earners, own 36.4 per cent of the entire income available to Mexican households. On average, though, a household in this top 10 per cent will earn around US$5,000 per month (INEGI 2008).

The Mexican upper-middle class is composed mostly of white-collar workers (Goldthorpe et al. 1980) and averages an income of around US$2,000 per month (INEGI 2008). Incomes below this fall rapidly. For example, a household in the middle 10 per cent of the population averages around US$700 per month, while a working-class household of the lowest-earning 10 per cent will bring in less than US$200 per month. As is usually the case with averages, these have to be viewed with care. Mexico's high inequality means that average household incomes can be deceiving. Mexican society is so unequal that it is not uncommon to find at one end of the country levels of deprivation similar to those of the poorest nations and at the other end wealth and development beyond any developed Western nation. Within this context, this book explores how trusting relationships are managed in an environment of very scant State protection.

This chapter has set out the theoretical frame of reference for the upcoming chapters. Signaling theory helps us to understand how potential kidnapping victims make decisions based on trust when hiring employees to work in their households. In a context of very high crime rates and a weak rule of law, trust becomes central to most activities, if only to avoid victimization. Signaling allows us to explore how people manage risk in these kinds of environments. Vertical integration compliments our framework and provides a tool to understand other mechanisms used by employers to successfully protect themselves from crime. Ultimately, what this book seeks to accomplish is to provide an illustration of the mechanisms people use in their interactions with others to protect themselves from crime. Before we delve into these relationships, the next chapter will illustrate the history of crime in Mexico, linking the country's political economy to the advent of one of the harshest and longest-lasting crime waves the country has ever seen, which included a sharp increase in kidnapping. Then, in Chapter 3, the book will detail the evolution of kidnapping from its political beginnings in the 1960s and 1970s to its modern version as an (at times petty) economic crime.

# 2

# Crime, Kidnapping, and Liberalization in Mexico in the Late Twentieth and Early Twenty-First Centuries (1994–2015)

The last three decades have seen profound changes in Mexico. Its social composition, demography, and economy are all radically different from what they were even two decades ago. During this time, crime has also evolved in many different ways. Unfortunately, it has become more common and now affects a significant amount of the population. In this chapter, I will set the context for the core of this book. I will explain how the process of democratization and liberalization that took place in Mexico from the late 1980s had the non-intended consequence of higher crime rates and heightened social volatility that we see today. The rise of kidnapping (and of most types of crime) since the mid-1990s is intimately tied to political economic processes that were gripping the country and the Latin American region at the time. They are in fact, as this chapter will show, a by-product of deep economic and political changes. This is the main thrust behind this chapter. It aims to provide the reader with a solid context on which to situate the analyses of kidnapping and trust provided later in this book.

There is a clear link between crime and violence and a level of socioeconomic development (see, among others, Cotte Poveda 2011; Lagrange 2003; Parsley 2001; Soares 2004), and this is certainly found in Mexico. During a period of around twenty-five years, the country transformed from an authoritarian political system based around one-party rule to an imperfect democracy and from a closed, import-substituting economic model to one that embraced deregulation and free-market reforms in tune with

Intimate Crimes: Kidnapping, Gangs and Trust in Mexico City. First Edition. Rolando Ochoa © Rolando Ochoa 2019. Published in 2019 by Oxford University Press

the near-global adoption of the neo-liberal model in the 1980s. This was, and still is, a long process fraught with crises, contestation, and protest that mostly emanated from sectors of the population which 'lost out' during this time of reform, such as indigenous peoples (Trejo 2012) and the rural and urban poor.

During this process, crime saw an increase due to not only the soaring inequality brought about by liberalization, but also the loss of control over the underworld established by the political elite under authoritarianism. The political party Partido Revolucionario Institucional or PRI (Institutional Revolutionary Party, in English) ruled Mexico—at least at the federal level—from 1929 to 2000. It was created by revolutionary leaders as a way to 'institutionalize' the country after years of revolutionary bloodshed.[1] In its heyday, the PRI controlled much of the Mexican political economy through networks of patronage, repression, and corruption and the establishment of sub-national authoritarian regimes sympathetic to the regime. The processes of state formation in Mexico, while important to the narrative presented herein, have been thoroughly and much more deeply described and analysed elsewhere, from many different perspectives, by Cordova (1972), Garrido (1991), Knight (1985; 1990a), and Padilla (2008), among others.

## The Transition to a Market Economy

In the mid-1980s, Mexico was at the gates of change the likes of which had not been witnessed since the Revolution (1910–21). In the next quarter century, the country would become almost unrecognizable, its social structure changing momentously. Before this time, Mexico had been a somewhat prosperous nation, exploiting its resource wealth, which included significant oil reserves and mineral deposits. Mexico is the world's largest producer of silver and one of the top providers of copper, gold, and zinc. As a result of this commodity abundance, Mexico achieved stable and significant growth. The country's GDP grew by 2.9 per cent per annum in the 1930s and jumped to 7.0 per cent in the 1960s, before levelling off at 5.5 per cent in the 1970s (Looney 1985: 3).

[1] Its first two inceptions were known as the National Revolutionary Party (PNR, in Spanish, 1929–38) and the Party of the Mexican Revolution (PRM, in Spanish, 1938–46).

During this time, the country also relied on an inward-looking Import Substitution Industrialising (ISI) scheme as its model of economic development. Quotas on imports were implemented, local industries were heavily subsidized—if not outright owned—by the state, and centralized planning based on oil prices was common. ISI as a model of development was originally set up to allow the country to industrialize and thus build a solid economic base. However, this over-protection resulted in a rapidly growing but highly inefficient national industry sector, which in turn exacerbated regional inequalities within the country (Sánchez-Reaza and Rodríguez-Pose 2002). Another side-effect of this process was the decimation of the rural sector in Mexico, which saw investment and production fall as industry received the favours of government support (Looney 1985). Support for national industries was heavily reliant on income generated by borrowing money on high oil prices.

The collapse of oil prices in the early 1980s, coupled with chronic mismanagement and corruption, led to a major financial and debt crisis in 1982, which sank Mexico into one of its deepest recessions to date. During this time, Mexico suffered a very rapid decline in international reserves, which forced the government to devalue the local currency (the Peso) against the US dollar. Eventually, the Peso would lose 50 per cent of its value. This in turn triggered further capital flight, leaving the country literally cashless. In September 1982, the Mexican government advised their creditors that the country would be unable to service its debt, which amounted to around US $80 billion, including private and public sector debt (Buffie & Krause 1989). The recipe of borrowing against oil revenue had finally become undone. Mexico then received close to US $3.5 billion in immediate cash loans to relieve pressure. In addition, the country would receive further economic support from the International Monetary Fund to the tune of US $ 3.8 billion, among other support programmes (Barkbu et al. 2011). A key component of this support package, and a central factor in what would happen in the country in the future, was that the support was tied to a commitment from the Mexican government to enact a series of free market reforms which were already being promoted by institutions such as the IMF.

In 1986, Mexico became a member of the Global Agreement on Tariffs and Trade, a first step in what would become a wave of liberalizing moves as the country embraced the free market.

At the time, the effects of the 1982 crisis were still being felt and the economy had not yet recovered from the financial upheaval (Sánchez-Reaza and Rodríguez-Pose 2002). However, the days of ISI were numbered. As the country recovered from the debt crisis, it became clear that a new approach to economic development would become necessary.

The process of liberalization in Mexico would reach a high point when in 1994 Mexico signed the North American Free Trade Agreement (NAFTA) with Canada and the United States. This would create one of the largest free-trade economic zones in the world, comprising close to 400 million people. The government of the day pushed this trade deal as the gateway for Mexico to finally deliver on its economic promise and resolve its poverty issues. NAFTA came into effect on 1 January 1995.

Unfortunately—and perhaps predictably—the start of the trade agreement was beset with difficulties. On the same day it came into effect, the Zapatista Army for National Liberation (EZLN in Spanish) declared war on the government in the southern state of Chiapas. Headed by the charismatic Subcomandante Marcos, the EZLN uprising was the result of decades of ethnic mobilization in Mexico. The demands of these groups ranged from the political to the economic and ethnic (Trejo 2012) and put the spotlight on the plight of indigenous Mexicans, who account for the most disenfranchised and poorest populations in the country, and make up around 10 per cent of the total population. As Jung (2003: 4) has argued, the issue of identity is a 'condition for participation in a global political dialogue' and the Zapatista movement was, thorough its ethnic demands (constitutional recognition and autonomy), looking to be finally included in a dialogue from which it was barred for many decades, or indeed centuries.

The Chiapas uprising sent shockwaves through the political establishment, whose reaction was mostly repressive, but at times they responded to the EZLN's demands (e.g. by incorporating indigenous rights in the constitution and recognizing the indigenous peoples of Mexico as the foundational elements of the nation). This 'inclusion' would mostly remain on paper and, twenty years after the uprising, many of the grievances put forward by the EZLN remain; impunity, poverty, repression, and deprivation are common in indigenous areas of Mexico and it is no coincidence that some of the poorest areas of the country also have the highest concentration of indigenous inhabitants. In 2012

(CONEVAL 2012 poverty among indigenous people (76.8 per cent) was almost twice as high as for the rest of the population (43 per cent); extreme poverty was almost five times higher (38 versus 7.9 per cent).

The start of NAFTA was overshadowed by yet another economic crisis later referred to as the Tequila crisis of 1995. The reasons for the crisis are varied and have been extensively researched. The main explanations for the collapse of the Mexican economy in late 1994 and the early days of 1995 are, among others, an overvalued currency and deficit, and a speculation-fuelled payment crisis capped with a self-fulfilling panic which drained national reserves (Lustig 1995; Sachs et al. 1996). The results of the crisis were in many ways catastrophic and raised 'a number of questions regarding the sustainability—and even the merits—o market oriented reforms in Latin America and other regions' (Edwards 1998: 1). Despite complying with neoliberal reform agendas (deregulation, privatization, stabilization, and a somewhat general and at times imposed consensus on the benefits of the reforms), the 'catastrophic' (Calvo and Mendoza 1996: 1) crisis brought the economy to its knees. Faced with an overvalued currency, low reserves, and a lack of transparency, in late December 1994, the government decided to devalue the Peso by as much as 15 per cent.

Faced with this and very little in the way of further information or supporting programs, investors took their money out of the country in a panic, shearing US $4 billion in just one day from the Mexican Central Bank (Edwards 1998: 28). In this situation, Mexico was at a heightened risk of defaulting on rapidly maturing debt. It was at this time that the US government, the World Bank, and the International Monetary Fund sprang into action again, making close to US $40 billion in credit lines available to solve the country's solvency problem (Edwards 1998). This quick influx of cash allowed the country to avert what would have been an even more disastrous (and potentially international) economic crisis. Eventually, the country would begin a slow road to recovery and regain growth and some macroeconomic stability.

However, this somewhat quick recovery did not have the results originally expected. While overall poverty and extreme poverty have seen reductions, these have been small. For example, in 2012, with regard to income, 52.3 per cent of Mexicans were considered to be poor. That same measure in 1992 was 53.1 per cent, which only amounts to a reduction of less than one percentage point. In 2012, 45.5 per cent of the population was classified as poor when using a compound measure which includes access to food, education, and income (CONEVAL 2014b). Moreover, inequality has continued to be a serious problem. The country's GINI coefficient (used to measure the levels of income inequality, where zero is perfect equality) has been only marginally reduced from 0.562 in 1990 to 0.500 in 2012 (CONEVAL 2014b).

The 1994 Zapatista uprising and the 1995 Peso crisis put in stark contrast many of the contradictions of modern Mexico: a country which was (and is today) attempting to insert itself into the global markets and play a solid international role, while at the same time facing important internal issues. These would evolve over the next three decades from the merely economic to a host of social issues related to crime, drug trafficking, corruption, and a weak rule of law, among other issues, which still plague the country today. Kidnapping is but one of many manifestations of these issues. How did crime behave during this period?

## Crime in an Open Market

The economic crisis of 1995 detonated an increase in overall crime rates and began what would eventually become the most significant crime wave Mexico has ever seen—a wave that continues in many different forms today. As will be explained in later chapters, it is at this time when kidnapping made the transition from a rare (and sometimes politically motivated) crime to a much more common and economically oriented activity (Ochoa 2012). The period from 1995 to 2006 would see a steady escalation in the levels of kidnapping and other crimes all over the country. Interestingly, homicide actually decreased during the 1990s and early 2000s; it then exhibited explosive growth (Zepeda 2004) at around the same time that kidnapping was on the increase.

The financial crisis of 1985 not only exacerbated economic disparities, but also signalled an end to what had been, until then, a sort of marriage of convenience between organized crime and the government. It has been argued that up until the late 1990s and certainly not after 2000, the government had 'predictable' (Campbell 2009) relationships—based on corruption—with ever-expanding criminal organizations. It was precisely this close relationship that allowed what was then a powerful central government to control criminal activity and provide a certain peace. The 1995 crisis and the ongoing political processes of democratization signalled a change in these relationships, as the government no longer had the resources, both economic and political, to maintain them.

Mexico's slow process of democratization played a part in this (Morris 2009. Mexico had been for the better part of the nineteenth and twentieth centuries a country controlled by a hegemonic party, the PRI, which ruled Mexico under a form of authoritarianism described as 'the perfect dictatorship' by author Mario Vargas Llosa and 'at once tragic and brilliant: Tragic in that it forces citizens to accept massive corruption, low levels of government service, and highly inefficient policies; brilliant in that it forces citizens not only to accept these features, but to play their role in maintaining the system' (Diaz-Cayeros et al. 2000: 3). The PRI exercised fiscal and political control with the sole goal of self-perpetuation, which meant scant delivery of public goods, very high levels of corruption, and impaired development as Diaz-Cayeros and colleagues state:

> In short, the PRI's principal goal of party maintenance leads it to harness the resources of the Mexican state for partisan, electoral purposes. Economic development conflicts with this goal: funds targeted to win elections crowd out funds for economic development; and because the PRI draws its greatest strength from poor areas, fostering growth hurts the PRI. (2000: 55)

This form of governance not only made radical power-grabbing moves (such as coups etc.) unnecessary, but it also gave off an aura of stability to the outside world which was not reflective of the reality inside the country. However, democratization moved painstakingly forward, the opposition gathered strength, and an increasing number of local governments were won by parties other than the PRI. Thus, as the party weakened its death-grip on the political process, it also loosened its control of the underworld (Morris 2012) and of its own forces of law and order, which were then able to act independently of the government and also to compete with each other for control of illicit markets. This allowed criminal organizations to become stronger and eventually challenge the government's control over them. This was made easier by high levels of corruption. This situation has been called Mexico's 'security trap' (Bailey 2014). Lack of monetary resources in policing institutions meant that many of its members saw in kidnapping a secure way to increase their incomes with little risk of being caught due to a very weak rule of law.

The process of democratization came to an important climax in 2000 when, for the first time in Mexico's modern history, a party other than the PRI won a presidential election. Vicente Fox of the right-of-centre Partido Acción Nacional—National Action Party—(PAN) came to the presidency among record participation and on an agenda which sought to consolidate Mexico's democracy and put an end to PRI hegemony. This moment was a significant turning point for Mexico and a remarkable result of the democratization process which had been taking place for many decades. Rightfully, Mexicans were then hopeful for the future, having witnessed the possibilities of democratic participation. Fox promised much during his campaign and expectations were high. Economic growth was on his agenda and, following his party's intentions, he sought to further integrate Mexico into the international economy. Crime was already a concern for the population and he also made promises to tackle this. The PRI's exit from the height of federal power sent shockwaves through the party's state and local structures, and the party lost further control. These newfound openings allowed organized crime groups and other criminals to operate autonomously, 'ending their subordination to the government' (O'Neil 2009). The Fox administration was characterized by the consolidation of many new organized crime groups. This was the result of Fox's policy to destroy old and well-established criminal organizations such as the Juarez and Tijuana cartels. This brought about a fragmentation and dispersion of the cartel members, who then coalesced into new groups (Abadynski 2000; Bagley 2012). During this period, Mexico also experienced an increase in general crime rates even though homicide was at the time showing a downward trend which would reverse by the end of his tenure (Zepeda 2004). It has been argued that this was due to the sudden weakening of the PRI's control over criminal activities in the country, which came as a result of their waning political and economic power (Ochoa 2012), and their control over vast networks of corruption and organized crime (Shelley 2001).

The situation deteriorated throughout the Fox administration; many states in the country fell into cycles of drug-trafficking-related violence, including the western state of Michoacán, which was the scene of terrible conflict between drug cartels. The situation would only worsen in coming years. Graph 2.1 shows the behaviour of homicide since 2000. Most common forms of crime such as robbery, assault, and theft also increased, as shown in Graph 2.2.

**Graph 2.1 Homicide in Mexico 2000–2017 per 100,000 People (INEGI 2018)**

Note: All INEGI data is of crimes *reported* to local authorities. It is safe to expect, given the numbers mentioned regarding non-reporting, that actual figures for all crimes are much higher.

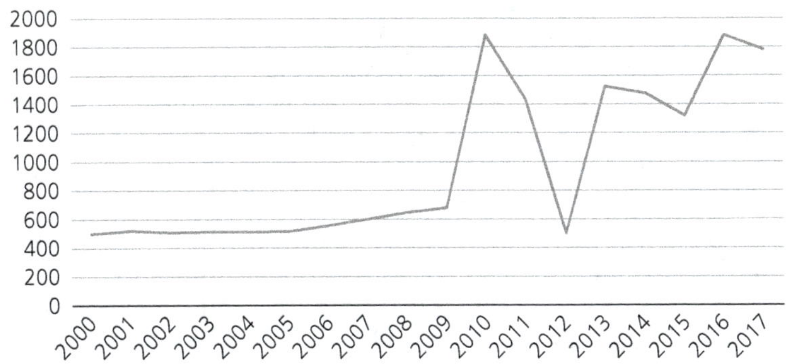


**Graph 2.2 Theft in Mexico 2000–2017 per 100,000 People (INEGI 2018)**

## The War on Drugs

In 2006, the incumbent PAN won the presidency for the second time, defeating a disarrayed opposition and a fledging PRI candidate whose claim to fame was not only his humiliating defeat at the ballots and allegations of corruption when governor of the southern state of Tabasco, but also his well-documented cheating during the Berlin marathon, when he stopped after running a few kilometres, then drove to the finish line to cross it, arms held high. Felipe Calderón, the PAN candidate, came into office in December and soon after began what would become the flagship, for better or worse, of his administration. By then, crime and particularly organized crime had become the key issue for the electorate. Polls began showing that Mexicans were then more concerned about safety and security than they were about jobs or the economy. The National Institute of Statistics and Geography, a government institute, has carried out victimization surveys on this topic every year since 2011. Since then, Mexicans have consistently stated that security is the greatest challenge in their state or region (INEGI 2017). In the last iteration of the survey in 2017, the number of Mexicans reporting that security was their main concern stood at 61 per cent. Clearly, the state had been unable or unwilling to provide what is one of the cornerstones of any society, namely the safety of people's personal integrity and property. By even the most libertarian of definitions of the state, public safety and legal certainty are still key for a successful society, and at this point it was becoming clear to many Mexicans that they had neither.

President Calderón pledged to fight this situation, and fight it he did. He almost immediately commanded the army first to take control of what was a rapidly deteriorating situation in his home state of Michoacán, where violence had escalated and order was deteriorating as local gangs fought for control of drug-trafficking routes. Over 7,000 soldiers descended upon the state. The situation there would worsen to the point where, in 2008, in the central plaza of the state capital Morelia, unidentified men threw grenades into a crowd celebrating Mexican Independence Day, killing eight civilians and wounding over 100. This was the first time that organized crime had targeted civilians in such an explicit manner and many saw this as a signal to the government of their power and willingness to use violence to defend their positions and territory. The carnage in Michoacán was, unfortunately, a sign of things to come. The first military incursion into Michoacán would be the beginning of a period of violence which is ongoing. The central strategy of the Calderón government was to confront, in military fashion, the cartels which had established themselves during the Fox administration. Both the army and the navy were called upon and they became the principal enforcers of Calderón's government drug policy. Large swathes of Mexican territory became militarized in a way that had not been seen since the early days of the 1994 Zapatista insurgence. Spending in the criminal justice system and the military soared. Police corporations and the military at times almost doubled their personnel numbers and public security spending grew 'five times faster under Calderón than it had under Fox' (Morris 2012: 37).

Corruption only added an extra layer of complication to a situation which was already very difficult. It has been well documented that many drug cartels are staffed by former or acting members of the security forces. Indeed, many of the original kidnapping gangs discussed in the Chapter 3 also began their careers in the police (Ochoa 2012). It has been documented that the infamous cartel *Los Zetas* (The 'Zs') started out as a Special Forces army corps before they defected and transferred their skills to organized crime. The Zetas are known to be keen on a diversified income stream, which includes people trafficking and kidnapping. The lines between law enforcement and criminal activity have always been blurred in Mexico and as the relationships between crime and government agents were increasingly documented, it became clear that they were not only circumscribed to the local, municipal level, but went all the way to the very top of the political pyramid.

In 2008, a former director of the Specialized Prosecutor in Organised Crime Investigation (Subprocuraduría Especializada en Investigación de Delincuencia Organizada or SEIDO, in Spanish), Noe Ramirez, was arrested for allegedly receiving up to US $450,000 from drug cartels in exchange for protection. Three of his subordinates admitted to being in the cartel's pockets and went into witness protection. Ramirez was freed in 2012 citing 'lack of evidence'. These stories are not uncommon and make up a substantial part of the ethos of corruption in Mexico. Fieldwork conversations with government officials carried out as far back as 2008 confirmed that Calderón's government estimated that up to 90 per cent of municipal governments were infiltrated by organized crime. Unfortunately, as mentioned above, corruption has been built into the narrative of the Mexican State since its inception. Police corporations were designed initially not as a tool to deliver a public good, but as a means of political control (Ochoa 2012). In this context, it is actually unsurprising that the insecurity situation has deteriorated and that, despite the preoccupations of ordinary citizens, the government has been unable to deliver this most basic good.

Law-enforcement institutions have been notoriously difficult to reform. A 2008 law aimed at implementing oral trials (leaving behind the paper-based, accusatory system of old), ridding the prosecutors and courts of useless procedural burden, and giving them actual capacity to investigate crimes has shown only a fraction of potential results and remains implemented in only a minority of courts. Technical capacity remains a huge challenge. Prosecutors and their staff are notoriously undertrained, often lacking the basic capacity to investigate the simplest of crimes.

Research I carried out in 2008 at the prosecutors' offices of one of Mexico City's most prosperous districts revealed shocking situations.[2] Prosecutors in Mexico follow a very tight paper-based script that tells them what to do when a crime is committed. This is literally a step-by-step set of rigid instructions (or *diligencias*, diligences). Failure to comply to the letter can cause serious trouble for the prosecutors. The result of this is that not much happens away from a desk and there is little investigation (police basically choose when to do this based on their own interest), resulting in most convicted criminals being both petty and always caught red-handed. As a junior prosecutor confessed, if a case does not arrive on her desk with a person already detained, it goes straight 'into the file' (a box that eventually ends up in a warehouse). There were at the time only two certified forensic experts on locks (who were able to determine and certify if a lock had been forced etc.) in the entire city—a city of 8 million people. A prosecutor spoke of how they had to wait sometimes for days or weeks for one of

[2] I was a participant in a research project investigating practices within the prosecutors' offices in Mexico City. The project was organized by the Centre for Economic Education and Research (Centro de Investigación y Docencia Económicas or CIDE, in Spanish). I am grateful for being able to participate in this project.

these experts to work on one of their cases. When they did get hold of them, they had to pay for their transport and food, and sometimes give them cash.

In the same prosecutor's office, police officers had to pay for the privilege to use a patrol, motorcycle, or Jeep,[3] as well as for gas and to fix the vehicles when they broke down, which was often. Corruption is also a problem in prosecutors' offices. . One of the most revealing experiences there came from witnessing a junior and a senior prosecutor debating (in front of the researcher) how they would make a case of robbery stick by creating false charges and producing fake witnesses to make sure the accused would be convicted. They planned to fabricate assault charges in the case of a petty robbery of a grocery store, and would use a member of staff to sign in as a witness to the fake assault. The same senior prosecutor spoke of his anger at 'the human rights people' who were always on his case and did not let him 'do his job'. To reiterate, this was a prosecutor's office in one of Mexico City's most economically developed districts. It is not difficult to imagine what may happen in other municipalities or districts.

The legacy of Calderón's drug war has been terrible by any measure, and has resulted in the deaths and disappearance of over 200,000 and 25,000 people, respectively. A topic which has not received as much attention is forced migration and displacement. Estimates state that close to 250,000 people have been internally displaced by the drug conflict, as entire towns are emptied when people escape the violence brought by the cartels. A report released in 2016 (Consejo Pro Defensa del Migrante/American Friends Service Committee (CPDM/AFSC). 2016) states that, at the northern border, NGOs are facing a changing migration environment. Historically, individuals who made their way to the border were leaving their homes in search of economic opportunity. Today, most of the migrants arriving at the northern border (with the United States) are fleeing because of violence. The same report states that in a survey of new arrivals at a well-known shelter, 73 per cent of those polled said their reason for leaving was violence. This violence also has an important gender perspective as, tellingly, 79 per cent of new arrivals at the shelters are women (CPDM/AFSC2016).

[3] The prices were set by the desirability of the vehicle, with Jeeps commanding the highest prices.

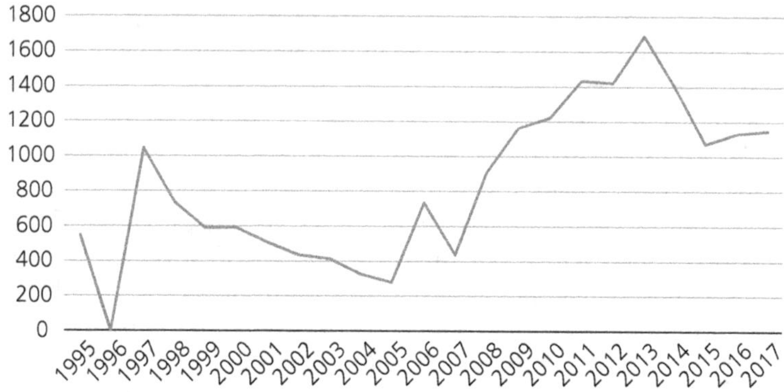


**Graph 2.3 Kidnapping in Mexico, 2000–2017 (SESNP 2018)**

As can be clearly seen in Graph 2.1, homicide rates exploded after 2006 and have seen a minor drop in 2012. 2013–14 figures tentatively show another drop, but in informal conversations with people familiar with the figures, there seems to be a growing concern that these figures have been 'cuchareadas' ('skimmed') to reflect lower than actual figures. The years 2015 and 2016 saw an increase in the overall homicide rate, as clashes between government forces and cartels intensified in many regions of the country, and overall crime rates also increased, particularly in urban areas (Morfin et al. 2016).

The impact of the War on Drugs on other kinds of crime has yet to be fully researched, but evidence suggests that they have been displaced as cartels and other criminal gangs move into kidnapping, extortion, and other illicit activities to supplement their income (Enamorado et al. 2016; Rios 2013). This can be seen as a direct effect of the War on Drugs, which has increased the cost of drug trafficking, but has not closed the door on other illicit activities. The fact that Mexico has a very weak rule of law means that for some criminal groups it is easy to move from one crime to another without incurring significant costs, and this may explain why, after an initial decrease in the early 2000s, there has been yet another increase in kidnapping from around 2006, as can be seen in Graph 2.3. This is related to the fact that, as Chapter 3 will explain, in the early 2000s, the government—under pressure from wealthy communities—made fighting kidnapping gangs a top priority. This led to smaller, less professional gangs taking their place, which then contributed to the mid-2000s increase.

## Mexico Today: A State in Crisis

Mexico's weak rule of law, which allows for corruption to thrive and impunity to reign, is a key issue that enables us to understand the current situation. The historical issues of impunity, corruption, conflict of interest, and crime did not magically materialize. They are the product of historical institutional and political arrangements which are deeply engrained within the state. These processes have had nefarious results. In Mexico, around 90 per cent of crimes are never reported to the authorities according to a 2017 victimization survey (INEGI 2017). In terms of kidnapping, estimates suggest that only around 30 per cent of these incidents are reported (Mexico Evalua 2010). There are a few reasons why this is so; surveys have revealed that the main reason people do not report crimes is because of a deep distrust of the criminal justice system, which leads them to believe (with good reason) that nothing will come out of the process of disclosing a crime. A 2011 survey from Latinobarometro[4] shows that 45.3 per cent of people do not trust the police *at all* and 35 per cent have *very little* trust in the same establishment. Thus, in total, this suggests that almost 80 per cent of Mexicans have little or no trust in the police. The same survey states that close to 70 per cent of those polled have little or no trust in the government in general; close to that same percentage respond that they trust the judiciary very little or not at all. Mexicans exhibit a high level of distrust not only in their justice institutions, but also in the government in general. At the time of writing in 2016, the federal administration commanded approval rates of under 20 per cent—the lowest rates since recording began in the mid-1990s. This is reflected well in the way in which citizens react when a crime is committed against them, which is normally to ignore it, and try to move on. The high rates of non-reporting illustrate this well. One recent study shows that up to 93.6 per cent of crimes in Mexico are never reported (ENVIPE 2017). This becomes much more shocking when we know that 32.4 per cent of Mexican households contain at least one crime victim (INEGI 2012). When crimes are reported, the story does not change

[4] The Latinobarometro survey is carried out each year. It has representative samples of adults in eighteen Latin American countries. The total sample size is approximately $N = 20{,}000$.

much: 97 per cent of serious crimes (homicides, assaults, kidnappings) result in no conviction (Acosta 2011). This is due in part to the lack of capacity in the criminal justice system (CJS) to investigate serious crimes. This, Acosta argues, generates misguided incentives to convict petty criminals so that the CJS is seen as doing its job. In the past, judges were allocated sentencing quotas, which fuelled these practices. This results in a very high conviction rate of petty crimes, resulting in jails being populated with small-time criminals, while the 'big fish' are never caught.

During the same fieldwork at the prosecutor's office mentioned above, I came into contact with a person who had been accused of theft. At the time, he was being held in a small closet in the prosecutor's office basement where those recently arrested were confined due to lack of space. The entrance to the closet was blocked by an old desk. The closet was dank, full of old, mouldy papers, and measured roughly 1 by 1.5 metres in size. About four people were being held in there at the time. This individual drove a delivery truck for a fast-food company and on one delivery he had taken a packet of biscuits which, he argued, were broken and would have to be thrown away. He was observed doing this by a manager, who called the police. He was promptly arrested and charged. When I met him, he had been under arrest for around twenty-four hours and had not yet seen a lawyer[5] or had any food. Surveys of incarcerated individuals (Bergman et al. 2002, 2005b, 2009; Perez Correa et al. 2012) show that, in many cases, people are convicted without ever speaking to a judge (up to 75 per cent of respondents) or having competent legal advice (up to 51 per cent claimed not to have had legal advice before their trials)—a clear violation of their human rights and the basic principles of criminal justice. This individual had called his boss at work who had promised to show up to help, but never did. He readily admitted to taking the goods, but said he was otherwise clean and had never committed a crime. When asked, one of the officers working on the 'case' simply stated that the most likely outcome would be that the accused would go to jail for two or three years. This case exemplifies the unfairness and many of the fundamental injustices and malpractices of the Mexican justice system.

[5] Mexican law states that police can detain a person for forty-eight hours before they charge him or her. If no charges are filed, the person is released. As this case shows, though, once arrested, the rates of conviction are very high.

This environment of impunity and perverse administration of justice has changed little over the last thirty years and is today one of the key challenges facing the country. Perceptions of insecurity confirm this grim reality. People in Mexico do not feel safe, nor do they enjoy the freedom that safety affords or the certainty that can be achieved with a strong rule of law. In Mexico City, 85 per cent of people report not feeling safe living there (ICESI 2007). Moreover, nationwide, 67 per cent report having changed their habits and activities due to feelings of fear and insecurity (Jaime et al. 2010). The situation in Mexico today, with regard to the rule of law, crime, and even kidnapping, is not very hopeful. After the initial seven years of the War on Drugs unleashed by President Calderón, little in the way of change or achieving peace the country has occurred. The levels of violence experienced by Mexicans in recent years have traumatized society and generated an environment of distrust.

## The New PRI

In 2012, Enrique Peña Nieto of the PRI was elected to the presidency. After twelve years in opposition, the PRI had managed to produce a top candidate. Peña Nieto was groomed since his days as a governor of the state of Mexico, a large industrial state, politically vital and controlled historically by the PRI. His youth and 'good looks' made him an ideal candidate for the media. He was also married to a popular *telenovela* actress. Indeed, he was constantly criticized for being a 'product' without much depth, and more suited to TV. His candidature rested heavily on a promise to tackle insecurity and make safety a principal goal. It also brought back memories of the relative peace under the PRI of the past, a time that many had begun to wish for. He toured the nation, making statements and signing symbolic promises to deliver security and change the course of the War on Drugs. Peña Nieto won largely on this platform and as a result of the population's general dissatisfaction with the incumbent PAN and their extremely unpopular war.

Unfortunately, things did not go as planned: the situation deteriorated soon after the election. During his first two years in office, Peña's presidency became characterized by opacity (his office, unlike that of his predecessor, stopped reporting homicides related to organized crime) and a general continuity of Calderon's reliance on force to deal with crime. His administration's key policy during the campaign was the creation of a centralized *gendarmerie* (a military-style police force) to deal with organized crime instead of the military. The initiative never took off and was mired in conflict as both military and civilian forces fought for its control. It was seen as a waste of money: there already existed a unified Federal Police Force. The strategy was soon abandoned in its original form. Today, the Gendarmeria Nacional has become an appendage of the Federal Police Force, with unclear mandates. The unravelling of what was the government's flagship idea for combating crime was a clear sign of the Peña government's lack of impetus and ideas regarding security. Conversely, Peña's administration put all its weight and influence behind passing a series of economic reforms—mostly aimed at opening the oil industry and other areas of the economy to foreign capital.

To the outside world, these latter reforms gave Peña's government an aura of international credibility, which those in power were very happy to enjoy. Thus, Mexico continued its progression towards liberalization and a free market economy, a process which by then had been in place for three decades. At the time, hopes were very high, especially abroad, about the new presidency's potential. Peña seemed to do no wrong and evidently enjoyed the full support of the US government, with President Barak Obama referring to him as his 'amigo'. *TIME Magazine* gave Peña Nieto the cover of their 24 February 2014 issue, with the headline 'Saving Mexico'. The response to this attention and validation within Mexico itself was less enthusiastic. By this point, it was becoming clear to many that the president was more interested in pushing his economic agenda than he was in delivering the much-promised security. Exactly why the government gave such scant attention to what was clearly a priority for everyone in the country remains somewhat of a mystery, and is likely a central cause of the PRI's humiliating defeat in the 2018 presidential elections.

The urgency with which the government pursued economic reforms was never seen in the security agenda. Perhaps there was a misguided belief among the higher echelons of government that economic reform would bring about the holistic change needed—a sort of trickle-down effect—much in the way that there had previously been a sort of blind faith in the Washington Consensus, as described by Naim (2000).

The security situation seemed to unravel further when, in 26 September 2014, forty-three students at a teachers' college in the town of Ayotzinapa in the south-western state of Guerrero were abducted by police and disappeared. To this day, their remains have not been found. The students had gathered together in their municipality of Iguala for a funding drive—part of a cycle of protests around the commemoration of the infamous 1968 student massacre in Mexico City. What happened next is contested and very much depends on whose version of the facts we believe. It has been argued that the students' activities were allegedly disturbing an official act headed by the mayor's wife. They were confronted by police a number of times, shots were fired, and six people died at the scene—some of whom were passers-by, like the taxi driver who just happened to be there at the time the protest was taking place. After the altercation, local police officers were seen bundling students into patrol cars and other police vehicles. This was the last time anyone saw them. In total, forty-three students—all aspiring rural teachers around 20 years of age—were taken. One student's dead body later appeared on the street, his face skinned and his eyes removed.

What was relatively new about this episode was the open, brutal, and cynical targeting of civilians by uniformed members of the police force. It is known that a number of these institutions in Mexico have been co-opted or infiltrated by organized crime. Through fear and threats or money, criminal groups have managed to infiltrate local governments in many regions. In the case of Iguala, it has been argued that the police acted on orders from the mayor, whose wife was a known 'operator' for one of the local criminal gangs: *Guerreros Unidos* (United Warriors, in English). They allegedly handed the students over to said gang and the students were subsequently murdered. Since then, the picture of a region not only captured but completely controlled by organized crime has become clearer. The Iguala police chief was allegedly receiving up to US $53,000 per month from organized crime. The mayor's wife was related to key cartel members, some of them already deceased.

Over a month later, on 8 October, the Federal Prosecutor announced that the students' remains had been found, pending DNA testing, burnt and disposed of in plastic bags in a river near a rubbish dump. Families of the students have voiced their lack of trust in the finding and the government itself. Some forty arrests were made among the police force and gang members, as well as the mayor and his wife. The governor of Guerrero went on administrative leave. International organizations, including the Organization of American States, Amnesty International, and the United Nations, have voiced their concern over the situation. Under such pressure, the government brought over a team of highly skilled Argentine forensic experts to investigate. When the Argentine team began questioning the official version of events, they were invited to leave the country immediately after presenting their final report, which was largely ignored by the Mexican government. In it, the forensic team hinted at the involvement of the military in the disappearance and questioned whether the bodies found in the tip actually belonged to the students. To this day, there is no agreement on what actually happened, and most people do not believe the official story.

The federal government's response to the disappearances, much like in its authoritarian past, was slow and apathetic. Eleven days passed after 26 September 2014 before the president even mentioned the students (some critics pointed out that it took him 10 minutes to express his sadness at the death of a famous Mexican comedian). This gave the impression that he had more important issues to worry about, such as pursuing his economic agenda. At the time of writing, he has yet to visit Iguala.

The response brought about memories of the 1985 earthquake, which killed thousands in Mexico City and left large sections of the City in ruins. At the time, the response of the government was so slow that it gave rise to a veritable army of volunteers who, with private means, rescued survivors, collected and distributed medication, food, and other basic goods, and ran shelters. After this, a new generation of urban social organizations was born, mostly out of the need to pressurize the government for support after the earthquake, but which would develop into a solid, pro-democracy movement. The earthquake has been described as one of the key moments in Mexico's democratization, when the population realized their own power and potential for organization (Hiskey 2012).[6]

[6] On 19 September 2018, another earthquake shook the City and other states, which caused close to 400 deaths and left nearly 250,000 people homeless, among other significant damages. Once again, civil society was seen rescuing people from the rubble, organizing shelters, and running food distribution centres. The government has in turn been accused of misusing reconstruction funds. Some things, it seems, don't change.

Back in 2014, the Federal Prosecutor further enraged people when at the press conference announcing that the remains of the students had been found, he cut off questions from the assembled press by waving his hands and stating 'ya me cansé' ('I am tired'). Parents of the students were present at the conference. This was taken up very quickly by civil society (the hashtag #yamecansé was born) to level harsh criticisms against the government. This kind of detachment only reinforced the general perception that the government simply did not care about these issues.

Beyond the PR disaster that was the government response, there was also evidence of something that has been known to researchers of the Mexican justice system for a long time. Mexico lacks the capacity to investigate even the most salient and terrible crimes. Forensics in this case had to be carried out by an Argentine team. DNA tests had to be completed in Austria. Most of the prosecutor's case was constructed on the basis of confessions from alleged killers. In a country where the rule of law is so weak and due process is routinely disregarded, it is wise to take these 'confessions' with a pinch of salt. It is not unusual for police and prosecutors to extract confessions under duress from alleged perpetrators, hence their apparent dislike for human rights, as expressed by a prosecutor interviewed in 2008.

The Ayotzinapa/Iguala case was in many ways the straw that broke the camel's back. In a way not seen in probably two decades, Mexicans took to the streets to voice their outrage. Over a period of many months, protests took place in Mexico City and in almost every other major city in the country. The case has sparked a number of international protests in close to eighty different countries as diverse as India, Australia, and Germany. The students' case became a catalyst for many of the frustrations present in numerous Mexican homes. The protests began demanding the return of the students. The protests were extremely peaceful, with families and children present among the tens of thousands. There were, however, a few violent incidents: in one instance, the door of the National Palace in Mexico City's historic central plaza was set on fire; and the state government building was set on fire during the protests in Guerrero. However, these were smaller incidents in what was a major, peaceful mobilization period.

Once again, the state's response straddled the line between apathy and authoritarianism. The president ominously warned of the government's faculties for the use of force. At a major protest in Mexico City's central plaza on 20 November, federal and local riot police charged the crowds in an effort to clear out the square. People documented on social media how police assaulted women and the elderly at random. A well-known documentary filmmaker and her sister, whom I interviewed later, were beaten by police. The stories and images of random police violence spread on social media. Eleven students were arrested during this protest; they were accused of serious crimes, such as attempted murder, and were sent almost immediately to maximum security prisons far from the City. Human rights groups denounced they had been denied access to legal representation and had been forced to sign confessions. The prosecutor included as evidence against them the fact that they called each other *compa* (mate, buddy). They also justified the injuries some of them presented by stating that they were self-inflicted by the students purposely banging their heads against the police riot shields. This did little to appease protesters and only served to reinforce the notions that the government was not listening. The demands began to evolve to include even the resignation of the president himself and the liberation of the eleven students. They were freed some days later as protests continued.

For the first time since Peña Nieto's inauguration, the presidency was also suffering abroad. The foreign media picked up the case of the forty-three students and was still writing about it months later. Most, if not all, writing was highly critical of the Mexican government and its inability not just to address the students' disappearance, but the security issues overall. During Peña Nieto's visit to a G20 summit in Brisbane, Australia, the admittedly small Latino community—and even smaller Mexican community—in that country organized protests in almost every major city.

Faced with increasing legitimacy problems, things could hardly get worse for the administration; however, they did. An investigative piece by a respected Mexican journalist broke the news that the private residence of the president's wife—a US $7 million mansion in Mexico City's most exclusive district—was financed and owned by a contracting firm which had gained significant contracts from the president while he was a governor and also during his presidency. The 'White House' scandal (names thus due to the chosen colour of the mansion) spread like wildfire, and was also picked up by the international press. This most obvious conflict of interest was yet another example of government cronyism, corruption, and overall untrustworthiness. The administration tried to bury the scandal, first stating that as this was the First Lady's house, it was unrelated to the president and thus not bound by transparency laws. Then, in an infamous video, the First Lady scolded the nation, told of how *Televisa* (the massive Mexican telecommunications company) had paid her millions of dollars (even though she had not worked since 2007) with which she planned to buy the house. She then said she would sell the house, so her honour would not be in question. Needless to say, this convinced few people. A few weeks later, the president appointed a new anti-corruption czar and tasked him with investigating the White House affair. The appointee was a close friend of both the President and one of the cabinet ministers, and an old PRI member. Not surprisingly, he found no wrongdoing during his investigations.

The president then announced a ten-point plan for dealing with crime and insecurity (no mention of the 'White House'). The ten points made no mention of kidnapping specifically, although they did address 'everyday security'. The plan went from the vaguely promising to the ridiculous, and included the following:

- A law against criminal infiltration of municipal authorities. While a good idea in principle, this measure seems to, on the one hand, shift all responsibility for infiltration to the municipalities, ignoring the large-scale corruption that takes place at higher levels of government, and, on the other, it adds to the already existing (and large) host of laws passed previously, such as the law against organized crime. The problem here would be enforcement. If the country does not have the capacity to enforce existing laws, what good is a new one?
- Clearer definitions of jurisdiction of all levels of government to combat crime. This is a much-needed initiative, but one that ultimately fails to deliver what is most needed, which is deep structural reform of the criminal justice system and anti-corruption structures.
- The creation of thirty-two unified state-level police forces to replace the municipal police. While also a good idea in principle, it remains to be seen how centralizing policing to state-level government, which is notoriously corrupt and tends towards authoritarianism, will solve any problem.

- A '911' national emergency number. For reasons mentioned above (e.g. corruption, ineffectiveness, and lack of technical capacity), this initiative has no real meaning. While the forty-three students were being taken away by local police, an army garrison was stationed not 200 metres from the scene. It could be said that perhaps some state police were also in Iguala. None of them moved to help the students. A 911 call would not have changed this.
- The creation of a unique, national, personal ID to enhance transparency and streamline government procedures. This was also intended to help law enforcement to identify people more easily, thus aiding in the investigation of crimes. A similar ID basically already exists in the form of the voting card: perhaps this could be the base for the new initiative.
- A special security operation in the area of Guerrero most affected by crime. This sounds very similar to the original initiative designed by President Calderon for Michoacán (mentioned above). Such operations tend to be short-lived, which may even have a displacement effect: they may solve the problem in one place, only for the same problem to emerge elsewhere soon after.
- A series of initiatives to strengthen 'everyday justice'. These initiatives need clarification and also go to the root of many of the problems discussed in this chapter. A weak rule of law affects all citizens and this must be tackled—not by the creation of new laws, but by the creation of mechanisms of enforcement and the promotion of new social norms geared towards legality and respect for the law. This applies to the criminal justice system in particular.
- To improve and build on the human rights system. This has been an ongoing process since the creation of the National Commission of Human Rights in 1992. To date, it can only issue recommendations, and has been criticized for 'lacking teeth'. Strengthening and giving it power to prosecute would be a possible avenue.
- To give federal backing to a national anti-corruption system and other initiatives. This seemed, indirectly, to respond to those who criticized the government's lack of transparency and conflicts of interest. It remains to be seen which mechanisms will be put into place so that the fight against corruption

can be taken to where it is needed, regardless of who is at the heart of it.
- To strengthen 'open government' initiatives and bolster transparency in public administration. As with some of the other points, it remains to be seen which mechanisms will be designed to make this work.

There is a theme for the criticism of the points listed above. Insofar as structural reforms are not enacted to tackle and redesign the entire criminal justice system, and end impunity and corruption, crime policy is doomed to fail. At the time of writing, these proposals have largely not been implemented and the security situation in Mexico continues to deteriorate as conflict between the armed forces and cartels—as well as between cartels themselves—intensifies. Scepticism about the case of the forty-three students remains high and it is safe to say trust in the political establishment has suffered perhaps irreparable damage.

Unfortunately, the winding-down of the Peña Nieto administration did not bring about much good news on the crime/security front. 2016 (Peña Nieto's term ended in 2018) saw significant increases in homicide rates, even compared to 2015. Reports show that crimes and violence overall are on the rise, especially in urban areas (Morfin et al. 2016). Mexico City, once heralded as the only place in Mexico where cartels did not interfere, has seen a rise in crimes in general and the presence of organized crime is more heavily felt than ever. Kidnapping is once again on the rise in the City, as is homicide. There is a growing consensus that the security situation in Mexico has in fact deteriorated since 2012—the year when Peña Nieto was elected largely on promises to tackle violence. In July 2018, the incumbent PRI suffered its worst electoral defeat in its history, losing control of Congress and the presidency, as well as several governorships. At the federal level, the PRI's presidential candidate received only 16 per cent of the popular vote, ending in a distant third place to the left-leaning candidate Andres Manuel Lopez Obrador, who won with 53 per cent of the vote.

Gender-based violence has also become a key part of the social discontent. Violence against women reached an all-time high during the Peña Nieto administration. Figures suggest that between the years of 2013 and 2014, seven women were killed every day in Mexico. The numbers of femicides—as they are referred to—have been on the increase for fifteen years. Perhaps not coincidentally, the state of Mexico, where Peña Nieto was governor before becoming president, has one of the country's highest rates of femicides (INEGI 2013). Thus, we arrive at the near-end of the Peña Nieto administration in a context that at best is deeply problematic. In January 2017, the president's approval ratings hit a historic low of 12 per cent and opposition to his administration was mounting. The Trump administration was yet to begin and its certain impact on Mexico was still not felt. However, it is safe to say that, in the international arena, Mexico's dealings with the United States were to become more strained.

## The New Role of the Military

Since the War on Drugs was launched in 2006, the military has taken on a very important role on the Mexican security scene. Ideally, Mexican soldiers do not leave their bases unless a threat to national security calls for them to act, although historically they have been used to exercise political control. This was clearly the case during the 1968 student protests, which ended with the infamous Tlatelolco massacre, in which hundreds were killed by soldiers. Another example of this was the 2005 Zapatista armed uprising in the southern state of Chiapas, which led to the militarization of large swathes of the Mexican south-east (Trejo 2012). It is important to state that—particularly in that region—soldiers were routinely used to intimidate or eliminate political dissent for many decades (Trejo 2012).

Today, the armed forces are involved in many policing activities in Mexico, and this pattern only seems to be getting stronger. The army and the navy are routinely involved in the fight against drug cartels and are a fixture on many cities' streets on a daily basis. The military has slowly, over the last decade, inched its way into the arena of civil policing. New regulations and laws have also strengthened their position vis-a-vis the government, which now relies heavily on them for the provision of law and order. The War on Drugs has indeed been a boon for the military. Over the last ten years, the armed forces' budget has risen by almost 100% per cent (Arande 2011), and the number of active soldiers has increased from around 93,000 in the 1970s to around 212,000 today, an increase of about 3,000 soldiers per year (Nieto 2013). For example, military judges can now issue search warrants to investigate civilians suspected of crimes. More worryingly, in mid-2016, a new law was proposed which would allow the military the power to investigate crimes, generate arrest warrants, carry out forensic work, and basically supplant the civilian prosecutors' offices. The argument behind this proposal is that civil police forces cannot deal with the task of tackling organized crime due to their inefficiency and corruption. The proposal also aims to give juridical certitude to the actions of the military. Critics of the proposed reforms argue, correctly, that this would give undue power to the military, an institution already well-insulated from oversight, since by law civil courts cannot police the military. It also entrenches the military into the civil realm, an area in which it was not created to act. It would also remove any incentive of the civil police to reform and improve on their work.

Military encroachment into civil policing has resulted in an increase in the lethality of armed encounters, as well as an increase in human rights abuses. The national prosecutor has reviewed up to 4,000 complaints regarding torture since 2006 (only fifteen of these have resulted in a conviction). Research published in 2015 states that the army kills more people than it injures, as does the navy. The former killed 10.4 civilians for every one it injured, the latter 16.8 in the period 2007 to 2014. These numbers are extremely high; in fact, generally, the number of injured people should be higher than that of the dead. This points to an exaggerated and illegal use of force (Silva-Forné et al. 2015).

In late 2016 and early 2017, the military demanded that the civilian government provide them with a formal legal framework (thus giving them legal justification) in providing public security. The armed forces effectively demanded to take over public safety from other agencies and thus legitimize their long-term presence on the streets. Academic experts (especially in constitutional law) declared this to be a soft coup, which would justify further militarization of the country and provide enormous political clout to the armed forces. In 2018, newly-elected president Andres Manuel Lopez Obrador went a step further and institutionalised the militarisation of public security—against all expert advice—with the creation of the National Guard. This is a branch of the military which is now in charge of public security. All of these factors have resulted in a conflict-rich situation. The process of liberalization and democratization which took place in Mexico for the last three decades has brought about, at best, very mixed results. While economic growth was constant (save for the 1995–97 crisis), today

Mexico faces enormous challenges. Corruption, a weak rule of law, poverty, and very high inequality are pervasive. Violence, especially related to organized crime, along with kidnapping, remains a key issue, and so far, the policies intended to curtail these have had little success.

Alongside the processes of liberalization, democratization, and economic growth, kidnapping has undergone significant changes. In fact, it is possible to trace the history of kidnapping through Mexico's political economic history. Chapter 3 will examine the historical development of kidnapping, as well as the root factors which made it such a prevalent crime in Mexico City, the gangs in operation, and how the police worked for or against them. This lays the groundwork for the subsequent analysis of trust-based relationships.

# 3

# Kidnapping

## A History of Gangs, Police, and Policy

'I dare say that in two years we will be at levels where we will see, at most, ten, or fifteen kidnappings a year, at most, if really exaggerated.'

José Luis Santiago Vasconcelos (1957–2008)
Mexican Federal Prosecutor for Organized Crime
November 2003

Kidnapping has experienced many changes since its first appearances in the 1970s. It has gone from existing only as a political tool used by radical groups—mostly left-wing militant organizations—to promote their struggle or raise funds for their cause, to a crime that is simply economical in nature. Kidnapping today is mostly an income stream for regular and organized criminals in Mexico. My research found no politically motivated kidnappings after the 1970s. There is evidence today that kidnapping has experienced a qualitative change that means it has now become a crime that, counterintuitively, affects mainly the working and middle classes as opposed to its traditional wealthy victims. The history of this crime is tied intimately to macro processes of modernization, democratization, and liberalization, as well as to micro processes of social interaction, decision-making, and trust in Mexican communities. Thus, the processes described in this book should be seen as parts of a whole, which interact with each other constantly.

Before moving on to the history of kidnapping, it is important to understand that information on kidnapping in Mexico, especially data, is not easy to find and, when it is available, it

Intimate Crimes: Kidnapping, Gangs and Trust in Mexico City. First Edition. Rolando Ochoa © Rolando Ochoa 2019. Published in 2019 by Oxford University Press

presents some problems of verification and inconsistency. Data at the district level is rare—even if this has recently improved considerably—and is many times non-systematic, and thus some claims about kidnapping must be made carefully. In the last two or three years, the available data has substantially improved, even if there are still doubts over its accuracy. At the time when the bulk of the research presented in this book was undertaken, the government would not publish consistent numbers with regard to kidnapping, particularly at the municipal or district levels. This secrecy in holding back kidnapping numbers was, I believe, meant as a political strategy to subtract importance from the issue by making its true scope unknown. By the same token, under-reporting presents an important problem. In 2014, the percentage of crimes that went unreported in Mexico was estimated at 92.8 per cent (INEGI 2015). This tells us that the actual number of crimes—including kidnapping—that take place in Mexico are *substantially* higher than indicated by the official figures. Having said this, improved data, triangulation, and interviews, as well as the use of the news report database, allows for a recreation of the narrative of this particular crime, as experienced by the population of Mexico City in particular. Recently, crime data has shown significant improvements, especially in homicide measures.

This chapter presents a first attempt at a methodologically sound history of the crime of kidnapping. Much of the information presented here was extracted first from the Kidnapping News Reports Database (KNRD 2009) which was described in detail in the methodological section in the Introduction, and the information was triangulated with sources in law enforcement through interviews in order to corroborate the information as accurately as possible. For a crime that has created so much noise in the country, we actually know very little about kidnapping itself. There is scant documentation and almost no publications about the subject. On the academic front, we find very little research on the topic. Studies of kidnapping are very rare. This chapter attempts to make sense of the vast amount of information and, sometimes, confusion that prevails surrounding this crime and its development.

Mexico has one of the highest kidnapping rates in the world. Along with countries like South Africa, Colombia, and Brazil, its (reported) figures reach well into the hundreds, even thousands, every year (Briggs 2002). In fact, victimization surveys and other studies (e.g. ICESI 2008 as well as Ortega 2008) put the actual figure well into the thousands in Mexico City alone. In 2017, there were 1,390 *reported* kidnappings nationwide (Secretaria de Seguridad y Proteccion Ciudadana, 2019) ICESI 2011.[1] Taking into account Mexico's extremely high proportion of crimes not reported, it is safe to say that the number is much higher.

Kidnapping is a common topic of discussion and the fear generated by this crime is also one of the main reasons why people in the City feel scared when going about their daily lives. Most of my fieldwork respondents—indeed, 98 per cent (victims included)—voiced a special fear of this particular crime over others, such as robbery or carjacking. Interviewee OF7 (academic, 37, female) referred to it as the 'most horrible crime of all'. It is not unreasonable to believe that the prospect of spending what could possibly be one's final days locked in a room in often inhumane conditions would create a very deep kind of fear based on the uncertainty of regaining one's freedom. Interviewee victim EV2 (businesswoman, 37) described being taken:

> Then they got me into the house, and I saw other men, I don't know how many. They got me up the stairs and stuck me in a little room, a child's room, I remember perfectly it had a Mickey Mouse quilt, and Pluto, blue, and they had a TV on and the light on … and they put a towel over my head, so I could not see and God knows what … when I got to that room I did say to myself, shit, I am trapped …

The media has also had a very important role in the creation of kidnapping paranoia. Stories abound in the newspapers and news channels about the conditions and horrors endured by kidnapping victims. One such piece, for example, tells the story of a botched police rescue operation in which the leader of the kidnapping gang, upon discovering that the police had entered the safe house where the victim was kept (apparently because of the noise they made on arrival), opened fire, killing two officers and the victim (a middle-aged woman who worked for a drug rehabilitation centre),

[1] In Mexico, only about 25 per cent of crimes are ever reported and 97 per cent of those remain unsolved (Magaloni and Zepeda 2004). A debate about the 'real' crime rates is ongoing (ICESI 2009, 2010). Some sources put the number at almost ten times the reported figure (Magaloni and Zepeda 2004; Ortega 2008). It is not possible at this time to know the actual number of kidnappings, but it is safe to say that the actual figure will be higher than the reported one.

and then shot himself (KNRD 2009). These types of stories are common, as exemplified by the number of news reports gathered on the subject of kidnapping for this research (just over 1,700 for a ten-year period),[2] and fuel people's perceptions of the City and their place within it.

Teresa Caldeira (2000 19) introduced the notion of the 'talk of crime', understood to mean 'everyday conversations, commentaries, discussions, narratives and jokes that have crime and fear as their subject' and which are used in everyday interactions to explain the harsh reality of fear and crime. This kind of talk generates and maintains the perceptions and prejudices that, Caldeira argues, produce opinions and explanations which set the stage for social interactions. At home, in the office, normal conversations are peppered with anecdotes and stories about crime. This type of talk is very well exemplified by one respondent: '(the situation) is dire, and I'll tell you why, I mean, you don't have freedom to go anywhere, you go around in fear all the time, I mean, absolute distrust of the whole world' (ENV3, retired, 50s, female). The commonality of this kind of expression is staggering. Of all the interviews I was able to record on audio, 70 per cent of people agree that they have some sense of fear permeating their everyday lives in Mexico City. This is consistent with the findings of national-level surveys (such as the one undertaken by ICESI in 2007), which place the same figure at around 74 per cent. Indeed, most people with whom I have had contact in the City consider crime to a greater or lesser extent in their everyday decisions, such as where to live, when to go out, and other such choices.

Among all this 'talk of crime' (Caldeira 1998), kidnapping has become part of the country's cultural baggage. Although this crime has been present for many years (it was used during the Revolution and other periods of Mexican history), it was not until the mid-1990s that it achieved the widespread notoriety now accorded to it. Kidnapping was a very rare occurrence after the revolutionary period and, as such, it was rarely reported (Ortega 2008). During the 1930s to 1960s, Mexico was a relatively stable country, with low levels of crime. Kidnapping resurfaced in the 1960s. I will label this period the 'modern history of kidnapping'.

[2] Refer to the Appendix for a detailed table on the number of news reports, as well as details on the people interviewed.

The modern history of kidnapping in Mexico can be divided into three waves. The first of these, what I call its political phase, took place during the late 1960s and 1970s. During this time, kidnapping was almost exclusively used by militant left-wing groups as a source of cash and as a form of political mobilization. The second stage took place from the late 1970s to the mid-1990s—a transition period that also encompasses a period of deep change in Mexico, in both the political and the economic arenas (electoral competition and economic liberalization being some of the main structural changes discussed in Chapter 1). In this second stage, kidnapping was reconfigured after the defeat of the guerrillas by the government, but it never disappeared. It was during this period that rampant corruption in the police forces set the stage for the formation of the most prolific and professional kidnapping gangs that would take centre-stage years later. These gangs saw their beginnings as part of the police force. Since then, rumours have circulated of a secret brotherhood among city police that continues to operate to this day in the City's criminal rings; there is, however, no proof as yet that this brotherhood actually exists. The third and current wave takes place from 1995 to the present day. It began during the financial crisis of 1995, when it became evident that the economic reform that had by then swept the country had not been accompanied by the necessary social reforms—a state of affairs which would indirectly lead to a rise in crime rates (Lustig 2001) and the destruction of the old police-originated gangs. In this period, less well-organized, younger, and family-based gangs began to fill the positions left open by the sophisticated gangs already destroyed by the government. This made the face of kidnapping change from a rare, well-organized crime carried out by 'professionals' to one that became routine for many gangs that viewed it as a complementary source of income to their other illegal activities, such as car theft and drug dealing.

## In the Beginning: Left-Wing Radical Groups, Planes to Cuba, and Kidnapping as a Political Statement

As stated earlier, kidnapping made its first appearances on the national stage in the 1960s (Ortega 2008).[3] At this time, the

[3] Kidnapping has existed for a long time in Mexico, dating back to the highway robbers of colonial times. For the purposes of this book, we will focus on the 'modern', post-World War II era.

country was experiencing the legacy of the decade's political turmoil, especially the pro-democracy social mobilizations that led to the massacre of perhaps hundreds of students in a Mexico City plaza on 2 October 1968, the year the Olympic Games came to Mexico City (Pensado 2013). As was the case in many countries in the region, Marxist thought (in its many interpretations) was taking hold of certain actors in the political spectrum (Bethell 1995; Escobar 2018). These actors, mostly students, teachers, radical blue-collar workers, and peasants, were set against the authoritarian style of government of the time, and managed to organize sectors of the population for political mobilization. The ruling party (Partido Revolucionario Institucional or PRI) had by then been in power in one form or another since 1929[4] and many actors in society, especially those of a more progressive nature, began demanding more democratic openness. Workers' unions and peasant organizations joined the students in their opposition to what they saw as an undemocratic regime completely intolerant of dissent. The tensions between the status quo and those who wished to change it, as well as the constant repression, forced many members of the social movements to seek a more radical avenue for the achievement of their revolutionary designs, both in the cities and in the rural areas of Mexico. During this time, several radical armed groups appeared on the scene, most of which were of communist extraction. They were the product of the merging of radical political idealists, students, and mobilized organizations which already operated in Mexico (Bellingeri 1993). Most of these groups were composed of left-wing hardliners who believed armed struggle to be the only way to depose the government. The perceived success of the Cuban Revolution and all its cultural iconography was the very influential backdrop for these groups' actions (Bellingeri 1993).

Clandestine Armed Groups (Grupos Armados Clandestinos or GACs, in Spanish), as they were known then, used kidnapping as a means not only of raising much-needed funds for their attempts to overthrow the government, but also as a form of political protest, by targeting economic and political elites. One of the most active GACs in terms of kidnapping was the Clandestine

[4] The party would not be defeated in a presidential election until the year 2000.

Workers Revolutionary Party and People's Union (*Procup*). This group operated in the poor and mostly rural south-western state of Guerrero and claims to be the direct predecessor of the People's Revolutionary Army (Ejercito Popular Revolucionario or EPR, in Spanish), an armed group still active in many areas of Mexico that as recently as 2007 successfully bombed and destroyed several state-owned oil and gas pipelines, causing hundreds of millions of pesos in damages and forcing the army to evacuate thousands of people. The *Procup* are known to have carried out a number of kidnappings throughout the 1970s and 1980s. Indeed, most of the kidnappings recorded in the 1970s were carried out by the *Procup* and other similar armed groups (Ortega 2008). Mobilized peasants were not the only ones using kidnapping as a political tool; the Communist League 23 September,[5] an amalgamation of radical student groups and teachers that operated in urban centres nationally, were also involved in kidnapping.

The Communist League kidnapped a number of businessmen in the 1970s in order to pressure the government into releasing students/activists held in prison for dissent from the late 1960s. In 1973, the *Fuerzas Revolucionarias Armadas del Pueblo* kidnapped Terrance Georges Leonhardy, then US consul in Guadalajara, demanding the release of student prisoners and their transport to Cuba. In another instance, the League of Armed Communists (LCA) kidnapped a number of young people, demanding a plane to Cuba and 4 million pesos. The case of the LCA became a source of national embarrassment when it transpired that on board the plane to Cuba were the two sons of a governor, as well as a US consul. Added to this was the fact that the delivery of the money was televised: it was delivered by the Chief of Police wearing nothing but his underpants, as demanded by the LCA (Castellanos 2008). In all, towards the end of the 1970s, close to thirty dissident armed groups operated in Mexico (Castellanos 2008). Most were unceremoniously dealt with by the government through military operations, forced disappearances, and repression (Aviña 2014). Others simply ran out of revolutionary fuel and vanished. The Communist League 23 September and the *Procup* wedged themselves in the national

[5] The date in the group's name refers to the date of a guerrilla attack on a military barracks in 1965.

imagination and are still remembered today, not least because they also formed part of the basis for the Zapatista indigenous movement which gained international renown with its 1994 uprising in the southern state of Chiapas.

The Mexican government's first reaction to this first wave of politically motivated kidnappings was to give in to the dissident groups. Then-President Luis Echeverria implemented a policy of payment and negotiation, providing money and the fabled planes to Cuba without fail. The victims were always important people: businessmen, politicians, and other major actors in Mexican society. The government did not want to have the death of any of these people on their hands. On 17 September 1973, this would change. On that date, the Communist League 23 September attempted to kidnap northern businessman Eugenio Garza Sáda, then one of Mexico's wealthiest men, a well-liked philanthropist and the founder of one of Mexico's largest universities. Garza Sáda was shot dead at a road intersection when resisting the abduction; two people who accompanied him were also killed. Garza Sáda held a very important place in the business community and their organizations and was heavily involved in industrial growth in northern Mexico.

In a significant break from their well-scripted relationship with the government, a cosy arrangement that allowed massive fortunes both political and economic to develop, the business community aggressively blamed the president for this attack. At Garza Sáda's funeral, a very close friend of his gave a speech blaming his death on the lack of leadership in the government and on the president's recent populist verbal attacks on the business class, which stated that they did not pull their weight in Mexico. President Echeverria was backed into a tight spot. For the first time in his presidency, he was facing a very angry economic elite who also saw an opportunity to let him know they could not be embarrassed in public. Echeverria vowed never to negotiate with kidnappers again. Instead, he decided on the implementation of an 'extermination policy' (Castellanos 2008) against these groups.

This decision would be tested only a few months later when, in December 1974, in Guerrero, one armed group—the Army of the Poor and Peasant's Brigade against Injustice, led by mythical Mexican revolutionary Lucio Cabañas—kidnapped a senator and gubernatorial candidate. At around the same time, in Guadalajara, the People's Armed Revolutionary Forces (Fuerzas Armadas Revolucionarias del Pueblo or FARP) kidnapped none other than President Echeverria's father-in-law. This presented the best chance for the government to act or be publicly embarrassed. Echeverria stood by his word. He sent up to 16,000 troops to the Guerrero mountains to hunt down Cabañas and rescue the senator. The manhunt yielded the expected results and the senator was rescued (and then went on to become governor). The FARP was chased all over the state's notoriously inaccessible mountainsfor weeks. Cabañas committed suicide as he was about to be captured by the army (O'Neil 2009; Turbivillie 1997).

In the case of the president's father-in-law, 'repression landed in the popular neighbourhoods of Guadalajara' where the urban guerrillas operated. This is yet another example of the selective use of the army by the Mexican government to supress social mobilization. Little is known about these operations, but what is known is that the captive was liberated without fanfare (Castellanos 2008). At the time, Echeverria also strengthened what became known as the 'dirty war', a direct and clandestine war on GACs and other social movements orchestrated from the presidency's inner circles, which resulted in one of the largest waves of systematic human rights violations in the modern history of Mexico. Echeverria, decades later, would be subpoenaed on human right violations charges in front of a special court. The dirty war was carried out by secret armed groups (sometimes referred to as 'white hawks'), which operated with impunity throughout the country.

The Eureka Committee, an NGO dealing specifically with the issue of disappeared persons, has 530 disappeared persons' files from 1969 to 1980 (Comité Eureka 2007). While not comparable to the levels of violence left by other Latin American regimes in their wake, the Mexican violence is distinctive for its selectivity and secrecy. The dirty war ended for all practical purposes the political phase of kidnapping. In those times, the power of the state and its intelligence organizations was still very firm and it had many resources at its disposal, which meant that many of the guerrilla groups, whether urban or rural, were no match for the forces of an authoritarian state.

## The Heyday of the Black One: Police as Criminals and the Formation of the Perfect Kidnapping Gang

During the 1980s, kidnapping became more common, although it was still a marginal crime by all accounts (Ortega 2008). During this time, criminals and mainly organized crime groups were in the process of discovering that kidnapping was a very profitable business. Ortega (2008) has counted 'little more than 300 kidnappings in Mexico from 1970 to 1985'. The 1980s in Mexico were characterized by rampant corruption, economic crisis, and the blurring of the distinction between government agents and criminals. The development of kidnapping is closely related to the internal dynamics of the police forces during this period. The Mexico City police is a particularly important actor in this process.

During the PRI's authoritarian rule from 1929[6] to 2000, the police forces were often used to help maintain the political status quo (Azaola 2006). In fact, the enforcement of the law came second to the keeping of the political order. In essence, the police institutions were not really created to protect the populace, their goods, and their property, but rather to serve as part of the political machinery that helped maintain the same party in power for over seventy years. They were, above all, a source of social control. In this context, the police institutions became, as did most government establishments, subservient and fully dependent on the power of the Federal Executive, who single-handedly decided who the heads of the different police institutions would be, as well as how long they would remain in the job.[7] This was based on the extreme powers of the Mexican President, which went far beyond the constitutional powers accorded to him and have been called 'meta-constitutional

[6] The PRI was not always known as such. After its foundation in 1929, it was known as the National Revolutionary Party, and it then changed its name to Party of the Mexican Revolution in 1936 after an internal power struggle. It gained its final name in 1946.

[7] During this time, the president not only chose the heads of the police, but also most political positions, governorships, candidacies, and almost any post in the government. He also decided the next PRI presidential candidate, and as such the next president through a process commonly known as the *dedazo*, an expression that can be loosely translated as 'hit from his finger', whereby he chose, from his inner circle, the next in line. This was always shrouded in a democratic veil through elections that the PRI would always 'win' through a host of interestingly named practices such as 'rollercoaster voting', whereby PRI voters would be taken

powers' (Carpizo 1978). These powers emanate from the fact that the PRI was created as an 'institutional instrument' (Wiarda and Guajardo 1989) in 1929 by the winners of the Revolution (1910–21), and basically performed this same function with each president, gradually losing power and cohesion through economic mismanagement and pressure from organized society from the mid-1980s (Meyer and Aguilar Camin 1993) until its electoral defeat in the federal elections in 2000. Throughout this period, the police became a corrupt organization, serving politicians and the wealthy elites and, in their spare time, pursuing criminal careers as drug dealers, kidnappers, and bank robbers shrouded in corruption and government tolerance for their activities (Conklin 1989).

One of the most salient examples of police involvement in crime—and the origin of some of the most notorious kidnapping gangs—is the career of Arturo 'El Negro' Durazo (his nickname means 'the black one', allegedly given to him due to the colour of his skin, but also attributed to his deeds). Durazo rose to national prominence when his good childhood friend José López Portillo became president (1976–82) and as a prize for his loyalty made him Chief of Police of Mexico City. This was back in the days when Mexico City was only the seat of the federal government and all its authorities were designated by the president. No City authorities were voted in at that time. It was not until 1996 when the City was granted autonomy through a constitutional reform and elections finally took place there. This lack of democracy generated an environment of unaccountability that was skilfully exploited by people like Durazo to carve out infamous criminal careers for themselves.

During his six years in office, Durazo became notorious as one of the most accomplished gangsters in the country, and kidnapping was one of his sources of income. Such were his powers that he gave himself a military title (General), even though he never had

in trucks to as many polling stations as possible to vote as many times as they could; there was also the 'ballot box impregnation', when a PRI official would show up at the polling station and stuff the ballot box with pre-filled-out ballot papers, all in favour of the PRI; last but not least were the 'racoons' or PRI sympathizers, who would show up and steal ballot boxes where there was evidence of opposition advantage, to sometimes return them filled with PRI votes; dead people also had a knack for showing up to vote for the PRI. These are only some of the many practices used by the PRI machinery to win elections. Much more sinister ones included the intimidation and co-optation of opposition leaders and the curtailment of political and free speech rights (Carpizo 1978; Weldon 1997).

a military career, much to the dismay of the army, who received no answers when they complained about it.[8] He amassed a huge fortune (well into the hundreds of millions of dollars) through kidnapping, outright stealing of public funds, and drug trafficking (Gonzales 1983). He is, among other things, credited with starting the tradition of the *entre* or a monetary 'cut' demanded (or, rather, extorted) by higher officials in the police, on a regular basis (weekly or daily) from those in their charge. A junior officer interviewed during fieldwork (LE19, junior prosecutor, male, 30) confirmed that this practice is still prevalent in some areas of law enforcement, notably the police. He spoke of how officers must pay to have access to patrol cars and how better cars (such as Jeeps) command higher prices. The same, he argues, applies for extra firearms and most other equipment. Durazo also created the Directorate of Investigation for Crime Prevention (Direccion de Investigacion y Prevencion del Delito—DIPD, in Spanish), an investigative police unit notorious for harbouring the most corrupt and violent elements of the force, handpicked by Durazo himself. Members of DIPD were also known as *Madrinas* (godmothers) to many criminals. This basically meant that DIPD members sold protection to criminals. A criminal would then have his own personal *Madrina* who kept him informed of police movements and also turned a blind eye to his activities. Arrangements between *Madrinas* and their godchildren was so deeply ingrained that, in some cases, criminals would even let themselves be captured by their *Madrina* only to be secretly let go afterwards, thus paying for their protection not only in money, but also in prestige for their protectors, who would then be rewarded with pay raises and more important jobs. The concept of the *Madrina* has now evolved and generally also refers to people who are not members of the police force, but 'work' with actual members of the force, or just people (mostly criminals) who mimic being in the force by presenting fake police documentation. The phenomenon of the *Madrina* and its evolution in recent times deserves, by itself, much deeper research.

Durazo created an empire of crime throughout the country by being literally untouchable. As we have seen, not even the army

[8] The fact that not even the army, one of the nation's most powerful actors, could stop this shameful episode gives us an idea of the power wielded by Durazo over the president, who was willing to annoy the armed forces for the sake of his friend.

could approach him. People in the City (myself included) still have memories of his power. His motorcade is an excellent example of this. An advance detachment of police motorcycles would close the entirety of his predetermined route, sometimes for hours, so he would face no traffic. This could be at any time and could cut off some of the main avenues of the City. After this, a motorcade of no less than eight new black cars, many more motorcycles, and helicopters would cruise slowly through the City as bystanders and other drivers looked on. Gonzales (2002), a former bodyguard of Durazo, describes how he used the police force as his private labour force. Policemen served his guests drinks and food at his infamous parties held in his many multi-million-dollar mansions. One of them, high on a hill overlooking the ocean on the pacific coast of Mexico, was a replica of the Greek Parthenon, with a replica of the legendary New York nightclub Studio 54 inside. The grotesque palace still stands and, for a few pesos under the table (this is Durazo's home after all), the guard on duty will let people in to take a look. Durazo was also known to send his bodyguards to empty out entire restaurants so he could eat comfortably with his family. No one could say no to him. However, beyond his more colourful actions, Durazo managed to create a criminal empire that generated millions in revenue. It is widely believed that, during his time, the foundations of Mexico's now legendary corruption and criminal collusion were laid, especially with regard to the police (Azaola 2006). He institutionalized criminal practices and protection schemes (robbery and the *Madrinas*) to such an extent that these still survive to this day. When his mentor, Lopez Portillo, left the presidency in shame after presiding over one of the most corrupt and inefficient presidential terms in history and leaving the economy in a shambles, he was tried by the next administration and convicted of corruption, spending nine years in jail (Wilkie 1989).

In terms of kidnapping, Durazo's legacy is clear. Under his auspices, some of the most accomplished kidnappers learned the ropes of a sophisticated crime. Alfredo Rios Galeana, one of Mexico's most notorious bank robbers and kidnappers, worked directly under Durazo in the mid-1980s (Ortega 2008). His criminal career spanned two decades and included some of the era's most notorious crimes. He started his career as a policeman, but quickly turned to crime when his police unit was disbanded in 1981. He created a gang consisting mostly of former policemen and policewomen. He was captured at least three times and escaped on all occasions, once being rescued from a courthouse by an armed commando. He would personally then go on to train at least two of the most important kidnappers who became active in the 1990s. He disappeared in 1986, only to be finally arrested in Los Angeles in 2005. It is unclear how many kidnappings he perpetrated, but it is known that part of his business (after large-scale robberies) was the kidnapping of wealthy individuals (KNRD 2009). He is indeed, along with Durazo, one of the godfathers of modern kidnapping. In a sense, he is the ideal criminal for this: well-connected in the police force, highly trained in the use of violence, armed, and with access to trained recruits. The important legacy of this man, specifically for the development of kidnapping, is discussed below.

## 1995 Onwards: From the Ear Chopper and the Colonel to the Inexperienced Gang

In 1994, Alfredo Harp Helú, one of Mexico's richest men, was kidnapped and subsequently freed after an unknown but surely substantial payment (KNRD 2009). This was arguably the beginning of a new era of kidnapping, in which wealthy Mexicans became the main target of what had by then become a non-political crime that was mostly driven by profit. Kidnapping became a business pursued by gangs whose leadership was in many cases trained in the police forces under Durazo, as is the case of those under the command of Alfredo Rios Galeana. These gangs were well organized from the start. The environment of unaccountability and corruption prevalent in the City's police forces up until this point was the perfect laboratory for the birth of these groups. In 1995, Mexico experienced a deep economic crisis that exacerbated existing social tensions and helped increase crime rates all over the country (Kelly 2000). Table 3.1 shows the number of kidnappings reported to the authorities in the period from 1995 to 2012.

Table 3.1 shows that kidnapping at the national level exploded after 1995 (548 reported), to peak in 1997 at 1,045. From then onwards, we see a steady drop that reaches a low of 334 in 2004. A slow but steady economic recovery, as well as local elections in Mexico City, which brought in a strong legitimate local government, may explain this decline. From 2004, however, we again see an increase in the kidnapping rates to a high of 1,317 in 2012. This increase at the national level can be attributed to the ongoing War on Drugs (Guerrero-Gutierrez 2011; Ochoa 2012). This increase is,

**Table 3.1 Reported Kidnappings in Mexico, 1995–2017**

| Year | Kidnappings |
|---|---|
| 1995 | 548 |
| 1996 | N/A |
| 1997 | 1,045 |
| 1998 | 734 |
| 1999 | 590 |
| 2000 | 591 |
| 2001 | 505 |
| 2002 | 435 |
| 2003 | 413 |
| 2004 | 323 |
| 2005 | 278 |
| 2006 | 733 |
| 2007 | 438 |
| 2008 | 907 |
| 2009 | 1,162 |
| 2010 | 1,223 |
| 2011 | 1,433 |
| 2012 | 1,421 |
| 2013 | 1,688 |
| 2014 | 1,395 |
| 2015 | 1,069 |
| 2016 | 1,131 |
| 2017 | 1,149 |

Source: SNSP (2018).

as we shall see, reflected more in other states and not in Mexico City. Regionally, ten of the thirty-one states of Mexico are where 75 per cent of all the kidnappings take place. Table 3.2 shows this pattern. These states are not concentrated in any particular region of the country and are well distributed in the north, south, and centre. The state that stands out is Mexico City, which has almost 30 per cent of all the kidnappings in the period 1997 to 2009. This may be because of the high concentration of population in the City.

**Table 3.2 Kidnappings in Mexico, Top Ten States, 1997–2009**

| State | Percentage of Total Kidnappings |
|---|---|
| Mexico City | 27% |
| Edomex | 13% |
| Michoacán | 9% |
| Tabasco | 9% |
| Guerrero | 8% |
| Jalisco | 8% |
| Tlaxcala | 8% |
| Oaxaca | 7% |
| Baja California | 7% |
| Sinaloa | 4% |

Source: ICESI (2009), with data from PGR (2007).
Note: Today, close to 60 per cent of all kidnappings take place in the state of Tamaulipas, one of the worst affected by drug-related violence and cartel activity.

On average, there were 1.4 reported kidnappings a year per 100,000 people in the City for this period. The neighbouring State of Mexico (Edomex), which also shares a large part of what is considered the Greater Mexico City area, itself contains 13 per cent of kidnappings. Almost 40 per cent of all reported kidnappings take place in these two states. Data concerning the exact location of the Edomex kidnappings is not available; however, qualitative information from interviews with law enforcement agents and prosecutors in that state tells us that many of these do take place within the Greater Mexico City area (LE23, state kidnapping prosecutor, 60, male), which has a large population concentration.

## Kidnapping in Mexico City

In Mexico City, the story varies from the national-level data. As kidnapping rates fell nationally, those in Mexico City rose steadily throughout the late 1990s and early 2000s. This was especially noticeable in 1999, when a 100 per cent rise was reported. This can be related to the fact that 1999 (and part of 2000) was an electoral year (at both the federal and the City levels) in which the ruling

PRI party would lose power at the federal level for the first time in over seventy years. The weakening of the traditional institutional framework and the further loss of patronage to many social actors that this brought about, as well as the uncertainty of what would happen when and if the PRI lost, could have meant that a window of opportunity opened for criminals to maximize their income in this period. Going back to the data, although in 2005 and 2006 there was a decrease in the number of kidnappings, the numbers again rose in 2007 to 112 and again to 139 in 2008 (KNRD 2009). Surprisingly, the number of kidnappings fell to eighty-five in 2009, a decrease of almost 62 per cent (see Table 3.3).

**Table 3.3 Kidnappings Reported to the Authorities in Mexico City, 1997–2017**

| Year | Kidnappings |
|---|---|
| 1997 | 22 |
| 1998 | 66 |
| 1999 | 120 |
| 2000 | 141 |
| 2001 | 148 |
| 2002 | 144 |
| 2003 | 136 |
| 2004 | 145 |
| 2005 | 103 |
| 2006 | 92 |
| 2007 | 112 |
| 2008 | 139 |
| 2009 | 85 |
| 2010 | 80 |
| 2011 | 54 |
| 2012 | 65 |
| 2013 | 60 |
| 2014 | 78 |
| 2015 | 62 |
| 2016 | 54 |
| 2017 | 50 |

Source: Secretaria de Seguridad y Proteccion Ciudadana. 2019.

## A Shift in Kidnapping

Information gathered during fieldwork points towards an interesting development in kidnapping. It would appear that the wealthy ceased to be the only victims of kidnapping in Mexico City, meaning that, even as rates decreased at the national level, they tended to increase in the City (save for 2009). This book does not deal with kidnapping at the national level and as such cannot pose a solid answer to why this is so. Further research on the behaviour of kidnapping in the country as a whole is necessary to establish the causes of this. As Carlos Castillo Peraza, a centre-right intellectual and politician, put it as far back as 1999 in an essay entitled 'Kidnapping as Distinction' (Castillo 1999):

> Until a relatively short time ago, a 'kidnappable' was a person whose great riches constituted a certain promise of payable ransom. Or maybe someone whose social or political position was reasonably considered as sufficient cause for an abundant payment, not from the victim's pocket but from that of his friends, partners, followers or fans. Well, it could be said that kidnapping was a sign of distinction of the victim ... As we know things are no longer like this ... for a few pesos criminals take even the least wealthy and the least powerful.

## Not Just the Rich: Kidnapping at the District Level

In spite of the lack of district-level data, I was able to gather enough to construct Table 3.4 (KNRD 2009). This table was created using the news report database where I found press releases and other information released by the City government. Indeed, the National Institute of Statistics and Geography recently released information regarding the number of people sentenced for different crimes, controlled by the place where the crime was committed at the municipal/district level. In this way, I was able to ascertain how many kidnappings had led to at least one arrest in each district. Evidently, the trustworthiness of these data is questionable; we do not know if perhaps more than one person was arrested for each crime. However, it does give us seven data points for each district and from those points we can clearly see a trend emerging: while the number of kidnappings dropped in Miguel Hidalgo, one of Mexico City's wealthier districts that historically had a high kidnapping rate, they rose in Iztapalapa, a fully

**Table 3.4 Kidnapping at the District Levels in Two Mexico City Districts, 1997–2008**

| Year | Miguel Hidalgo | Iztapalapa |
|---|---|---|
| 1997 | 25 | 19 |
| 2001 | N/A | 30 |
| 2003 | 10 | 4 |
| 2004 | 16 | N/A |
| 2005 | 0 | 1 |
| 2006 | 2 | 7 |
| 2007 | 3 | 31 |
| 2008 | 1 | 40 |

Source: KNRD and author's own (2009), and INEGI (2009).

working-class district with no wealthy areas. This gives us a general idea of a possible shift in the behaviour of kidnapping.

The year in which this trend is most evident is 2007, when there was only three kidnapping reported in Miguel Hidalgo and thirty-one in Iztapalapa. We do not know if the only kidnapping for that year was actually of a wealthy inhabitant of the Miguel Hidalgo district or of a working-class person (there are working- and middle-class neighbourhoods in the district). However, the fact remains that kidnapping has steadily risen in a 100 per cent working-class area and dropped in a wealthy area. Indeed, if that one kidnapping was of a working- or middle-class person, it means that no wealthy people were kidnapped in Miguel Hidalgo. More data needs to be collected in the future to prove or disprove this trend. For now, all we can rely on is qualitative evidence from the mouths of City authorities. For example, by the year 2000, it was widely reported and admitted by the City's authorities that one of the most active kidnapping organizations in the country, *El Coronel* (The Colonel), had 'as its main area of action the zone of Iztapalapa' (KNRD 2009). This new trend was also voiced by the kidnapping czar for the City, Jesús Jimenez Granados, in 2002:

> The situation is not one of psychosis … however, any citizen is now susceptible of being kidnapped … among the improvised gangs … we have registered cases in which someone is deprived of their freedom for

a ransom of $5,000 pesos,[9] which means that right now in kidnapping the targets are not just businessmen ... and their families ... with high monetary power. (KNRD 2009)

This could potentially be explained by the fact that it seems that success of the government's policy towards the highly organized kidnapping gangs was overshadowed by the fact that, as a side effect of this, victimization increased in working-class areas of the City, as less sophisticated gangs took the place left open by the older, better organized gangs.

It could be argued that the higher kidnapping rates in Iztapalapa are a function of its population size. Iztapalapa has a population of 1.3 million and Miguel Hidalgo about 550,000. This issue may be addressed by looking at the numbers of kidnapping as a percentage of the district's population. As the numbers of kidnappings are low, these percentages tend to be very small. For Iztapalapa, in 2007, it amounts to 0.002 per cent of the population, and for Miguel Hidalgo, it amounts to 0.0003 per cent. In order to visualize this better, the number of kidnappings for every 100,000 people can be calculated. These figures tell us much more, as they show that the kidnapping rate in the working-class district is significantly higher. Table 3.5 shows this important difference from the data available by district. We can see that there is a considerable difference between the two when controlling for population.

Furthermore, in a press conference in 2008, the Federal Prosecutor revealed that ransoms had devalued from previous years. Now, he said, the *highest* ransoms hover at an average of US $24,000. In the mid-1990s, they *started* at US $250,000 (KNRD 2009). This further highlights that victims are no longer extremely wealthy. This downward trend would continue unabated (Ortega 2008 to the present day, resulting in an increase in the kidnapping

**Table 3.5 Kidnappings for Every 100,000 People in Two Mexico City Districts, 2007**

| District | Kidnappings for Every 100,000 People | Percentage of Total Kidnappings, 2007 |
|---|---|---|
| Miguel Hidalgo | 0.2 | 0.67% (1) |
| Iztapalapa | 1.7 | 20.77% (31) |

[9] This is equivalent to around £250.

rates of people in working-class areas. As I will argue later, this is in part related to the success the government had in dismantling (be it by arresting or killing) the older gangs.

## Actors in Kidnapping

### *The gangs*

The story of kidnapping in the second half of the 1990s belongs to a small number of gangs that became known throughout the country. These gangs carried out many of the kidnappings in the City and areas surrounding it (KNRD 2009). They were specialized criminal groups victimizing wealthy members of society such as businessmen and the like. They were spearheaded by strong leaders who, in some cases, had previously been members of the police or the military. In a style concurrent with the behaviour of other organized crime groups (Reuter 1985), these gangs often competed with each other and 'passed the baton' between themselves over time, or briefly overlapped. When one was successfully destroyed by the police, another one surfaced to take its place. This was the case with the three most renowned gangs of the late 1990s and their story illustrates very well the dynamics of kidnapping.

Daniel Arizmendi, aka *El Mochaorejas* (the Ear Chopper), a former state policeman, was the leader of a particularly vicious gang known to cut off its victim's ears and send them to his or her family as a means of pressuring them into paying. Over 200 kidnappings are attributed to his group according to the then Federal Prosecutor Jorge Madrazo (KNRD 2009). However, Arizmendi's notoriety was also at the root of his downfall. His exploits and seemingly untouchable status made kidnapping the most talked-about crime in Mexican society. This has been ascertained consistently over the last ten years of field research I have carried out on the topic. The sheer number of news reports on kidnapping found in the KNRD also attest to this. One of his preferred target groups was the wealthy Spanish community of businessmen (KNRD 2009); some of the oldest fortunes in Mexico belong to this group. The notoriety he acquired mostly through extensive media coverage of his activities and the police hunt that ensued had as a side effect an increase in social demands for his capture. The Federal Police, using special faculties, took up the case and Arizmendi became one of the country's most wanted men, along with the most dangerous drug barons. His arrest became a top priority for the government; he became a political issue to an administration that was still then recovering from financial meltdown and a sceptical electorate who saw in Arizmendi all that was wrong in Mexico (KNRD 2009). Here was a former police officer engaged in kidnapping and murder, operating with impunity in plain view and doing so with particular viciousness.

Following a successful Federal Police operation involving phone tapping, the cooperation of many of his victims, and a protracted legal process, Arizmendi was arrested on 18 August 1998 as he was preparing to collect a ransom from the family of a victim his gang had already killed (KNRD 2009). His son and wife were already in jail on kidnapping charges. Secondary evidence gathered suggests that he could no longer afford to extend his known network of protection within the police to the Federal Police once his case became a political and not simply a police issue (KNRD 2009). Even though his gang had an important influx of cash, they could not afford the same protection enjoyed by drug traffickers, and were thus unable to corrupt the higher echelons of the Federal Police for support. Furthermore, his capture became of such paramount importance for politicians that the police had no choice but to do their job properly.

As we have seen in the example of the *Ministerios* (prosecutors' offices), the only thing that trumps the status quo is political need. The Federal Police in this case were able to organize their resources and use them to their full capacity to capture a known dangerous criminal. This case begins to illustrate an important point, namely that, given certain circumstances, the police are able and willing to do their job. Sadly, this seems to happen only when political leaders step in to demand this, under pressure from their wealthy friends. In an interview, a district attorney in Mexico City admitted that political cases are almost always given priority under orders 'from above' (Interview LEI1 Prosecutor, Mexico City)). That is to say, then, that the police seem to know their job is determined by hierarchy rather than the actual crime itself. The justice system is still used as a selective political tool, as opposed to an instrument for the universal protection of citizens—a state of affairs that continues to be to the detriment of those who have no resources.

Arizmendi's baton as the foremost kidnapper in Mexico City was promptly picked up by a man by the name of Andres Caletri, a career criminal with some links to state police forces who had already been jailed twice under charges of homicide, robbery, and illegal gun ownership; twice he escaped from prison—in 1986, and then again in 1995. It is unclear when exactly he became a kidnapper, but his first known case was the kidnapping of businessman Eusebio Carranza in December 1996. Among his victims, we find a high-ranking Chrysler executive named Elliot Margolis kidnapped in 1998, and two members of the Zaga family, the owners of a Mexican textile and clothing manufacturer and his son.

Unlike Arizmendi, Caletri did not have police training and his career evolved from petty crimes to robbery (he is said to have robbed at least two banks) to kidnapping. His career is also illustrative of how criminal markets and actors evolve in response to outside pressures. Caletri learned the ropes from one of the most famous criminals in modern Mexican history, Alfredo Rios Galeana, who used to work in Durazo's DIPD. He was a former police commander who in the early 1980s became a full-time criminal, forming a dangerous gang that carried out some kidnappings, bank robberies, and murders (KNRD 2009). Caletri was one of his associates during the early stages of his criminal career (KNRD 2009). He operated in a more sophisticated way than Arizmendi. In what can be seen as the perfecting of kidnapping, he formed independent criminal cells in Mexico City and elsewhere and sub-contracted victim research and 'storage' to other gangs, with no direct connection to himself or one another (KNRD 2009). This points to a level of organizational sophistication that is more akin to the structure of organized crime groups and even terrorist groups than mere gangs (see Krebs 2002; Sanderson 2004). Furthermore, his case also highlights the fact that, as actors that held a near monopoly on a criminal activity (be it drugs or kidnapping) are eliminated from the scene, this creates a vacuum that is quickly filled by other actors wishing to enter such market.

Caletri stepped up his kidnapping game just when Arizmendi's gang was in the process of being neutralized by the actions of the Federal Police. Again, this is consistent with findings in other criminal markets (Reuter 1983, 1985), such as the drug trade. Caletri's victim profile is also consistent with that of Arizmendi: executives, wealthy manufacturers, and ranchers in neighbouring states and other rich victims were preferred. Although he possessed a long criminal career, his kidnapping career was much shorter than that of Arizmendi. Caletri was arrested in February 1999, only six months after Arizmendi. A specialized unit made up of seventy officers from the Yaqui specialized group (a group made up of highly trained officers with secret identities), the Federal Preventive Police, the Federal Judicial Police, and the Special Organized Crime Unit, many of whom had worked in the capturing of Arizmendi, were solely devoted to the capture of this one man and his associates (KNRD 2009). The resources employed in the capture of Caletri point towards the seriousness with which the government responded to this particular threat.

*El Coronel* quickly followed in his predecessor's footsteps. An old member of one of Caletri's cells (KNRD 2009), he also used a decentralized structure to achieve greater efficacy. At the time of his arrest, the Federal Prosecutor claimed that he was in charge of at least five criminal cells operating in diverse sectors of the City and other states (KNRD 2009). In this way, *El Coronel* was never directly involved in the kidnappings, but served as the brains behind those gangs, also collecting most of their income. His organization, like those before him, mostly targeted wealthy businessmen and their families, especially those in the jewel trade. Many of its victims were members of the Jewish community of Mexico City. Evidence gathered in fieldwork points out that this particular gang, headed by a man named Marcos Tinoco Gancedo (who presented himself as a former army colonel, hence the nickname *El Coronel*), was behind at least nine kidnappings of members of this community, for which he allegedly received up to 30 million pesos in ransom money[10] (KNRD 2009). According to the Federal Prosecutor, this gang was involved in at least eleven kidnappings in 1999 alone (KNRD 2009). The victims of these gangs included the son of the owner of a famous restaurant chain, the owner of a textile company and his son, and other wealthy individuals. The elite police group responsible for the capture of Arizmendi and Caletri was also tasked with the capture of *El Coronel* and his

[10] This is equivalent to around US $3 million today.

inner circle. Again, the Federal Police used its specialized units to acquire this target and finally arrested him in 2000.

In the space of three years (1998–2000), the three most notorious, specialized, and effective kidnapping gangs in recent Mexican history were dismantled. This was achieved by a combination of mobilization, like the massive protests against insecurity which took place in 2008 and 2014, and demands form very powerful actors (the Spanish and Jewish communities have close relations with political elites). The decision of such political actors to act and resolve a problem and, very importantly, the ability of a small group of law enforcers at the federal level who were able to remain away from the influence of these criminal organizations, led to these gangs being effectively investigated and prosecuted.

Whatever their specific activity, the thread joining all the victims of these gangs together was wealth. Reports suggested that the ransoms demanded by these gangs started at a minimum of a quarter of a million US dollars in this period (KNRD 2009). When they were arrested in 2000, members of the gang of *El Barry*, another well-established kidnapper, were in possession of two victims, for which they were demanding US$3 million in ransom (KNRD 2009). After the destruction of these criminal organizations, we see the beginning of a shift towards more numerous kidnappings.

The success of the Federal Police in dismantling highly organized and efficient gangs opened the way for other gangs to appear. With the leaders and lieutenants of the large kidnapping gangs largely behind bars, new kidnappers with new strategies surfaced. However, these new actors were not as sophisticated as the original criminals. The new gangs comprised younger elements that 'evolved' from other crimes such as car theft, robbery, etc. and saw a new, profitable market opening in kidnapping.

In June 2003, Jose Luis Santiago Vasconcelos, Federal Organized Crime Tsar, declared that 'this crime phenomenon (kidnapping), in maybe two years, will no longer be a topic to discuss in press conferences' (KNRD 2000). By 2007, Jesús Jiménez, now the Specialized Kidnapping Prosecutor, talked about the complete disappearance of highly organized kidnapping gangs; instead, he stated, he saw 'copycat kidnappings' carried out by young petty criminals who were 'inexperienced and abuse the use of force'. He also mentioned what he called the 'treason phenomenon' in kidnapping, where family members or close collaborators of victims (workers, neighbours) perform or are instrumental to the kidnapping. This phenomenon is behind the decision to study the hiring process of household employees. In the prosecutor's own words, 'I can assure you that the big kidnapping gangs are practically extinct; there will be some groups that are better armed and more sophisticated, but the constant is young people, rookies, people close to the (victim's) family' (KNRD 2009). In the following chapters, I will discuss how communities in Mexico City reacted to the threat of kidnaping and sought to navigate the risk of actually being kidnapped by someone close to them.

### *The state*

One of the most important objectives of the State is to provide protection for its members' personal integrity and property. When a government cannot provide this ideal service (Varese 2001), it faces a serious challenge to its legitimacy, for what good is a state that cannot fulfil its most basic function? The Mexican justice system is afflicted with this problem. Corruption and inefficacy, together with a weak rule of law, allow for crime to remain a profitable and somewhat safe activity. In an interview, a high-ranking prosecutor admitted to knowing who under his command was involved in protection rackets with car theft gangs, as well as to knowing how they operate and how much money they were making off the racket. However, he was unwilling to risk his life or job security to do anything about it (LE3, senior state prosecutor, 47, male). In another case, a protection racket was arranged by the investigative police, who received payment from criminals on a monthly basis to refrain from carrying out arrest warrants against them (LE5, prosecutor, 30s, male). As was the case with the car theft racket, this happened with at least the knowledge of higher-ranked officials, with most of them having no intention whatsoever of dealing with the problem. This corrupt deadlock is a common occurrence in Mexico. Corruption is so rampant that it has indeed become part of the country's structural existence and permeates all areas of life (see Varese 2000). In this light, the state is unable to provide a secure environment and the corruption of state officials is one of the most important fuels for this situation.

On a more specific level, studies by the Secretary of Social Development (2006) show that around 97 per cent of crimes are unpunished in Mexico. If crime ever pays, it definitely gives a good return in Mexico City. Furthermore, when the judiciary does act, it seems to convict mostly petty, non-violent criminals (Bergman et al. 2005a). The incentives, Bergman's study shows, are for police and judges to dole out prison terms, as they are rewarded by the quantity and not the quality of the criminals they capture. Their rewards include promotions, recognition, and simply the fact of being in their superiors' good books, a resource that may prove useful in the future should lay-offs occur or opportunities for promotions arise. Therefore, it is clear why 50 per cent of criminals in the states in Bergman's study (2005b)[11] are in prison for crimes that have the monetary equivalent of up to only $2,000 pesos (or roughly US $150). It is also evident that many high-ranking criminals are not caught and those who commit crimes of a high monetary value tend to remain free, although this may not be exclusive to Mexico, or indeed the developing world.

Although it is not the lowest nationwide, it is worth noting that, out of the very small percentage of crimes reported in the Federal District, only 33.1 per cent are efficiently investigated by the *Ministerios Públicos* (Magaloni and Zepeda 2004). This leaves 66.9 per cent of crimes *reported* that are not investigated up to regular international standards of quality. Observations of this process made during research in prosecuting agencies or *Ministerios Públicos* in Mexico City during 2008 and 2009[12] revealed that, in most cases, prosecutors tend to follow strict bureaucratic guidelines that impair criminal investigations. These guidelines are firmly set in the organizational culture of the *Ministerios* and those who stray from them are usually informally punished. Following the guidelines religiously actually allows the MPs to act in an unaccountable way, as they can always argue they do exactly as they are told. Therefore, there is no incentive to actually solve a crime, but rather the bureaucrat in charge needs to fulfil a checklist of *diligencias* (orders, steps) before passing the case to the next bureaucrat along the line. The result of this is that, in cases where actual police investigation is necessary (i.e. where

[11] Mexico City, Morelos, and Estado de Mexico, which all border one another.

[12] This was as part of a project that sought to evaluate the work practices within the *Ministerios*. The project was coordinated by Professor Ana Laura Magaloni of the Centro de Investigación y Docencia Económicas in Mexico City. I am deeply indebted to Professor Magaloni for allowing me to join her team.

the perpetrator of a crime is unknown), most of the cases end up in a file box.

In fact, prosecutors rarely leave their office, leaving most investigations to the Ministerial Police, who de jure should only follow the prosecutors' orders, but who de facto design and implement investigations according to their own particular preferences and strategies. While at times this situation opens the door for more rapid and creative investigation by the police, it mostly means that the only corporation within the justice system that can exercise any control from the state over the criminal world is the Ministerial Police (also known as the *Policía Judicial*). They choose who to arrest and who not to, when to serve a warrant, and when and how to investigate an offence, being kidnapping or another crime. It seems from this perspective that the Ministerial Police is an almost autonomous body, whose goals at times coincide with the goals of the state and at times do not. In the words of one Ministerial Police Commander, 'we basically tell the MP [prosecutors] what to do' (LE12, investigative police shift commander, 44, male).

A notable exception to this rule is when politics are mixed up in police work. When a high-profile case arises, for example, if the son of a politician has been robbed or kidnapped, the case is usually given full attention, a proper investigation is carried out, and often the culprits are found (LE2, district official, 36, male). This is done when 'the *Procurador* (Chief Prosecutor) phones' (LE2) and orders the case to be treated as a priority. In this case, all actors within the force cooperate neatly (the *Minsterio* agents, the police, and the coroners). It is not difficult to understand why this happens. All actors have an incentive to cooperate and solve the high-profile cases because this will mean not only good publicity for them (they are doing their job), but also that, once the case is solved, this institution can go back to business as usual.

Corrupt exchanges, in a narrow sense, involving at least one member of the state, take place every day in Mexico City. Bribery is common at many levels of government and especially among the judiciary and law-enforcement agencies. We find two main types of corrupt exchange: those that seek to obtain special treatment from the authorities and those that aim for said authority to perform its normal functions (Varese 2000). On the other hand, one finds exchanges in which special treatment is bought from a government agent. An example of this is the payment of *mordidas* or 'bites'[13] to an official in order to influence a decision, avoid a fine, or give special expediency to a bureaucratic process.

### The law

Mexico City, was, until 1997, under the direct rule of the federal government. The *Regente* or head of government was directly appointed by the president and there was no local assembly, with the president also appointing the Chief of Police. An important constitutional reform enacted on 22 August 1996 set the grounds for a significantly more autonomous City. The reform provided for the direct election of a *Jefe de Gobierno del DF*, basically a mayor/governor, and also for a local assembly much like the ones operating in other states in the country. From that moment on, the City was in large part responsible for public security within its borders. It is interesting to note that the DF authorities adopted the Federal Penal Code as their own and published it with barely any changes in 1999; it was not substantially changed until 2002 (Parés Hipólito 2007: 57). All policing, crime fighting, and prevention were thus carried out based on the Federal Penal Code (Parés Hipólito 2007: 57), which later became known as the New Penal Code for the Federal District. Kidnapping was described as a crime since the early inceptions of this law both at the federal and City levels. At this moment, kidnapping became a *local* crime to be prosecuted by local City forces. However, as this crime became more prevalent, it became necessary to change this law to encompass the diversity of this particular crime. As organized crime had achieved a wider presence in Mexico, the federal government passed through Congress, also in 1996, the Federal Law against Organized Crime (Ley Federal Contra la Delincuencia Organizada—LFCDO). This law was designed to allow the federal government to prosecute organized crime groups more effectively. In the specific case of kidnapping, the crime will be a federal offence when:

- it is carried out by persons involved in groups who are engaged in the trafficking of drugs, guns, people and organs or terrorism and counterfeiting;

[13] Widely used Mexican slang for 'bribe', hence the also popular expression that refers to policemen as '*mordelones*' (i.e. 'biters').

- the victim is a foreign diplomat, a federal public servant, or a foreign public servant;
- in both cases, the Federal Prosecutor must exercise its *faculty of attraction* and decide explicitly to investigate the crime.

The law then defines organized crime as:

> When three or more people agree to organise or organise themselves to commit, in a permanent or a reiterated fashion, conducts that by themselves or together with other conducts have as an end or result the commission of one of the following crimes, they will be sanctioned by that fact alone, as being members of organised crime: robbery ... kidnapping ... child trafficking ... (LFCDO 2017)

In all other instances, however, the crime of kidnapping is a *local* offence and is prosecuted by the City authority. It is unclear when exactly a kidnapping is not committed by an organized group, but the current agreement in the courts (*jurisprudencia*) is that, in order for the crime to become a federal offence in the light of the LFCDO, it must be committed by an identified criminal organization and the Federal Attorney's Office must decide to *attract* it. Although the DF has its own Law Against Organized Crime that makes these crimes a local issue (as do other states, but not all), the practical consensus is that all organized crime acts are of a federal nature. It is beyond the scope of this book to delve any further into the legal implications of this.

Within this legal framework, the Mexico City government, with ample assistance from the federal administration, has since the late 1990s been attempting to implement successful policies targeting kidnapping. As a response to the citizens' demands for better security and specifically for protection against kidnapping, the City Government attempted to destroy the gangs that operated in many parts of the City and victimized its wealthy inhabitants. Evidence gathered throughout this research reveals that, especially after 2005, the police were able to carry out this objective with a measure of success, especially when the federal government attracted the cases.

## The Role of the States

Mexico is a federal country, divided into three levels of government: federal, state, and municipal. Despite the strength of the central government, it is necessary to acknowledge the key role played by state governments—and governors themselves—in Mexican politics. Indeed, most crimes committed in Mexico are still 'local'-level crimes. That is, they are under the jurisdiction of state governments. As mentioned above, kidnapping is no exception. Thus, state and local police (much like the Mexico City police) deal with most kidnappings. This makes them central to any crime-related policy. States have traditionally been the key political operators in the Mexican political system, especially as it relates to the perpetuation of PRI power at the federal level. States traditionally bring in votes for the PRI in exchange for money or career-making. Democratization has meant that the power of the states has eroded, but it remains very strong. An example of this is the lack of prosecutions of governors accused of corruption, who are normally protected by the party system.

Many states in Mexico have dire rule of law issues, particularly those which have the highest rates of poverty. Governors are routinely accused of corruption, conflicts of interest, links to organized crime, and running the state for personal gain. In this sense, local elites can be detrimental to the fight against kidnapping. It is therefore important to understand that politics and sub-national regimes matter. While it is not the goal of this book to expand on the impact of federalism on crime, it is important to underscore it nonetheless.

This chapter has presented the reader with a detailed history of the behaviour of kidnapping in Mexico and in Mexico City in particular. I have explained how, from a sophisticated, resource-intensive crime whose victims were the very wealthy, kidnapping became a more common crime, affecting middle- and working-class people. This is the result of: first, the reaction of wealthy communities to the kidnapping of their members, which included political and economic pressure on the government; second, the government's surprising success in destroying those older gangs; and, third, the fact that Mexico's weak rule of law allowed for new, less experienced gangs to take the place of the older ones. Thus, Mexico City found itself in the unenviable situation where kidnapping saw an increase. Chapter 4 focuses on the first factor mentioned above. It analyses, in general, how wealthy and upper-middle-class communities reacted to kidnapping. The analysis moves from the macro-community level in Chapter 4 to the micro level in Chapters 5 and 6. It is in these chapters where the analysis of trust-based relationships takes place and where the book explores how individuals avoid being kidnapped by someone close to them—an intimate crime.

# 4

# Survival Strategies

## Wealthy Communities React

Mexicans have, over time, developed a number of strategies and actions that are designed to avoid the risk of becoming victims. This is the product of a steep learning curve that began with the second wave of kidnappings described in Chapter 2 and was compounded by the government's lack of response to crime issues. As a result of being victimized or perceiving that there was the potential for this to happen, wealthy individuals and their families devised a series of survival strategies aimed at avoiding victimization. This particular social class has considerable resources at their disposal, both political and economic. Moneyed elites have historically had a cosy relationship with Mexico's politicians and government structures, which at times results in an important conflict of interest. This has been referred to as an 'allegiance for profits' (Purcell 1981). It is this closeness, embedded in a context of weak rule of law and inequality, which allows this social class to pool resources and manipulate or capture government action to their benefit. This chapter deals with the ways in which these communities have dealt with the risk of kidnapping.

These informal relationships between government and elites also fuel inequality in access to justice and due process, as well as other forms of state protection. At the same time, this allows elites freedom to act in non-institutional ways, as well as to capture the actions of the state and use them to their collective benefit. In the case of kidnapping, this is reflected in their ability to demand extra protection from the government. As the president of a tenants' association in a very wealthy gated community told me in 2008, 'we have a direct line to the [Mayor of the] City'. With regard to crime, their clout has allowed them to gain preferential protection from the state, many times to the detriment

Intimate Crimes: Kidnapping, Gangs and Trust in Mexico City. First Edition. Rolando Ochoa © Rolando Ochoa 2019. Published in 2019 by Oxford University Press

of other groups, particularly the poor, further entrenching informality and injustice. Unfortunately, *successful* mobilization in this area comes harder to middle- and working-class actors and groups. Their lack of economic clout as well as scant access to decision-makers means their demands, in this case of protection from kidnapping (or other forms of crime as well), many times fall on deaf ears. This is certainly something working-class and even middle-class Mexicans are unable to do. In fact, besides the act of voting, middle- and working-class Mexicans have little access to or say in how the government delivers public goods, when it does. To an extent, wealthy people's strategies—political lobbying and buying private security, among others—have been successful, in that they are today less victimized, and kidnapped less often, unless of course one counts being locked in gated communities and investing huge sums in private protection as a kind of victimization. Thus, we see that it is the poor that are victimized more often. This chapter will illustrate the community-level reactions that have been developed by wealthy Mexicans in order to protect themselves from kidnapping.

## The Elite Learn to Protect Themselves

After the initial rise in crime and kidnappings against the wealthy in the 1990s, in Mexico City, these people began a slow and not always successful process through which they acquired protection via a host of different strategies. The fact that they are less victimized today is evidence of their success, but this has come at a cost in lost space, segregation, and substantial monetary investments—all of which no doubt affect their quality of life and also perpetuate some of the social ills that plague Mexico. Indeed, the fact that they are still at times victimized speaks to the imperfect nature of these protection, or survival, strategies.

During the 1990s and 2000s, wealthy individuals in the City realized that they were the ones who were better positioned to provide themselves with protection from crime. This partly explains the explosion in growth of private security firms during that period, which will be discussed later. Interviewees at times described how government inefficacy led to a kind of class awakening, where they realized that they had the means to avail themselves of protection, through both economic and political means.

There are many examples of this kind of mobilization; indeed, they are everywhere, today permeating life in the City at all levels. This chapter will use examples to illustrate the processes described above. While not exhaustive, it is hoped it will give the reader an idea of the immense effect crime—and particularly kidnapping—has had on a particular group. Clearly, survival strategies will vary from group to group and from social class to social class, and they all are deserving of analysis; however, for reasons of time and space I will focus on the 'ideal-type' kidnapping victim, namely, the upper- and upper-middle classes. For clarity, I will divide this sub-section into two parts. First, I will discuss how *communities* dealt with the threat of kidnapping; I will then narrow down the focus to a 'meso' level where I look at how *family* units changed their behaviour to protect themselves from crime.

## Privatizing Security and Self

In the mid-1990s, several wealthy communities in Mexico City were repeatedly victimized by kidnappers. The wealthy Spanish and Jewish communities were particularly badly hit. As security became a fundamental issue for wealthier individuals, communities began to organize and alter their behaviour and environments. In other words, their 'survival strategies' changed (Migdal 2001). As noted by Caldeira (2000), in Brazil, higher crime rates caused a process of self-segregation on behalf of middle-class, upper-middle-class, and wealthy people that remains to this day. This process of self-segregation is ongoing and has generated even more social separation in the City, with the wealthy only ever interacting with anyone from a different social group in a service capacity.

One of the first reactions communities had was to remove themselves as much as possible from the perceived risk which was often associated with being outside or in public spaces. It cannot be overstated how pernicious this can be to the life of Mexico City. Thus began in Mexico the popularity of the gated communities that are now a central part of life in many countries (Caldeira 1997, 2000;). This self-segregation continues to the present day and has indeed spread to other social classes. Once only for wealthy families, the gated community has trickled down to middle- and lower-middle-class communities. Middle-class neighbourhood associations all over the City banded together to build gates and pay private security firms to look after their communities. The appearance of high-security, walled communities became a fixture of the City, not just in Mexico, but also in most Latin American countries. The physical spaces of the City were changed dramatically as the line between public and private space became blurred; the former encroaching increasingly into the latter.

A certain level of paranoia was also to blame for this privatization process. As 'talk of crime' (Caldeira 2000) spread through Mexican society, what was once unthinkable, or at least unreasonable—to close off one's street to outside transit or to hire private security firms—became an increasingly feasible option. As Caldeira (2000: 19) herself states, 'talk of crime ... helps produce segregation (social and spatial)'. Over time, it became normal to see fences and *casetas* (small private security booths) springing up, literally from one day to the next at times, at the entrance of streets that were once public spaces. This was in many cases illegal and lead to confrontations between the government and those communities, as the government tried to remove the fences. Mostly, in the case of smaller streets, the government adopted a *laissez-faire* attitude, allowing many streets to be closed off by those who lived there. This was not only circumscribed to streets and housing developments: buildings both public and private were finally closed to the public and made safer with private security personnel, video cameras, and electric garage doors. Thus, the mere act of living in the City became securitized and surveillance of all kinds became a priority.

Safety became a way of life in the City and a priority for many communities. Caldeira argues that this process of spatial segregation brings about higher inequality, as justice and citizenship rights become contested as individuals jostle for control of spaces and access to security (Caldeira 2000: 40). It is certainly the case that building walls generates a strong *us and them* mentality; walls are meant not just to keep people out, but also to keep people in. As a mechanism for protection, this may be useful, but the social cost of such behaviours, as argued by Caldeira, is high in terms of segregation and inequality. In the case of the neighbourhood of Polanco, the focus of much of the fieldwork presented here, a survey of thirty apartment buildings there revealed that all but one had extra security measures (private security, electric doors, controlled access, CCTV, etc.). Thus, one of the first reactions of the wealthy/wealthier Mexicans was to remove themselves from public space and privatize their security, as well as the physical spaces they inhabit.

Private security deserves a special mention here. As trust in the government and its security forces fell during the 1990s (ICESI 2003, 2005b), the number of firms offering private security to the City's population grew. The City's Minister of Public Security (Secretaria de Seguridad Pública del Distrito Federal or SSPDF, in Spanish) had registered 2,820 private security companies in Mexico City alone (SSPDF 2009), although, it says, only 514 are actually active and properly registered according to government protocol. The National Directorate for Private Security (Direccion General de Seguridad Publica—DGSP in Spanish, a government agency) estimates that between 2010 and 2015, the sector (as in number of registered private security firms) grew by 49 per cent, and the number of people employed by them by 76 per cent (SeguriLatam 2016). The sector employed (in 2007, when the latest figures are available) 11,892[1] people and had over 7,000 clients, including residential areas, industry, commercial establishments, homes, and individuals. The same report from the SSPDF states that this industry also uses 1,366 vehicles, 765 of which are armoured or bulletproof. The SSPDF has also licensed nine such firms to use 8,111 firearms.

Income figures for the private security industry for Mexico City are unavailable, but at the national level in 2008 the private security industry reported an income of 40 billion pesos (about US $3.5 billion), making it one of the top-earning industries in the country. Today, the industry associations estimate the worth of the sector at about 1 to 2 per cent of GDP (SeguriLatam 2016). These figures may be taken with a pinch of salt, but they illustrate just how big this industry is in Mexico. The period of bounty that these firms have enjoyed and profited from has become exacerbated by the ongoing War on Drugs. An increasing number of

[1] This number is still minuscule compared to the size of the Mexico City Police, the largest in Latin America. Its Preventive Police branch (uniformed policemen/women who patrol the streets) has 30,800 officers. To this, one must add the 44,950 officers that make up the Auxiliary Police, which services financial and commercial institutions, as well as manufacturing industries. This is a total of 75,750 police officers in the City. This number does not take into account the Judicial (Investigative) Police, which has 3,964 members of its own, or the Federal Police, which may at times work in the City.

people are resorting to hiring these services as they see levels of insecurity rise.

These figures do not include the high number of illegal or informal 'security' companies that exist, especially at the municipal level. These are non-registered outfits which provide services locally and are not regulated by the government. These organizations present a problem for the state, as they constitute a sizeable portion of the private security market (Müller 2010). While this cannot be confirmed at this point, it would be reasonable to expect that many organized crime groups would have an interest in participating in this semi-legitimate market, as they have the training and the means to provide this service with low start-up costs. Thus, we arrive at today, a scenario where private security has become yet another actor in the Mexican security arena, and one which has acquired more centrality as security deteriorates in many regions of the country.

It is common practice for wealthy communities to hire these private companies to provide them with extra security (Ochoa 2012). Gated communities are the living quarters of choice for the City's elite and property developers have jumped on the bandwagon by marketing smaller, less safeguarded communities to middle-income families that want to have the added protection. In one case (Ochoa 2006), a very wealthy gated community hired up to eighty private officers from a single firm to provide them with security. Their services included screening all access to the compound, patrolling inside the compound, maintaining control over employees of the homes in the compound (checking their bags when they leave and checking for identification), and identifying anyone who wishes to access the community. This community is totally walled in (a thick, 2.5-metre-tall brick wall) and has electronic gates that can be operated only by those in the compound; all other visitors must announce themselves at the gates and give their ID to the guard (which he keeps until they exit).

In an interview, the director of the tenants' association for the compound at the time (himself a famous actor) explained their choice of private security and how they function. Interestingly, this community did not hire the most expensive and sophisticated private security firm (money is clearly no problem in this community, with houses there selling for a minimum of US $1 to $1.5 million); the director, Mr Argyle,[2] explained that they did not want

[2] The director's name has been changed.

highly trained people there because 'they might be too bright and start getting ideas'. They felt safer knowing that whoever is caring for their security is good enough to do that job, but really has no other aspirations in terms of wealth or job prospects. This is an ingrained, if grossly classist, security policy for the community.

The same community also had a policy of exemplary punishment. Even the most minor incident (an employee steals something of little value, for example) is denounced to the police and criminally prosecuted, even if this process is many times more costly than whatever the person stole. The community regularly works with a law firm in these cases. Their lawyers' informal role, he admitted, is to intimidate those who break the rules—by threatening them with swift prosecution—and also to make sure the justice system does its job when they report a crime by applying pressure through informal channels. This community was very successful in making security available for all their members.

Their actions also had an unexpected spillover effect, in that it secured parts of the areas around the community which comprised a middle-class and a working-class neighbourhood (Ochoa 2006). This has been found in past criminological research into the diffusion of benefits of crime control policies (see e.g., inter alia, Clarke and Weisburd 1994; Guerette and Bowers 2009; Weisburd et al. 2006). Inequality and the urban geography in Mexico and most of Latin America mean that wealthy communities often coexist with working- and middle-class communities in very close proximity. Indeed, they often border on each other. This is contrary to the inner-city/suburbs divide of the North American city, which creates different social dynamics. This close interaction is also reflected at the household level, where employers and employees interact daily, but are from entirely different social strata.

In the case of the wealthy community described above, when they lobbied the government for better public lighting around their compound, they unwittingly made the surroundings safer for their neighbours. The same interviewee told me that they realized that they needed to offer something in return for the privilege of extra patrols around their area, which they did by offering to pay for water to be delivered to a working-class community near them which has long-term water access issues. He also spoke of instances when their private security guards were dispatched to help neighbouring communities when crimes were committed there, such as robberies or break-ins. This particular community understood their interconnection to the neighbours. He also readily admitted that they were aware that good relations with the communities around them were important in securing *their* community. This is not a coincidence as many of their household employees come from the working-class communities with which they share space, roads, and access. This feeds into the trust dynamics discussed later. The political economy of security in Mexico means that these relationships become very important, even as they may reinforce old class structures. In this particular case, the self-serving actions of a wealthy community had some positive side effects for the communities around them. This does not mean that this will be the case for other communities.

These spillovers come at a very high cost, namely, they make security for the larger population a good that is managed for the benefit of a few, or is dependent on the whims of the rich. This echoes research undertaken on the commodification of crime prevention and policing in general (Garland 1996; Loader 1999) which broadly argues that victimization is more likely for those who cannot afford to change their habits or acquire some form of protection. It is also important to point out that these groups rarely if ever lobby or use their power to push the government towards more general or inclusive policies (justice/security for all), keeping a more or less self-serving attitude in their agenda, which is reflective of their historic relationship with the state.

## Capturing/Shaping the State

Beyond the creation of private spaces and escalating segregation, there are other ways in which communities reacted to crime in Mexico City. One of the three communities under study was at the time very susceptible to kidnapping and, in fact, one of their members (a well-known television presenter) had recently been abducted and freed after a large payment. This proves that, at times, security arrangements do not work—evidence of the weakness of some of the informal security arrangements operating in these communities. As mentioned above, one mechanism that appears evident from such research, past and present, is that wealthy Mexicans decided to take advantage of their privileged position as a community to better protect themselves from kidnappers. This mechanism is rooted in the inequality persistent in Mexico.[3] As opposed to simply purchasing security privately, it is based on the fact that money can in many instances buy actions (or inactions) from state actors and on the willingness of wealthy people to use such power to their benefit. For example, wealthy communities can—via economic pressure or cronyism—pressurize the government into providing their communities with better security services, more patrols, or, indeed, better policing (Ochoa 2006). The negative impact of this dynamic on democratic development is well researched (see, inter alia, the work of O'Donnell 1998, 2004) and has largely concluded that the rule of law cannot be applied fully in such conditions of inequality.

In a system where pervasive corruption (Varese 2001) is present, it is easy for the wealthy to pressurize the state into certain behaviours, such as providing extra security services or lighting for wealthy communities, as noted in the section above. This exacerbates the inequalities explored by Holston (2007) and Caldeira (2001). Caldeira states: 'in recent decades security has become a product bought and sold on the market' (2). This applies not only to private security and protection, but also to the capacity, through corruption and other legal and illegal tactics, to steer government actors into certain actions or into remaining static.

These prevention strategies are not exclusive to the very wealthy. Many upper-middle-class interviewees also admitted to joining with their neighbours to hire security for their streets or small communities in an attempt to make them safer. While these communities did not have the same resources available as the very wealthy, they still were able to organize and purchase security from private sellers. In some cases, they paid a monthly fee to have a policeman (a public official) guard the entrance to their street (ENV13, dentist, 40, male). Others also provided regular serving police with 'tips' so that their street would be given preferential treatment on their patrol duties (ENV11, business owner, 45, female). Thus, the police are basically hired by individuals and communities to give them preferential service in protection. It is also common practice for Preventive Police (regular, uniformed

[3] This inequality has also led to an increase in crime, and has been extensively studied (Blau and Blau 1982; Fajnzylber et al. 1998; Frühling et al. 2003, among many others).

police) to 'ask' for a monetary gift from the places they guard. Most landlords comply, knowing that, if they do not, they risk being targeted by criminals or losing out on potential protection.

These protection rackets are an old and accepted way for non-wealthy people to have access to the best protection they can afford. The middle classes benefit from this, as it is usually cheaper than hiring a private protection firm full time. This also points to evidence of a racket in which police extort business owners with protection in a style similar to mafia groups elsewhere (Gambetta 1996 Varese 2001). Indeed, the police, as we have seen in Chapter 2, do tend to behave in ways that resemble a mafia group. They sell protection, extort, and engage in other crimes as well. More research is needed to establish how widespread this behaviour is and how exactly these rackets work on an everyday basis. What we do know now from fieldwork is that the police do offer their services on the private market by asking individuals and communities if they want better protection, and also by waiting to be asked by the same.

This scenario obviously benefits those with more resources to invest in security or payments to the police. Corruption thus allows for those with access to cash to privatize the services of public actors. This clearly presents a problem for democratic development as it entrenches privilege, cronyism, and in many cases conflict of interest between the private and public sectors (Ochoa and Graycar 2016). As we will see below, this is even more widespread in Mexico to the extent that the wealthy are able to shape policy and capture government action for their benefit.

An interesting case of these community-based efforts to acquire protection is the action of the Jewish community of Mexico City. After a long-running series of kidnappings victimizing members of this community (KNRD 2009), they organized themselves and decided to take direct action. The Committee for Social Action (Comité de Acción Social CAS, in Spanish) was created in 1999 with the sole mission of protecting the community from kidnapping and ensuring that cases that did occur were properly investigated, solved, and punished. The group is made up of around twenty-five volunteers from the community who 'include lawyers, psychologists and other specialists' (KNRD 2009). Their identities are kept secret for protection purposes. They also keep secret files on all the kidnapping gangs they research. In an interview, the head of the Central Committee of the Jewish Community in

Mexico said that members of the CAS keep a close relationship with the relevant police forces and that they are committed to following up on all cases without exception. They are a task force that becomes active once they learn of a possible kidnapping in the community; they work with the families of the victims and gather information about the kidnappers for police. They also perform informal investigations on kidnappings, lobby the authorities to carry out solid and thorough investigations of their own, and use their legal clout to make sure that once the kidnappers are jailed they never get out; as the interviewee stated, 'for us, someone in jail will remain there' (KNRD 2009). He also stated that, due to the efforts of the CAS, there are virtually no more victims within the Jewish community, with only two known cases in the last few years, both of which were solved and the culprits jailed.

Another interviewee (ENV8, marketing professional, 60s, female) in the same neighbourhood also told me that, beyond the actions of the CAS, the Jewish community had also carried out a strong lobbying campaign to pressurize the government into providing them with more security in their neighbourhoods (a large percentage of this community lives in the Miguel Hidalgo district). She told me that the community had been in contact with the government, stating that its members would start leaving the City and closing their businesses if the government took no action to prevent the kidnappings. The success of this strategy can be attributed to the extensive network of this community in the political sphere, as well as their economic power, which—as is the case with most wealthy Mexicans—affords them easy access to the justice system as described conceptually by O'Donnell (1998). In a country where the rule of law is weak, this kind of social organization seems to be one of the most effective responses. Their success needs access to important monetary resources and the political connections that come with it. Without this, they could not have the same level of contact with the government. Through these actions, it became very costly for kidnappers to victimize members of that community. The government did indeed respond to their pressure and now the Miguel Hidalgo neighbourhood is one of the most secure parts of the City. It is also one known for the constant presence of security forces. This group of victims probably presented to criminals the highest likelihood of being caught when compared to other social groups. At the same time, the state was busy putting together the elite police group that would destroy the old kidnapping gangs, as explored in Chapter 2. With their ability to organize themselves and cooperate as a community and also to influence the actions of the state, they achieved levels of protection that are not available to all members of Mexican society.

It is important here to make a distinction between self-defence and the concept of protection. It would appear that the CAS is a self-defence group. Self-defence appears to be a strategy used a posteriori, once the person/community is under attack; protection is normally acquired a priori, to avert a *likely* attack. The decision to get protection and/or work together is based, then, on a personal analysis of the likelihood that one will be attacked in the future. Within this distinction, the CAS is a case of self-defence; a group formed by a community under attack in order to better defend its members. Over time, however, it has become a protection agent, developing expertise to avoid future attacks, as its people still consider themselves to be likely victims.

This form of community organization may be contrasted with Banfield's notion of 'amoral familism' (1967), which argues that in some cases the economic interests of families will be detrimental to the overall development of the community in which they live—in that families have been able to work together to achieve a common goal, even if this means a poorer outcome for the City in general. In this sense, we may risk calling this type of action a form of amoral classism, where the nuclear family is replaced by social class and the actions of said class are at times detrimental to the overall development of the entire citizenry.

## Family-Based Protection

Here, we begin to head towards the micro-level analysis. Insecurity, or the perception thereof, affects different people in different ways, and we begin to see this at the family-unit level. While all families interviewed claim to have been affected by crime in terms of their behaviour, the intensity and direction of these effects are different from one unit to another. In most cases, interviewees freely admit that they find it difficult to be openly trusting, or at least as trusting as they were in the past. Thus, we see that this has made families change the way they relate to one another and how they interact with the world outside of the family realm.

Families and individuals have devised ad hoc strategies of protection. Everyone I interviewed admitted to changing their everyday activities and practices due to crime and specifically as a response to being victims of kidnapping or perceiving themselves as potential victims. This could be characterized as strategic behaviour (Gambetta and Hamill 2005), since individuals perceive themselves as potential victims and take measures to avoid actually becoming victims.

> I was never afraid before, I mean, I was very, I went to University came back at three in the afternoon, three in the morning, I went, I mean, no, no, no; as a matter of fact now I go at night and ... it transformed my life so much, well, I mean, I have worked it out, and ... I go out in the street and I walk all day, but I am very careful, I mean I am aware of who is around, and ... who is close to me, I am super aware, for example late at night, alone, I do not go out. I get home and I lock myself in, and, my whole life I planned it, it does not mean nothing will happen to you no? But I planned it, I live and work in a one-block radius.

These are the words of a kidnapping victim (EV1, architect, 35, female) describing the effect the experience has had on her in particular. She was taken with some friends after leaving a friend's house late one evening. They were kept for around twenty-four hours while the kidnappers negotiated with the families of one of the kidnapped group of four friends, who they assumed, had the most money. The interviewee described the kidnappers as 'incompetent' since they kept running out of cell phone credit and had to stop to buy more, and seemed confused and in disagreement with each other about what to do during the kidnapping. To her, it seemed like they had not done this many times before, if at all. This made the experience feel particularly volatile. Eventually, the kidnappers let the group go after collecting some money. They were left on a pedestrian bridge, in the early hours of morning.

While it is obvious that her experience and those of others like her is one of the most extreme cases of a life being affected by crime, it illustrates many of the feelings heard throughout the field research. It draws out a clear strategy to avoid being targeted. This particular victim reconstructed her world after being victimized so that she would have to travel as little as possible in her everyday life. She lived in a central area where everything was close and worked every day in an office she rented very near her home (a three-minute walk). These attitudes are echoed by people who have not been victimized in this way, but may have heard about instances and cases like this in their immediate social circle. For example, an interviewee (ENV12, academic, female, 62) explained how they had hired private security after suspecting that someone had been going through their mail, even though they had not been directly threatened or victimized. Another respondent (ENV13, dentist, 40, male) explained how he had made the decision to buy bulletproof cars, even though his family had never been targeted, and spoke of how their social habits had changed, as they went out less and less at night. Thus, victimization has long-lasting effects not only on the victims themselves, but also on those around them, and contributes to the overall narrative of insecurity and risk.

Another victim (EV5, art curator, 34, female) who was held for eight days made the more radical choice to leave the country after suffering intense post-traumatic stress disorder. This was triggered, she said, not by the kidnapping itself, but by years later being robbed violently in a Mexico City street: 'I thought, it has already happened to me, nothing can happen again.' The victim had constructed a sense of invincibility after the kidnapping as a coping mechanism, thinking that because she had been victimized once, it could not happen again. The experience of being robbed in broad daylight shattered a sense of safety she constructed after being targeted and, when it did, she decided to leave the country. She now resides in the United States and freely admits she is not certain she has any desire to return to Mexico. This case illustrates the incredible costs of kidnapping and one of the most radical decisions a victim can take in response to it. Even though it was not the kidnapping which triggered the decision to leave the country, it was certainly the *sine qua non* of the decision. Leaving family, friends, and one's home because of an experience like being kidnapped is an incredibly difficult choice. The interviewee did state that she missed all of these things, which made her life abroad sometimes difficult, but she could not deal with the thought of going back due to the stress and fear it caused her.

Since the mid-1990s, both victims and potential victims engaged in series of transformative practices that would alter the way in which they carried out their lives and would eventually also contribute to making them more difficult targets to attack. I have mentioned before how communities themselves organized to fight kidnappers and criminals in general through political influence, monetary capabilities, and community-based organizations. Individuals and families also engaged in these practices. Most of my interviewees claimed to have adopted safety measures to counteract the risk of kidnapping at one point or another. There are a number of protection mechanisms that are common to most people and families. The first of such mechanisms was that people *stopped sharing information* about themselves or their family. A certain level of privacy and secrecy is integral to most social groups or families. There are things people do not discuss outside of the family. However, casual social interaction, such as a chat with someone at the grocery store, at the park, or the petrol station, is an integral part of community life; this is how people connect and form a sense of community. This everyday activity has become suspect. Informal chats with strangers are avoided and casual social interaction generates suspicion; isolation ensues as these interactions are, in many cases, kept to a minimum. An interviewee explained her policy with regard to divulging information thus:

> I have forbidden my *muchacha* [maid] to give out any information, about the Señora, nothing, nothing. Who lives here, how many are we, nothing. Even I, when I answer the phone I say hello, who is this? Who do you want to talk to? If they say anything, I just say 'wrong number' and hang up; I do not give any information about anything. (ENV4, retired, 50s, female)

This is a version of many similar responses given when asking for specific protection strategies. Keeping family information as secret as possible is seen as critical for staying protected. Most, if not all, persons I have spoken to bring this up. One interviewee (ENV12, academic, 52, female) believed that her family was in danger because her bank statements had not arrived in the post as usual. Her fear was that someone was stealing them to assess her family's monetary value. She believed the threat to be so real that she took the case to the bank and investigated whether the statements had been misplaced or disappeared: 'the post did not deliver them, and it is the first time in a very long time that I see (this), on top of that, they were the envelopes (statements) of our most important investment account, and they disappeared' (ENV12). After a subsequent break-in (when no one was at home), the family decided to hire private security for their home; this included CCTV and a guard. The fact that this required a substantial expense for the family was not something which affected their decision.

Kidnapping in its 'classic' form was always based on good information. Gangs required extensive gathering of such information to choose their victim, plan, and execute the kidnapping. All members of the household in *all* of the interviews are under some form of instruction to keep basic information about the family secret. Clearly, a certain level of discretion about family affairs—anywhere—is always a given; however, the emphasis and the extent to which this practice is now carried out in Mexico City goes beyond this. A common practice is to give out false information (for example, lying about one's job or income when directly asked or giving out false addresses and telephone numbers when the necessity arises). This applies even in the case of providing information to government officials, like customs officers. This level of distrust makes the forging of new relationships difficult and also serves to further isolate these groups from others as they seek to protect their family above all other members of the community.

Other strategies include more practical matters, such as the purchase of bulletproof vehicles and guns. A businessman/dentist I interviewed talked about the need for this:

> Well, for example, we changed, and, and, our cars are bulletproof for example … Yes, that part is not nice, you have to make an expenditure that no, you should not be making … No, it should not be, hmmm, I do not know why it was [the decision to buy the bulletproof cars], it was someone, a case we heard of, a patient or something like that [who was victimized] and it was not the first one, so we decided [to get the cars].

This interviewee makes a point which is central to arguments about equity. He sees the purchase of the bulletproof cars as an expenditure he should not be making, but does so nonetheless. The cost of security arrangements can be prohibitively expensive. For example, a used 2011 armoured Chevrolet Suburban can cost up to US $90,000. These are not small expenses and, as the interviewee states, it should not be necessary in most environments. However, these are costs that an increasing number of people are willing to incur in exchange for safety, or at the very least peace of mind.

This peace of mind also applies to interaction with government officials, such as police, who are deeply distrusted in the City. The same interviewee told the story of how one night, coming home from a rare dinner out with his wife, he was stopped by police for what they argued was a routine check. He stopped the car and, refusing to open the window, only showed the policeman his ID from behind the glass. The police officer asked him to open the window and hand the documents over; he refused. As he recounted, 'I told the [policeman] "this is an armoured car, I am not going to open the window and I can stay here all night, but I am not opening the window and there is no way you can open it"'. This stand-off went on for some time, with the officer demanding he open the window and hand over his documents and him refusing. He was eventually waved off when the police realized they would not be able to convince him to get what they wanted.

This example not only illustrates some of the more salient aspects of the results of fear of crime in the City, but also points in the direction of a key issue affecting the quality of democracy in the City. People in Mexico do not trust the police, or the justice system for that matter. The fact that a citizen will refuse to talk to a policeman when stopped is indicative of these deep suspicions. This should not surprise anyone who is familiar with the history of the Mexico City police, as described in previous chapters. 'The biggest gang in town' is in fact a truthful reflection of the City police forces. While there are certainly honest elements within the police force there, as a whole, the institution is regarded as highly corrupt (Davis 2006b). Fear and distrust of authority (not only police, but also elected officials) is extremely widespread in Mexico. The current War on Drugs has only exacerbated this and in recent times there seems to be a further deterioration due to the increasing violence and evident collusion between drug cartels and the government.

Another case in point regarding the effects of crime at this level is that which opens this book. When I interviewed Mr X, he said:

> At some point, in our case, well, obviously, mmm, we entered the system of 'escoltas' [bodyguards] and guns, however, there comes a time when you realise that this is not the way in which you want to live and you break free of them, you break free of the 'escoltas' … you break free of the guns and you say: it is not that it will not happen to me, or that it will not happen to me *again*, simply, I will not be a hostage of criminals; so I changed the way I lived, to the way I want to live, if it happens to me it happens, if it does not it does not, I will be as prepared as I can if it does happen again, to defend myself with what I have within my reach, but I will not sacrifice my way of life …

He did, however, admit to taking precautions and to having changed some of his practices:

> In moments of risk … I take precautions and when I go to a restaurant I do not turn my back to the door, I see who is there and maybe I get stubborn and I leave … you do take certain precautions … but I have not accepted becoming a fearful person who modifies all his conducts.

Clearly, and with very good reason, this interviewee had modified his actions to a degree. He had implemented a set of mechanisms and strategies that are also common to other interviewees. First, people have developed a very deep awareness of their surroundings, becoming keen observers of people and situations around them that go beyond what could be considered 'everyday' precautions. Most people I have spoken to look keenly for certain signs/signals of danger, which include 'young men, kind of typical Mexican, thin, shortish, dark hair and baseball cap' (EV1, architect, 35, female). This is clearly a case of profiling, as many Mexican males could fit that description and clearly not all of them are criminals or violent people. This is deeply problematic, since the criminalization of young, mostly working-class Mexicans is widespread and high crime rates, as well as the War on Drugs, have only exacerbated this.

Other signs of danger may include 'four (men), black SUV, tinted windows, driving aggressively' (EV3, businessman, 55, male). This, again, is an image constructed on stereotypes of dangerous behaviours and attitudes. Many of these strategies are based on generalized interpretations of what is assumed to be dangerous. However, they are widespread and individuals act on them regularly. People spend considerable amounts of energy and time making these observations. Interestingly, after a time, they become second nature and are done reflexively and without much thought. Some interviewees alluded to the development of this 'skill' over time.

Another strategy involves avoiding going out at night to unusual and far-off places. As expressed by a number of interviewees, they rarely go out at night and prefer to stay home as opposed to risking an outing. This clearly limits the scope of the experience of living in the City. However, in many cases, this containment is purely for practical reasons, such as transport, proximity to services, etc., and security is not as central to the decision on where to settle and live or where to go at night. This is not to say that these large cities do not have areas that are considered dangerous by some—areas to be avoided by outsiders. What it does mean is that in Mexico, the decision not to go somewhere is many times made purely on security grounds. This particularly applies to people's participation in the night-time economy. By the same token, people have become accustomed to keeping their social activities to a clearly limited geographical area. As put by one interviewee, 'we don't go around everywhere at night' (ENV13, dentist, 40, male). Surveys (e.g. ICESI 2013) support the view that a high proportion of people in Mexico City have changed their routines and activities because of the fear of crime, and this is particularly true at night when many individuals choose to stay at home. Indeed, a national survey (INEGI 2013) shows that up to 23 million Mexicans (or about 20 per cent of the total population) have stopped going out to socialize or attend cultural or sporting events due to security considerations. This is not exclusively due to kidnapping, but to the overall sense of insecurity of which kidnapping is a part. Of those, about 1.5 million live in Mexico City, which accounts for about 20 per cent of the City's population.[4] This has serious implications not only for the people who choose to remove themselves from the City's entertainment and cultural life, but also for the City's economy in terms of lost clientele for restaurants and other such venues. It also affects the cultural character of the City, as night-time spaces become less populated and less welcoming. There is a clear tendency towards individual and group isolation in Mexico. Insular and segregated social classes have become even more so as insecurity increases and the spaces where different people interacted, such as parks, markets, and transport, become vacated or only occupied by those who cannot afford a 'safer' alternative. This, in turn, fuels feelings of alienation and insecurity, reinforces damaging stereotypes, and entrenches fear and distrust of the other.

The success of wealthy Mexicans in preventing and dealing more effectively with the threat of kidnapping is not just due their capacity to better organize and mobilize their resources. It is also tied intimately to Mexico's environment of inequality and corruption, which results in unfair access to government elites and undue influence in the policy-making process. The success of the

[4] The population of Mexico City is around 9 million people; that of the greater Mexico City area is around 23 million.

wealthy in protecting themselves and in garnering increased government protection also meant that, in Mexico's weak rule of law environment, the poor paid the price as kidnapping mutated into a low return, less organized crime. What can certainly be argued is that when protection is sold as a private good, those with access to wealth benefit more as they are better able to purchase this good—be it from the state or from private entities—in the open market. This chapter focuses on how elites have been able to devise strategies to protect themselves from crime from the community at the family level. Privatizing their environments and encroaching on public spaces is one of these tactics, as is the privatization of their security, which has resulted in the explosion of the private security industry. Alongside these unilateral actions, there have been concerted efforts to use economic and political power to capture and shape government action, thus gaining access to higher levels of state protection, to the detriment of other social groups. While this chapter has focused on the *macro* and *meso* levels of analysis, the following chapter will focus on the *micro* level by examining how individuals solve problems of trust and communication while navigating the risk of kidnapping.

As exposed in Chapter 2, kidnappings are often organized or facilitated by someone close to the victim, such as an employee. With this risk in mind, the following chapter will explore how wealthy individuals try to avoid this *intimate crime* throughout the process of hiring their household employees and illustrate how risk is managed in an environment of low state protection. The analysis is based on extensive interviews and field research, as described in the Introduction to this book.

# 5

# Avoiding an Intimate Crime

## What Is Trust Anyway?

During field research, I always asked people what trust meant to them. This question was posed to drivers, employers, police officers, members of the community, and almost anyone I encountered. What immediately stood out was that most people had a difficult time pinpointing what they thought trust was. Articulating a concise definition was challenging in most cases, independently of levels of education or socioeconomic status. Most people were unable to define it right off the bat, needing in many cases some prompting and explorations. Interestingly, only one person—a retired businessman—could provide a definition that in any way approximated the one found in the literature: 'when you know a person will do as you expect in a given circumstance'. Most interviewees have a very abstract notion of what trust is. In many cases, trust was described as a feeling, or a hunch, a gut feeling. The vast majority of respondents confessed never to have thought about a definition, even if trust is an integral part of their lives. This is not necessarily surprising, as many people do not think in academic terms. One interviewee (ENV9, retired, 70s, female) made a particularly compelling illustration of this. During one conversation on the topic of trust, she claimed she had very good 'instincts' and could make those decisions based on said instincts. We discussed this at length, trying to unpack exactly what these were. After a discussion of about thirty minutes on the topic, where we tried to unpack what factors triggered those positive or negative feelings, she concluded that perhaps there was more to it than just emotional reactions, although she was not 100 per cent convinced. This conversation, or a similar version of it, repeated itself countless times, pointing to the fact that many people choose not to reflect on trust itself, but rather take it as a sort of social given, a natural part of life. This is not surprising, as people have

Intimate Crimes: Kidnapping, Gangs and Trust in Mexico City. First Edition. Rolando Ochoa © Rolando Ochoa 2019. Published in 2019 by Oxford University Press

their own lives and do not necessarily have the time or inclination to ask themselves these questions.

This underscores some of the difficulties in researching topics such as these. Trust, as Seligman (1997) points out, is key to the functioning of societies; in fact, people in Mexico often talk about it. Yet, when confronted with the question of what trust is, many cannot find an answer. Trust in this case is a lived feeling and tied to a series of emotions, such as family bonds and friendship, many of which cannot be fully rationalized. This raises the question as to how researchers can construct a narrative on trust if it is such an intangible notion for people. More importantly, it tells us about how people experience their everyday interactions and decisions and how they interpret what may be complex cognitive processes. Some relevant questions arise here, for example: what is the weight of emotions in the establishment of trust? How can we discern the rational cognitive process from an emotional one, and is this even possible or desirable? Many scholars have delved into the interplay and analytic limitations between and among emotions and rationality. Elster (2004) has explored this at length and I direct the reader to his brilliant work. These questions remain open and inform some of the future discussions on trust.

## Drivers, Trust, and Signaling

A high percentage of kidnappings occur with the participation of either a member of the victim's family—what has been labelled the 'treason phenomenon' by the City police (KNRD 2009)—or a close employee, such as a driver, gardener, or business employee. This figure could be as high as 70 per cent according to press releases by the City police (KNRD 2009). It is clear why it is of the utmost importance for anyone who has employees in the family home (drivers, cleaning staff, and cooks are all common in higher-middle-income houses and above) to make sure that these people are trustworthy. In an environment of high kidnapping rates, it is important to underscore that one of the main roles of these workers, beyond their job description, is to protect a family's most basic information.

Why drivers? Many upper-middle- and upper-class families in Mexico have these types of employees. Exact figures of how many are not available, but qualitative evidence suggests that many families do employ them. All of my interviewees (employers) had a driver at one point or another. In some cases, this employment is part time. An example of this relates to a driver I interviewed (WNV12, driver/taxi driver, 40s, male) who, for a few days a week, freelanced as a driver for one of my other interviewees (he had been doing so for at least five years) and also drove a taxi the remainder of the time. This kind of arrangement is more common in middle-class homes. Upper-class households have more resources and are able to keep their staff employed full time. This may also reduce the risk of being victimized by locking in or vertically integrating household employment (Williamson 2005b). I will come back to the importance of these arrangements later. In a more or less crime-free environment where law enforcement institutions work efficiently (or more efficiently), drivers would have a small (if logistically important) role in a family's life. However, in an environment such as the one I have described in Mexico, where crime is common and kidnapping has become an important source of fear, these employees acquire a different role.

The driver of an *empresario*'s (businessman) children is the owner of information that kidnappers might pay handsomely for, possibly much more than his average monthly salary, potentially creating a strong temptation for the driver to default on his contract. The driver might also be forced by criminals to divulge this information against his will. This was the case in the kidnapping and eventual murder of a rehabilitation centre worker in 2009, mentioned earlier. A driver who worked for her became involved, through a personal friend, with kidnappers in his neighbourhood. They knew he worked at the centre and that he had access to information on potential victims there. They convinced him to facilitate their kidnapping by offering him money to give them information about the victim. They also attempted to intimidate him into cooperating. After having second thoughts about the crime that was about to be committed, the driver was then forced to stay quiet by the criminals, who threatened to kill him if he spoke out. He apparently made an anonymous call to the police to tip them off, but this led nowhere. The victim was kidnapped. Unfortunately, the victim was shot dead when the police attempted—and failed—to rescue her from the safe house where she was being held (KNRD 2009).

This story gives us an idea of the risk that hiring an employee may entail. This makes trust, and the establishment thereof, very important. Therefore, this relationship cannot be characterized only as a straightforward master–servant contract. The fact that the employee is, for all practical purposes, entrusted with protecting his or her employer's family makes these relationships much more complex. The protection of the sensitive information to which the driver has access must be cemented by significant amounts of trust and highly effective enforcing mechanisms. This is especially so due to the fact that there is a limited rule of law and credible threat of prosecution from the government should a default occur, a scenario described by Dixit as 'lawlessness' (2004). Recourse to an efficient and fair legal system that punished contract defaults would make trust somewhat unnecessary as a mechanism, since the threat of enforcement would ideally sustain the relationship. However, as Williamson (2005a) states, even in contexts where contracts are properly enforced by the state, there is a need for informal arrangements that cement and guarantee cooperation. Many of the relationships I examine here are of this sort. In Mexico, both employers and employees must resort many times to informal non-institutional mechanisms to sustain their contracts.

Thus, we see that the driver is not only offering his services as just that, but rather *he becomes an agent in the protection of the people he drives*. In other words, he is also employed to *protect information*. As one interviewee put it: 'trust (in the hiring context) means you are caring for something that is mine' (ENV8, marketing executive, 60s, female). This distinction is key because it allows us to establish drivers as providers of protection, even if this is not their real job description. This is not to say that they explicitly offer this service, but it is understood that in most cases the provision of such a good is expected as part of the employment agreement. The element of risk in this relationship makes it an ideal venue to explore trusting relationships and their development in an environment where there is no constant institutional enforcement.

Evidence from most interviews carried out with employers during field research (over 90 per cent of them) suggests that this security issue is the primary concern of the employer when hiring. If a driver is to enter a long-term contract, he must sell to his employer the idea that he is a skilled protector of information and worthy of trust. The employer must also be sure that his prospective employee is not a mimic (Gambetta and Hamill 2005), passing himself off as a fake driver, or someone who may be looking for information to use in the commission of a crime.

It is a driver's ability to protect this information that is his best asset, both at the time of the initiation of the relationship and also in further negotiations of their contract. In an environment of high crime and impunity, both employer and employee must reach a solid agreement because the costs of default can be very high for both.

There are two principal means of enforcement of a relationship such as this one. The first and ideal one is when the relationship becomes self-enforcing (Dixit 2004); this is achieved by reaching a situation in which it is in both parties' main interest to cooperate, mainly because the future costs of defection are larger than its immediate benefits (Axelrod 1984). If this is the case and actors are aware of such a mechanism, an equilibrium is achieved through which cooperation ensues. If an employee is to consider defecting from his employment contract and providing information to kidnappers, his pay-offs from this particular transaction must be higher than those he obtains from sustained cooperation. It is mostly the responsibility of the employer to make sure the costs of defection for his driver *always* surpass the pay-offs, since the state is not always there to arbitrate the relationship or punish defections. It is here where diverse mechanisms come vitally into play. The employer must make sure the correct motivations are operating for the potential employee.

The employer's first task is to figure out if the potential driver in front of him is governed by short-term 'raw' pay-offs or longer-term 'all-in pay-offs' that also take into account the employer's preferences and pay-offs (Gambetta and Hamill 2005: 4). That is, he must establish if the employee is motivated to engage in a long-term cooperative relationship or if he or she is likely to default. In most cases, the state plays the part of making sure that the costs of defecting are such that it becomes very difficult to do so. One such mechanism is, of course, the courts. If an employer and an employee enter into a contract, a defection on said contract can be punished by law. However, this becomes more difficult to achieve in a situation where we find a lack of enforcement by government institutions and prevalent informal relations.

The first task for the employer during the recruiting process is to establish whether he can trust his prospective employee before he hires him.[1] This is of paramount importance, as it is the first

[1] As mentioned above, the choice to refer to drivers as male is based on the fact that virtually all of them are. I have only ever met one female driver.

step towards entering into a relationship. The employer must establish whether the person presenting himself as a potential driver is who he says he is and has the intentions he claims to have. In this sense, they engage in a *basic trust game*, as explained in Chapter 2 of this book (Gambetta and Hamill 2005), and must solve both primary and secondary trust problems (Bacharach and Gambetta 2001).

As mentioned above, the employer must discern whether or not the potential driver will operate under his 'all-in' pay-offs or if he will not be able to resist the attraction of his 'raw' pay-offs (Gambetta and Bacharach 2001). In this relationship, the 'raw' pay-offs would be the immediate benefit of betraying the employer-truster and giving away his private information or facilitating a kidnapping. His 'all-in' pay-offs would ideally include sets of norms, values, and perhaps fear of punishment that would override the 'raw' motivation to defect, thus creating a protective environment.

The establishment of the driver-trustee's trustworthiness will be achieved by determining if he (the trustee) is in possession of a number of qualities or properties that the employer believes to mean he is trustworthy. In the case that concerns us, hiring, the process may be split into two steps. First, the employer must actually find potential employees. The second step requires the further establishment of a person's trustworthiness. All this is done through a process by which the employer screens the potential employee for signs or signals of certain properties. If the employee displays the signals the employer is looking for, it is then up to the employer to solve the secondary problem of trust (Bacharach and Gambetta 2001) and establish whether those signals he is watching are indeed true or just a front for a mimic or impostor.

## The Small World of Mexico City's Social Networks

The first step in the hiring process is to filter access through one's own network. This is related to the process of isolation lived by wealthy families referred to in the previous chapter. In the past, when safety was not such a concern, it was common to hire household employees through less secure channels. A common practice was to advertise for a position with a sign on one's front door. This would mean anyone—known or unknown—could apply for a job in the household. This has become mostly unthinkable today and speaks volumes to the way in which general levels of trust have decreased in Mexican society. Evidence of this process goes as far back as the mid- to late 2000s, when surveys showed that a majority of respondents stated they could not be as trusting of their neighbours as before (Ablanedo et al. 2008).

Interviewee ENV14 (businessman, 60, male) stated: 'Generally, my wife does not hire people she does not know, I mean ... she hardly would hire anyone who is a complete unknown ... someone who enters the house is not easy, normally it is people who know us.' Similarly, interviewee ENV8 (marketing, 60s, female) said, 'someone would have to recommend you ... (if you were to be hired)'. ENV3 (home, 50s, female), also said 'I got all my employees through friends, yes, all through my friends'. This is more so with regard to employers who have been victims of kidnapping. Victim EV5, a 34-year-old art curator, stated that 'now more than ever' she only goes through personal recommendations. These words echo the opinions of all the employers interviewed. In no case did any of the employers interviewed find a driver through any other means. Receiving a recommendation from someone in one's social group when looking for a potential employee is a necessary condition and cuts down on the costs of establishing how trustworthy this person is, assuming the individual recommending him or her is already worthy of trust. In this sense, a first trust-warranting property and the *only* way to enter into possible employment is by presenting or coming through a *personal recommendation* of a close friend or relative of the employer or someone in their direct network. Strong ties prove to be almost the only way to get a job in this situation. This is contrary to Granovetter's (1973) argument about the strength of weak ties, which he argues were more useful in transmitting information through a social network (information, in this case, about jobs) in the study he carried out. This is not so surprising and I would posit that the difference is related to contextual factors such as legal certainty, the rule of law, and levels of informality which could explain whether it is weak, or strong ties which prevail. Following this, we can picture Mexico City's social structure as a series of very dense networks, with few, or very weak, connections with each other. This further illustrates the way in which the City is segregated and divided, both socially and physically. It is interesting to note that through the process of hiring, one can observe two distant networks becoming connected. These two groups are employers and employees. In fact, these two groups are generally very socially distant, but through employment they become connected, and once trust has been established among the two groups, a weak tie is formed through which information may flow (about new jobs, for example) in the future. This process can be reinforced through a mechanism of vertical integration in household employment, which I will discuss below.

Thus, the first signal screened for is established; employers use their strong ties (Granovetter 1983) to search for potential employees. Explorations through people's weak ties may happen at times, but this is less common. As stated above, this particularity makes the process safer as it renders the transmission of information easier and access to jobs via a fake recommendation very costly if the employee does not have access to this network. People who do have access to it may display it at low cost, thus fulfilling the cost condition for a semi-sorting equilibrium (Gambetta 2009).

In any case, the close-knit social circles such as those prevailing in the Mexican upper-class group serve this purpose very well, since they are smaller networks where communication is very easily transmitted at a very low cost. Thus, the procedure for hiring a driver begins with an exploration of one's own networks. Asking friends or relatives if they 'know of anyone' will normally turn up one or two recommendations. The value of the recommendation rests on the already acquired trust of the person making the recommendation to the employer and sometimes *also* on the already acquired trust of an employee of the person making the recommendation. To put it simply, an employer will ask a close friend for a recommendation; said friend will then ask his employees if they know any potential candidates. This network of trust extends through two sets of employers and employees, or four clustered networks. The latter, having gained access to the network, and having proven themselves trustworthy, can then become a source of information for other members of the network. As mentioned before, the times when hiring was done through placing a cardboard advert on the front door are long gone. The process has become much more complicated and, in some instances, has also become safer.

Once a recommendation has come through the employer's network, the one-on-one hiring process begins proper. Clearly, having been backed by a recommendation, the prospective employee has already displayed a key sign of trustworthiness and, in fact, without this particular sign there is no chance of being hired. This is not, however, a final sorting equilibrium (Gambetta and Hamill 2004). Indeed, in this particular case, there is no such thing, as there is no fully sorting signal. The process must continue so that further vetting can occur.

Further screening takes place where the employer decides if he is to finally employ the driver. In this secondary screening phase, the employer seeks to establish for himself whether the employee possesses some of the other properties he deems to be signs of trustworthiness. In a sense, he is also double-checking that the recommendation he received is in fact a good one, and that the recommended person does possess the qualities or properties stated in the recommendation. At the same time, this verifies and reinforces their trust in their own networks, creating a type of feedback loop. The establishment of these links is not an easy task and is a process which occurs over a period of time. This involves making, as stated above, important changes to the process through which this sector of the job market works.

Most interviewees are aware of this process and ultimately accept the fact that changes to their practices are/were necessary. An interviewee (ENV6, businessman, 70s, male) told me: 'I believe that this situation [crime], hhmmm, forces you, regardless of your resistance to do so, to incorporate certain measures, changes, to avoid this kind of crime [kidnapping].' This echoes the feeling of resignation to which many interviewees refer. They subscribe generally to the idea that they do not want to build walls, spend money on security, or worry too much about their employees, but they must do it in order to feel safer. There is also an awareness of the fact that—ideally—that expense be shouldered by another actor, namely the government. As the dentist interviewee stated, these are expenses that one 'should not be making'. This also reinforces the context of inequality mentioned earlier, as it is clear that in many cases the access to security is dependent on a person's economic circumstances. Thus, the poor are left unprotected and to their own devices.

In this way, the process of hiring continues. Another major problem faced by employers is that some of the characteristics they look for in a driver can only be known over time or are not easily observed (Gambetta and Bacharach 2001; Gambetta and Hamill 2004). This poses a serious problem when making a decision that is potentially risky. When properties are only observable over repeated interactions, employers must look for proxies of these properties. Here, things can become more complicated as people often seem to rely on what many of them describe as 'gut feelings' to make these choices or assessments during the screening process.

What are the most common properties employers screen for? Over the course of over seventy interviews and countless conversations about the topic, Table 5.1 shows some of the most common properties that employers look for in a driver. *Discretion* tops the list of such qualities. This property is important not just for security purposes, but also in more general terms. Most employers tend to demand discretion to some extent of all their employees. This can apply to business information, family matters, etc. This also happens to be a very difficult property to screen for, especially in a short amount of time. It is possible to find out if someone is discreet when we have had several interactions with the person in which opportunities for discretion have arisen. These may include confiding private information to the person in question and being aware that they have not disclosed it later. While many interviewees had a hard time clearly defining the term, most were close to 'not disclosing family information' (ENV1, home, 64, female). Discretion can be simply described in this case as being able to withhold details of the employer's private life to which drivers have routine access; it also includes a reserved nature, being 'not nosy'. The information to be kept private includes work/life schedules of the whole family and a good knowledge of the level of wealth and income of the household, among other snippets of information that would be extremely useful for kidnappers. We will keep this simple definition for discretion henceforth, as it illustrates very well the employer's main concerns.

## Hiring

After the potential employee has been screened for discretion and he has been able to display it to the employer's satisfaction, he is hired and on most occasions the hiring process entails a test period. During this time (which can take from a day or two to three weeks, depending on who you ask), the new prospective

**Table 5.1 Most Common Properties Screened for by Employers**

| Property (from most difficult to easiest to screen for) | Mentioned by (%) | Sign | Screening methods |
|---|---|---|---|
| Membership in network/family | 100 | Recommendation | Verbal or written and verifiable |
| Discretion | 100 | Keeping information secure by not divulging it; proxies: being from outside the City, not too chatty | Very difficult to establish, relies heavily on recommendations and repeated interaction/ observation |
| Efficiency | 20 | Completing tasks quickly, without involving many people, and at low cost | Can be screened for only during test period |
| Helpfulness | 100 | Offering to do things in the household; volunteering for tasks | Only by observation |
| Age | 74 | Must be of a certain age, not too young and not too old (both unreliable) | Proof by observation and papers |
| Presence | 100 | Certain physical appearance: not too short, strong looking, muscular, clean-cut, also wearing a suit (formal) | On observation |
| Family man | 69 | By communication and official proof | Asking for children's birth certificates, proof of marriage |
| Knowledge of the City | 24 | Getting to places without asking, knowing good routes | Can be screened for during test period through tasks, sending him off to make collections, etc. |
| From another state | 25 | Documents, accent | Screened immediately |
| No criminal record | 100 | Police files easy to fake | Checking police files |

employee is observed and tested on many fronts. The largest variation found in this research was actually regarding the length of the test period; a businessman interviewee claimed to have a long test period in which the new driver would be entrusted with progressively more important tasks. Over the first few days, he would just be 'standing around' not doing much, and in this time he could show his helpfulness and initiative by doing things without being asked, like offering to help with certain tasks, or being available should a need arise in the household—all good signals of benevolence and efficiency. Eventually, he would be sent out to carry out minor tasks, such as going to the grocery store, and then he would be sent to the bank, eventually progressing to a level where the employer would be comfortable with him driving his family around. During this period, which could take a few weeks, the driver would be under observation; he would be assessed on all properties not immediately observable. Interestingly, the employer described how other employees would sometimes also participate in this evaluation by interacting and observing the new hire. In this way, the employer could protect himself in case the employee being screened changed his attitude when he was not around. This complex hiring process is rare and can only be achieved by someone with significant resources, or a sufficient amount to pay someone to stand around for a few days or weeks.

Other wealthy people, however, are more trusting from the start, or rather they have better screening processes. Interviewee ENV5, a businessman in his 70s, said: 'when you start [work] you start right away, you take money, people everything'. In his case, the hiring process was much shorter, which did not mean there was no screening—it was simply done in a faster (and perhaps more efficient) manner. This process usually would only take a few days and would include one or two interactions between the employer and the employee. It is important to say that these individuals were a minority in the interview sample and tended to be older. Their attitudes are perhaps a reflection of their past experiences with low crime rates, or a higher level of confidence in their screening methods. It can also be related, as I will explore later, to a practice of hiring members of the same family.

What determines the length of this observation period? This is linked to previous experience, and people's individual perceptions of the level of insecurity and risk at the time of hiring, as well as the resources available to them at the time of the hiring. Individuals with substantial resources may have the luxury of very long screening processes, an advantage that persons of lower socioeconomic standing may not possess. The employer's attitude to risk may also be a factor, with risk-prone individuals using a shorter observation period, as with the employer in the last example mentioned above. It is also a reflection, perhaps, of the levels of confidence people have in their own ability to make the right decisions, or in this case, to assess a person's trustworthiness. The fact that none of these businessmen mentioned had been betrayed perhaps attests to the success of their different strategies, regardless of the fact that the longer one is costlier than the other. Of course, both men mentioned have had negative experiences with employees with issues such as incompetence, rudeness, and similar problems, but none of this has resulted in any crime being committed against them. So which strategy is better? It depends on the resources available, and each employer will also make decisions based on this premise.

What all interviewees accept is that there is no perfect system, you 'do what you can'. In this, there is the implicit acceptance of risk, of the chance that, maybe, one will make a bad choice and be forced to face some future negative consequence. Another factor could well be the levels of trust the employer has in his or her own network. One could suppose that the higher the levels of established trust in the networks, the lesser the need for a long, costly screening process. This is because the potential employees will have already been selected from a reduced pool of candidates which already has some established trustworthiness.[2] Thus, a two-step process is established. It entails making decisions based on some public information (Spence 1974) in the form of the recommendation and a secondary screening process of variable length. Let us look at the particular signals employers look for and how they are screened for.

### *Discretion*

This property is very difficult to screen for and can only be established fully by repeated observation. This non-readily observable

[2] This also refers to vertical integration which will be discussed separately as a secondary mechanism for hiring.

trait is vital to every employer. Employers solve this problem partly through their recommendation system. Discretion is one of the traits they always ask for in a new employee when they search their networks. A recommendation as a discreet person from a relative or close friend of the employer is a very good mechanism to deal with this uncertainty. As mentioned above, it is very costly or almost impossible to fake a recommendation from a trusted source. This allows employers to minimize the job market uncertainty described by Spence (1974) and be better informed of the quality of the employee being hired. This is especially so when screening for a property such as discretion.

The recommendation process also has an important role for the person doing the recommending. In fact, they also run a risk in making a recommendation, as interviewee ENV13 (dentist, 40, male), who spoke candidly about the recommendation process, said: 'I think of these things … someone asks me to recommend someone and sometimes you don't even want to take the risk you see, you ask what if he does something, I better not even recommend anyone, so you are careful … you think about it'. This gives us an idea of the importance people give when asked for a recommendation; they do not want to recommend a lemon, so to speak, as their own reputation for trustworthiness and the safety of someone they care for, or at least have an interest in, will be at stake. Also, they may also be in a situation when they will be asking their network for recommendations in the future. In this sense, the people making the recommendation also engage in some level of screening, by trying to recommend someone who, to the best of their knowledge, possesses the qualities needed by employers. This feedback loop strengthens the relationship, making it a sustained cooperative arrangement. Discretion is a property which constitutes the first and very important filter for employers once the second part of the screening process has started.

As Table 5.1 shows, this property is tricky as it sometimes entails what could be called a non-signal, meaning that it is easier to assess it when the employee does the *opposite*. For example, a sign of indiscretion is being on the phone a lot. Respondent ENV1 (home, 64, female) described how they hired an employee who seemed (for them) to be on the phone 'all the time', always talking to someone. This made the employer suspicious, as they wondered what information they may be giving out. Clearly, this suspicion has some basis on simple bias: an employee should be able to do as he pleases in his spare time.[3] However, employers in the Mexican context tend to amplify the significance of certain signals, following a 'better safe than sorry' logic. This employee's over communicative style did not sit well with the employer and he did not last very long on the job.[4] Someone who is very chatty and talkative is also taken as probably being indiscreet. This was a concern echoed by other employers. The central logic behind this is that if someone is talking to everyone at work, they will talk to everyone outside as well, and this may pose a risk. These assumptions—particularly of someone who is talkative and expressive—are deeply steeped in Mexico's class structure, where to this day many wealthy people assume a role of superiority for themselves. There is an expression which exemplifies these attitudes perfectly. It is *igualado*; a pejorative word which is very difficult to translate, but basically it is used by people to refer to someone of lower socioeconomic status who speaks to and behaves towards them as an equal. In other words, it describes someone who does not show appropriate deference to the person of assumed higher social standing.

Being talkative and/or overtly open are only proxies of discretion. Therefore, there is no absolute sign of this property that leads to a fully sorting equilibrium. This is one of many imperfect signals (Gambetta 2009) that result in trust in these interactions. I did not find any one signal that achieved near perfection. However, silence can be a tricky thing. Employees must display the *correct* amount of silence, as someone who is too quiet can be seen as conniving and thus untrustworthy; the expression *ladino* is sometimes used to describe people like this. The term has historically referred to Spanish-speaking Mexicans during the colony era, and was used as a strong ethnic signifier to separate different castes or groups in the Spanish colonies. It also referred to white Mexicans (Gabbert 2004). The term has evolved and carries many meanings today;

[3] It is important to remember that, due to the characteristics of this kind of employment, even when not actively working, employees tend to be in or around the house, and drivers may have long periods during the day when they are simply waiting for their work to be required. During this time, they are easily observable, as are the employers. In the case mentioned here the employee may have been on the phone during those down times, which raised the employer's suspicions.

[4] As has been mentioned before, household employment in Mexico is mostly informal. This has many disadvantages (namely legal protection for both parties) and also means the relationship can be terminated suddenly, by any one party.

one of them is used to refer to someone who is a smart, conniving person. It becomes increasingly clear that achieving the right amount of discretion is, needless to say, a hard state to achieve for employees, especially the more inexperienced ones.

Respondent ENV2 (businesswoman, 60s) posed a further complication to screen for discretion. She stated: 'there is a saying: a new broom always sweeps well', meaning that once hired, employees will always try their best to showcase how good they are and it will take time for their real personas to come out. However, repeated and constant observation makes faking or mimicking complicated for someone who is not actually discreet. They will normally be betrayed by a number of expressions and even gestures and practices (Frank 1988). Frank argues that the effort required to maintain the emission of fake signals which go against established reflexes and practices would require levels of control which would be prohibitively costly for the mimic in the long term. He refers to these as 'telltale clues' (1988: 114), in that they betray the original nature of the signaller.

This reinforces the need for protracted observation, and most respondents boasted of being very good observers. Interviewee ENV2 (commerce, 50s, female) spoke of her training in psychology that, she claimed, she used to 'read' specific body language and attitudes in people. Some other employers do not have this training, but have also designed ways to measure and assess discretion. Most respondents describe a composite of many signs that tell them someone is discreet. As mentioned above, not being too talkative is part of this. Another factor consistently brought up is age; older people in a range from 30 to 50 are seen as more discreet (ENV2, commerce, 50s, female). This is due to the fact that they may have dependent family members and have achieved some degree of maturity. However, there are exceptions to this: employer ENV11 (business owner, 45, female) mentioned not hiring people over the age of 35, since she believed they are able to work less and have more of their time committed to family and thus less availability to work overtime or weekends, if needed. Even so, age was consistently mentioned as a sign used to screen for discretion. An advantage to this age requirement is that it is very easy to screen for. An employer only needs to have access to an official identification such as a birth certificate or voting card to screen for this. Age is thus a pooling sign, one that is easily on display and serves to 'pool' suitable candidates together.

The new employee's interactions with more senior, established employees are also important in helping the screening process. A mechanism which is sometimes used is that other employees will participate in the screening, especially those who have been employed for a long time and may have the full confidence of the employer. In a sense, they are used as agents, or grasses, observing the new arrival and reporting to the employer. This is an important source of information that is also related to vertical integration. We understand vertical integration here as the strategy to hire members of the same family, thus vertically integrating house labour. The impact of this in the relationships between employees was not lost during the research. There are times when there may be some suspicion or competitiveness between employees and sometimes senior employees have a significant say in whether or not someone stays employed, although this is not necessarily made clear to the new employee. One respondent (businesswoman, 50s) in a later interview (2015) spoke of how she discovered that a senior employee who had been working there for over a decade kept firing—or intimidating into leaving—younger, newer employees without the employer's authorization. This led to some problems with the senior employee, who had to agree to stop this kind of unwarranted intervention in the hiring process. This conflict among employees may be solved by using vertical integration.

If the household has vertically integrated its employees (Williamson 2005b), employing them full time, the screening of new members of the household becomes easier as they are under observation constantly by the employer or other employees, enhancing control and minimizing risk. This gives wealthy people an advantage over other social classes who may not be able to employ people on a full-time basis. Another expression of vertical integration relates to employment of members of the same family. This practice is common in Mexico: households may employ members of the same family or employers may recommend family members of their employees for work with one of their contacts. This can easily result in a network whose members belong to just a few families.

By displaying membership to a family, a driver may benefit from his family's reputation. Furthermore, he may also be tied up in a set of norms, moral codes, and behaviours that are kept and enforced by other members of the family. The employee has a greater incentive to be discreet if he knows that any indiscretion may bring shame and other costs to his family. The family of employees may also be able to deal with the threat of black sheep to their livelihood by a measure of self-policing. This brings us back to Fearon and Laitin's work on inter-ethnic cooperation (1996), especially with regard to in-group policing equilibria, whereby members of one group (in this case, the family employed) will deal with transgressors internally in order to avoid conflict with the other group (in this case, the employers). The employer knows this and is therefore more confident of the employee's cooperation. This is an effective way to avoid conflict between employer and employee. This in-group policing reduces the likelihood of opportunistic behaviour by any one of their members, by making punishment more likely and swift. This is beneficial to the employer, as it transfers the costs of enforcement and discipline to his employees.

Geographical origins are also mentioned as a sign of discretion. In many cases, originating from a poor rural area of the country (i.e. not having an urban background) is taken to mean the person is more discreet. This is based in the—many times racist—historical conception of rural people as noble, meek, and hard working. The City is here seen as the great corrupter and people who have lived there are believed to be more likely to be potential traitors, their trusting rural ways having been compromised by the City's dog-eat-dog environment. Having this 'pueblo experience', as interviewee ENV12 (academic, 62, female) called it, is considered to be an asset in this case. Whether this is true and people from outside the City are indeed more discreet, or if this is only a city folk prejudice, remains to be seen. It may turn out to be garden-variety snobbery. However, it is mostly taken as a fact by employers. For example, there is a rumour/preconception among the security industry that men from the southern state of Oaxaca make 'the best bodyguards' (law enforcement official, 40s, male) because of their apparent fierce loyalty and extreme fearlessness. *Oaxacos*, as they are at times referred to, have apparently built up a reputation for this. It is not clear how people from Oaxaca acquired said reputation. It is interesting to note, however, that that state has had a history of high levels of conflict, protest, and contestation that continues to the present day. It is also the most ethnically and linguistically diverse state in the country, with around eighteen different ethnic groups living in its territory, making up over 30 per cent of its population. It has also been, historically, a seat of PRI sub-national authoritarianism which survives to this day (Benton 2012). Whether these factors go some way towards explaining the Oaxacan's fierce reputation would require more, in depth ethnographical research.

There are around sixty-two different ethno-linguistic groups in Mexico, making up roughly 10 per cent of the population (Trejo 2012). Only one interviewee (ENV6, businessman, 70s) named ethnicity as a factor in the decision-making process. He stated: '[I am] racist ... and would not have an indigenous person as a driver ... they have their ... rights and all but in the driving of a motorized vehicle ... may be a little strange for them ... not something they are familiar with, [and that] is probably my fault! ... but it is a fact.' As surprising as this candid admission may seem, it reflects many of the biases and preconceived ideas held by Mexicans about indigenous people. The notion that indigenous people do not drive is clearly biased, and based on racial ideas perpetuated since colonial times of the superiority of metropolitan elites. These racial separations gave way to class divisions as the country developed (Knight 1990a), which persist to the present day.

Thus, we see that discretion is a property which is difficult to assess directly, but which can be screened for using a number of proxies and other mechanisms. Signals of discretion as described by employers include membership of a social network or a family of employees (the latter if the employees are vertically integrated). This is by far the best signal due to its cost relationship (Gambetta 2009). Other signals include the ability to communicate just the right amount (a very challenging signal), as well as certain geographical and ethnic considerations. The latter will be elaborated on during the discussion on presence later in this chapter.

### *Helpfulness and initiative*

Helpfulness and initiative were properties also identified as being screened for by all those interviewed. These are usually defined as a disposition to do things and carry out tasks. A helpful person will offer assistance even when it is not necessarily needed. As I will demonstrate, this is an almost costless signal to display, but like discretion, long-term interaction frequently brings out whether or not it is genuine. Interviewee ENV7, a real-estate agent in her 60s, stated: 'also he could have initiative, even though I do not tell him what to do … do X or Y, he does it on his own, without me saying anything … he could have this service attitude … that when I get home I notice things have been done without me asking'. As with discretion, helpfulness can only be identified through observation, although it is easier to identify and establish because it entails readily observable actions. Basically, the employee needs to keep active and offer assistance: this is a prime way for him to signal helpfulness. Interviewee ENV13 (dentist, 40s, male) spoke of helpfulness in this way: 'I realize for example when my wife gets home … if he goes and says "can I help you get your things out of the car?" … that attention [is important]'. Initiative is also getting the job done, as interviewee ENV13 put it: 'you are hired to do a job, and you do it, and I see you do it, then it works'. This underlines the importance of constant observation, and in the case of the driver, of signaling this by taking certain actions. Most people claim to be able to know if a person 'will work' very quickly after observing them only for a few hours or, at most, days. In the case of protection against crime, specifically kidnapping, initiative can be seen as a proxy of the employee being able to take matters into their own hands, of acting when necessary. Perhaps more importantly, it signals that the employee is not a pushover or shy. It signals confidence, which employers look for when hiring someone who will protect their family.

### *Presence*

Presence is another property found to be important. This means a driver must have a certain look, but also a certain physique. Initially, it would be easy to conclude that presence is simply a set of visual personal attributes, like the clothes one wears or the hairstyle one chooses. On closer analysis, it becomes clear that this property is more complex. There are two dimensions to this property: the physical and easily observable; and the intangible. Presence, as discovered in the field research, entails a series of attributes which form an individual's personality which go beyond what he or she looks like. Due to the fact that drivers are also hired, as established in earlier chapters, to protect the family and their information, having presence becomes more than just being presentable or good looking. This intangible force can also be described as the ability to stand out. In the case of drivers, this would be the ability to look confident, perhaps somewhat intimidating and serious. In other words, to be able to signal to the outside world that they were not to be messed with, and that they would be capable of violence if the situation arose (whether or not they actually would be if it indeed happened is another matter). Body language and even facial expressions are naturally effective tools to transmit this and this is a central part of Frank's analysis of emotions and strategy (1988).

On the physical side, a certain set of attributes are preferred when hiring and some interviewees speak of height as a good sign. Short men are not favoured as they are seen as being weaker and less intimidating than tall people. By the same token, men with larger muscle mass are also preferred. Thus, the ideal type for a person possessing the property of 'presence' would be a toughish-looking, large man, clean-cut, who wears suits. These are more signs than signals, as they are constantly on display regardless of the owner's intentions (Gambetta 2009). They also comply to a large extent with the costly-to-fake principle (Frank 1988). ENV7 (businessman, 70s, male) put it nicely: 'sure … you do not want someone coming looking like shit, all dirty; that puts you off right away'.

During an interview at a later date in Mexico City (2014, business owner, 60s, male), an employer told the story of a driver he had at the time (in line with the vertical integration line of thought, he also employed the man's wife as a cook). He trusted the driver very much and he had been employed for about eight years in the household. The driver emitted most signals discussed here. He wore a suit, was clean-cut, and was of large build. However, he 'looked too nice/gentle' as the employer put it. The driver himself was actually a very gentle person, according to the employer himself and other employees of the household (I can also attest to this, as I met him a number of times). This was not a deal-breaker for the employer, but he recounted how he tried to encourage his driver to 'look tougher' and to 'stop smiling to everyone he sees' when they were out on the street. I also interviewed the driver (who was in his late 30s at the time), and he was keen to humour his employer and tried—with varied success—to look 'tough', or at least not to look like too nice a person.

Thus, presence can be assessed along two different lines. On the one hand, there are signals of presence which are necessary, but do not comply with the hard-to-fake principle. Examples of this include haircuts and the wearing of suits. The relatively low cost of these signals is also why employers pay more attention to other signals of presence, such as body type or height, signals which are almost impossible to fake. On the other hand, we have some more intangible properties, such as courage, which are more difficult to fake. The above example outlining the struggles of a very good-natured driver to look tougher also indicate the difficulty in signaling consistently something *contra natura*. Even so, while presence is important for employers, there are certainly other properties they value more, such as discretion.

### *Age and other factors*

Age, a family, a clean criminal record, and a driver's licence are the next items that were most mentioned during fieldwork as clear signals of trustworthiness and a part of employers' crime prevention efforts. As mentioned earlier, age is a factor always mentioned and also a property costly to mimic. Men in their late 30s to late 40s are mostly preferred as they are seen as more responsible than younger men. They are perceived to have more stamina and the level of maturity required by the job. This is also compounded with the fact that men in this age group tend to be family men. Men with a family are seen as more responsible and with 'more to lose' (ENV4, retired, 60s, female) should they decide to betray their employer's trust. Again, having children is difficult to fake, especially if the employer is keen on cross-checking the information provided by the potential driver. Cross-checking information is also an option regarding police files and criminal records. No one interviewed bothered to make criminal record checks, perhaps because of the lack of faith in government institutions that issue such documents. In this case, the network recommendation seems to be good enough to vouch for the lack of criminal inclinations on the part of the potential driver.

All of these properties, as seen by their respective signs and deliberate signals, make up the bulk of the signaling game of hiring. Employers look for these signs in particular as they represent, for them and under these circumstances, the best way to ascertain a person's trustworthiness and thus their capacity to care for their family and information. Now we can construct the 'ideal type' driver. He would be a male in his mid-30s, married with children, of large build, from outside the City, clean-cut, articulate but not too talkative, and should readily volunteer for work.

He should also be able to portray seriousness and a capacity for violence through his presence. From the employer's perspective, we can see that the way to solve the problems of trust (Gambetta and Bacharach 2001) is to screen for a number of properties that, mainly, signal discretion. The recommendation system in place, which benefits from small, clustered networks prevalent in Mexico City, assures them that a minimum standard of trustworthiness will likely be kept as the recommendation itself is riding on the reputations not only of members of the network, but also their employees or families. This minimizes risk substantially. Once this has been achieved, the main goal is then to establish the trustee's trustworthiness via observation and repeated interactions. If successful, the relationship may last decades, as was the case in two particular families interviewed during fieldwork. It is important to underscore that this system benefits from, and reinforces, Mexico's social structure and in many ways perpetuates inequalities and biases. However, in Mexico's context of weak rule of law and relations-based economic markets (Dixit 2004, this is so far the most efficient way to secure employees and protect one's family against kidnapping and other crimes.

This chapter has explored the ways in which wealthy people navigate the risk of kidnapping through the hiring of drivers for their household. It showed how employers screen for different properties such as discretion and how they use vertical integration as a way to lower the cost and risk of hiring. What about the employees? The following chapter explores how employees access jobs and how they negotiate their relationships with their employers, and what strategies they use to communicate the properties for which they are being screened.

# 6

# The Employee's Perspective

In Gambetta and Hamill's book (2005), the focus is on how taxi drivers can establish their customers' trustworthiness. The authors deal in a section of the book with the other actor in the relationship, namely the client taking the taxi, or 'when the passenger is the truster' (Gambetta and Hamill 2005: 16). In it they recognize that sometimes the passenger is the one who has to make a decision about whether or not the taxi she is about to take is a safe bet. Mimics, that is, criminals passing themselves off as taxi drivers, do exist, but in the end, the authors argue, it would have proven impractical to focus on both sides of the relationship, especially since in their countries of study taxis are well regulated and so mimicking is difficult and thus somewhat rare. This is not the case in Mexico, where taxis are only loosely regulated and are quite often the vehicle of choice for robbers, rapists, and kidnappers. *Pirate* taxis are very common and government attempts at regulating them have so far produced mixed results. Lately, with the advent of ride-share services such as Uber, taxis (regulated and pirate alike) have struggled to compete as they are seen as the less safe option. Today, people in the City regularly use Uber as transport. This company will soon begin to accept cash payment in Mexico (as not everyone has a bank card). Recent conversations with Uber drivers (2016)[1] show they are reluctant to accept this as they believe they will be less safe once criminals know they have cash in their cars. *Express kidnapping*, which I have described before, is regularly carried out in taxis, making the taking of one perhaps just as dangerous for the user as it is for the driver. Further research on this would no doubt yield interesting outcomes.

[1] I spoke to about twelve Uber drivers over the space of a week in the City in 2016.

Here, I make an attempt to look at both sides of the issue. However, I focus more on how drivers signal their trustworthiness as opposed to how they decide whether or not to trust the employer.[2] The assumption is that employers will want to find a good employee, as we have seen in the previous chapter, and that employees will want to gain employment with a 'good' employer (there will be more on what 'good' means later). All of this happens in an environment of uncertainty about the other's intentions and abilities (Spence 1974: 6).

Driving work is by nature potentially dangerous. There is the risk of having an accident in which one could be hurt or, worse, killed. Mexico's roads are dangerous and sometimes poorly kept, which means accidents are common and the country is one of the top-ten countries worldwide for fatal road accidents (Milenio 2008). Moreover, Mexico City also has a serious drink-driving problem that exacerbates the number of fatal road accidents every year.[3] This has prompted the City Government to set up a breathalyser programme in the City's busiest streets, particularly on weekend nights. The penalty for being caught is a fine and twenty-four hours' detention in the police station.[4] According to the City, this has made driving there safer. However, driving in Mexico City remains somewhat risky in this sense.

Furthermore, as we have seen in Chapter 2, Mexico City has high crime rates. It is not uncommon to hear of drivers being hurt or killed during the commission of crimes such as car theft and kidnapping. In 2008, the 14-year-old son of a very wealthy Mexico City businessman was kidnapped on his way to school. He was being chauffeured by one driver and a bodyguard. They

[2] Although this is also a component of the process. I also focus somewhat less on the employee side of the equation due to space constraints.

[3] In 2017, there were 13.2 deaths by traffic accident for every 100,000 people nationally (INEGI 2019). For the sake of comparison, the United Kingdom had in 2006 a rate of 5.4 deaths per 100,000 people (Office for National Statistics 2009, accessed at http://www.statistics.gov.uk/cci/nugget.asp?id=1208), half that of Mexico.

[4] Sadly, as is often the case in Mexico, wealthier people manage to escape such punishments by virtue of corruption or by intimidating officers. The City has tried to fight this by appointing ombudsmen, who along with representatives from the local Human Rights Commission, are present in all checkpoints and make sure that corruption is avoided, as well as rights violations of those checked and eventually arrested. It remains to be seen if this has actually solved the corruption problem.

were driving in a bulletproof car and were stopped at a roadblock by individuals wearing uniforms of a Federal Police agency. However, these were not police officers, but kidnappers. They were then taken. The driver and bodyguard were soon found; the bodyguard was dead with signs of torture (his teeth had been pulled out), but the driver somehow had survived his injuries. After intense negotiations, a payment was agreed. The real amount is unknown, but different versions put the amount at anywhere between US $400,000 and $1 million. The boy was never returned. Nearly two months after the kidnapping, the boy's body was found in the trunk of an abandoned car (KNRD 2009). This vignette illustrates the very real risks that arise in the City, which in this case cost a child and his carer their life, and give an idea of the danger this kind of employment can have. The fact that drivers are regularly in the company of potential kidnapping victims makes their job risky and this is a factor they do take into account when performing their job. In interviews, most employees revealed that they considered their work to entail certain risks and that they kept an eye out for safety when out on the job, as we will see further ahead.

Regardless of these risks, the competition for these jobs is high. There is always a steady supply of labour in Mexico City, especially for this type of work. Driving jobs are well paid compared to others. On average, a driver in a wealthy household can make about US $800 a month—a good salary in a city where the lowest wage is around US $200 a month. In an interview (WNV6, 46, male), a driver admitted that he saw his work as a more sophisticated affair than just driving a car. He liked the fact that he was responsible for people and that, as such, his work was valued. In fact, this was a very common response by drivers. They saw a definite advantage in the fact that their work was recognized. He was also enthusiastic about the idea of taking care of the family, having contact with 'important' people, and driving good cars. In fact, almost all drivers interviewed saw these issues as a key aspect of their work. So, how do they get the job?

## All in the Family: Networks and Vertical Integration

In a similar manner to the employer trying to get access to employees, prospective employees attempt to gain employment through their own personal networks before entering the formal market. In this case, and contrary to Granovetter's propositions (1973, 1983), it is through the person's strong ties (i.e. family members, close friends) that jobs as drivers are most commonly accessed. Acquaintances are also used, but to a lesser extent. This is because, as we will see, a potential driver will often use a family member's good reputation to access a job. This is the first step in the hiring process. Of all drivers and domestic employees with recorded interviews during fieldwork (fourteen), only one did not get his job through this kind of network. Almost all the others gained their positions through a family connection. In one case (WNV1, driver/handyman, 30s, male), the driver was hired after he married the daughter of a woman already employed in the household (the daughter also worked for a time there). When asked specifically about this, he agreed that his job was a product of that particular link.

> I was three, four months unemployed [after he arrived from Tlaxcala, a state in central Mexico] then I tried to look through my family members, they tried to help me, they got me into department stores, well you know, the usual ... and my wife was already working here and she told me: you know if you don't mind what happens to you, you can work here, no? ... it was my first job in the City, I did not know how it worked, how the movement was ... I knew my wife worked here but I did not know the family.

The fact that all but one of the drivers got their job through strong ties is also illustrative of the broader argument with regard to the importance of people's close social networks in this regard.

In another case, a driver was responsible for recommending his cousin's husband, as well as other members of his close family (WNV6, driver, 46, male). Most drivers corroborated what employers had been telling me, namely that in order to get a job, the employee must have access to a certain network, mostly family-based, that allows them to be considered. The potential employee needs to have a close relative already working for the new employer or at the very least with a close friend or relative of the new employer.

Thus, we arrive at the first and probably the most important signaling mechanism through which a driver may prove his trustworthiness: *membership* of a certain family or group whose reputation has been proven over time by a number of different employees. Mexico's environment of informality and low contract enforceability by state institutions makes membership an important asset. This is mainly maintained through reputation. In the absence of functioning courts or contracts, a family's reputation is a vital measure of trustworthiness. By the same token, membership to a certain family is extremely difficult to mimic. One cannot pass oneself off as someone else's cousin when the 'cousin' in question is present in the room, unless they have a prior agreement to defraud the employer. One could think of someone marrying into the family to acquire the reputation and then committing a crime, but, even in Mexico, this seems too outlandish to be feasible and is certainly unheard of, at least in the realm of kidnapping. In general, the costs of mimicking or faking membership into the network are very high, if not prohibitive. This signal is taken to fulfil the cost condition fully (Gambetta 2009; Gambetta and Hamill 2005), or at the very least it fulfils it at a higher level than other signals. This further explains the importance of membership. This is strengthened by the fact that in order to get hired the potential criminal or mimic would have to not only fake membership into a family or network, but also potentially show their face for a significant amount of time, making the odds of being caught even more significant. Finally, because of the long-term character of the work relationship, even a very accomplished con artist would find it difficult to maintain the fake membership over the long term, as Frank has argued (1988). Members of the network are bound to catch on to him eventually and blow the whistle.

Thus, the first signal that must be emitted by a potential driver is membership of a family or a group of people that have proven over time to be good employees. This is consistent with the argument I presented about vertical integration (Williamson 2005b) as a protection mechanism. By vertically integrating household employees, the hiring process becomes more efficient and, ideally, the results are also safer. It is also a good thing for the employees, since they are guaranteed income as a family and are also less likely to be abused. Going back to Spence's work (1974), we can liken membership of this network to the act of belonging to a professional guild. If the employer is aware of the reputation of such a family because of positive past experiences he has had, he will welcome an employee who signals in a clear and verifiable way his belonging to this network through a recommendation.

The types of network discussed above are not easily formed. As I observed them in the field, they may span many families and a number of generations both on the employer and the employee sides. In a context in which the employer may not be able to observe the past behaviour of his prospective driver first-hand—a fundamental uncertainty in the job market as described by Spence (1974)—the observed past behaviour of other members of his family is a good enough proxy when added to other mechanisms that solve the problems of trust. In certain cases, this is also compounded and strengthened by the reputation of the person making the recommendation to hire the employee (i.e. a family member or close acquaintance of the employer). I understand reputation as a 'characteristic or an attribute ascribed to (a person) by his partners' that is based empirically on 'his observed past behaviour' (Raub and Weesie 1990: 629; see also Kreps and Wilson 1982). A positive reputation (of discretion, for example, as in: 'X is likely to be discreet in interaction Y') once acquired becomes a valuable asset for the person who owns it. A compounded family reputation may be even better and provide an incentive to maintain this reputation and also to make sure members do not tamper with it. Actors must take into account the fact that their current actions not only have an effect on the present, but also on the future, with 'longer term consequences due to the effect of his current decision on his future reputation' (Wilson 1985: 28).

A good reputation proven through signaling membership is only constructed over long periods of time. In some cases, I became aware of during research, the process began up to ten, even fifteen, years before, when in a different environment a person was given employment in a household. These 'pioneer' employees acquired good reputations with their employers through hard work and good work ethics shown in countless interactions in a safer and less demanding environment.[5] Indeed, in some cases, they became almost members of the family, sharing in their weddings and other important family events. Respondent ENV1 recalled how their more senior employees partook in their children's weddings and how they participated in their employees' important family events. Then, when another employee needed a driver or other household worker, it was the pioneer's good reputation that made

[5] Of course, the environment in question may well be such as the one I described when the social context in Mexico allowed people to openly hire in the market, sometimes by advertising for help.

them the sources for employment for their sons, daughters, sons-in-law, and other family members.

By virtue of genetics, a second generation of workers acquired a good reputation that they knew (as some mentioned in interviews) they needed to uphold or risk high costs not only for themselves, but also for their kin. In this way, wealthy employers and their employees, their families, and close friends become enmeshed in a complex but informal network that, over the space of many years, was created as a mechanism to: (1) secure safe employment on behalf of the employees; and (2) procure respectable employees who will be able and willing to protect a family's information and safety. Driver WV1 (a kidnapping victim's driver, 35, male) spoke in the following way about reputation when asked if being trusted in his job was difficult (parentheses are my own):

> In some cases, yes, but noooot really eh! I mean, more than anything, as, as I have arrived with a recommendation with some people, it's a bit less. Ok, you still have to earn the trust of these people, and [they] have to see how you work, so they give you more [responsibilities], but from the start you already have something that speaks for you, your image, no?

So, employees need to signal their belonging in a network in order to be considered for a job and vertical integration (Williamson 2005b) may well also help to explain this. By 'locking in' these employees full time, wealthy families reduce the risk of the employee defaulting or betraying their trust by raising the costs of future defaults. Using this mechanism, employers also reduce the cost they would incur when looking for a new employee, since they have a more secure in-house supply of labour; their risks are consequently reduced by not having to hire unknown people in the open market. These long-term linkages also allow, in many cases, for deeper, more personal relationships to be formed between the employer and the employees, which also make the environment safer. In one case (WNV4, cook, 50s, female), a worker who had been at a household for over a decade spoke of this relationship in these terms (parentheses are my own):

> Well, she [the employer] is always looking out for me, so the days I don't come to work she is phoning me: why did you not come? Well it is because I am sick, well I am worried [she says] that something happened to you; in case I get hit by a car or something.

In another example of this kind of relationship, a driver was even given a signature and access to a household bank account so he could take care of payments and other home expenses (WNV1, driver, male, 30s). This clearly denotes a high level of trust in the relationship and concretely in the person. The driver had two members of his own household working for the same family and he was the last to be hired eight years prior to the interview. While these examples may seem anecdotal, they serve to illustrate what the majority of interviewees displayed. During the fieldwork, all the employees I talked to had or were trying to develop this kind of relationship with their employers. The perception voiced by employers that this was a better way to do things was thus echoed by the employees. Both groups agreed that having this type of relationship makes cooperation more feasible and is also beneficial for all concerned when it functions properly. In the words of the same interviewee (WNV1, driver, male, 30s):

> … it is very important, and it is also more relaxed and secure for them [the employers] because they know there is someone who can respond in their household, whether they are here or not, I mean, with them … all their family have really good comments about me, like 'with him it's all good, perfect'. And for me this is very important and gratifying because then I can do my job better … in exchange for this I know that when I need something, like a letter of recommendation, it will be perfect.

From the employee's perspective, then, a vertically integrated work environment means gainful work for more members of their family (in one case I interviewed, up to four members of a household), which equals better earnings for the family unit as a whole. This situation also has the added advantage of reducing certain costs for the employees; these may include transport, as well as the more hidden but higher costs that finding a job outside the network would entail for other members of the family. An added advantage to this mechanism is that employee families may also be inclined to self-regulate if there are incentives to do so. A vertically integrated family of employees may find it in their best interest to deal with potential issues such as criminal risks within the family, before they affect their source of income and work (see Fearon and Laitin 1996). In terms of security, this is an important aspect of the employer–employee relationship and should not be overlooked. A betrayal by one member of the family may bring about consequences for all the members of the family employed there.

This may help answer a logical question: Why are more criminals not using/coercing employees to give out information for kidnappings? This would be cost effective for the criminals since they would not need to mimic or risk being identified. Working-class communities in Mexico City, especially those in the periphery—often in informal settlements—have some very particular social dynamics with regard to crime. It is very common that people there have direct contact on a regular basis with certain types of criminals. These may include drug-trafficking gangs and other such groups. In fact, contrary to some widespread perceptions which assume that criminals, civil society, and the state inhabit separate spheres, these groups have constant contact with one another (Arias 2006). They inhabit the same spaces, use the same services, and are well known to one another. As such, it would be feasible to imagine that co-optation or intimidation of honest citizens by criminals would be more common than it is. They could use employees as (willing or not) moles in the household; yet, this does not happen often and self-policing in these communities may offer an answer as to why this is the case.

However, this self-policing mechanism is not easy to uncover in interviews. During fieldwork, it proved difficult to discuss or assess the presence of this self-regulating mechanism in employee families. The closest mention of it was when a driver admitted to knowing people he had grown up with in his community who were involved in crime (he would not say what kind) and that he made every attempt to stay away from them and that they were normally ostracized from his family's intimate circle (WNV5, driver, 29, male). In terms of mechanisms of control, ostracizing someone from the family for criminal intentions or other negative behaviour was mentioned as a practice. In this sense, most of the punishment mechanisms are norm-based and may include denying the offender access to certain goods and benefits inherent in membership in the family, such as loans and other pooled resources.

Another interviewee (WNV10, driver, 30s, male) also mentioned that many people in his community knew who these individuals were and left them alone as long as they did not interfere with their regular lives. This included their jobs. This knowledge of criminals and their activities in working-class communities is not new in Latin America and elsewhere; Arias documents this phenomenon in Brazil (2006) and from my own research I can conclude that it is also a common occurrence in some of Mexico City's working-class neighbourhoods.[6] Self-policing in certain communities is not unheard of in Mexico. In fact, it is a common occurrence in many areas of the country and takes place in both urban and rural settings. Lynching as a form of self-policing is also somewhat common (Davis 2006a). All this evidence added to the information I gathered during fieldwork interviewing drivers could point us in this direction. I will not dig deeper into self-policing here as I believe more research needs to be carried out to successfully explore it. What can be said now is that self-policing seems to be present in some cases and is also used as a form of control by certain communities in order to secure their jobs and their environment.

## Signaling Trustworthiness

In order to secure a job, potential drivers and other employees must, besides proving membership of a certain family or group, convince their potential employers that they have the other trustworthy properties sought by the employers. All signals must then satisfy the cost condition particular to the interaction (Gambetta 2009). Their proving membership of a group or family does not mean immediate employment, even if it does get their 'foot in the door'. Because most signals in this case are semi-sorting (Gambetta 2009: 175), a set of various signals must be transmitted that will satisfy the employer.

Some properties sought by employers are easily screened for. This is the case with *gender* and *age*, which can be visually ascertained quite quickly. Some require documentation to which the employer can have relatively easy access, such as a *clean police record*, a *driver's licence*, evidence of his *geographical origins*, and

[6] This is reminiscent of the kidnapping case I described in the Introduction. The reader will remember that, during his investigations, Mr X discovered that many people in the community where his daughter was kidnapped and killed knew about the gang's activities, but did nothing about them. Perhaps the family's status as outsiders in the community (they only owned a weekend home there) made them easier targets. More research would be needed to explore and test this theory.

whether he has a family. Other properties are more difficult to screen for and to signal and I will focus some attention on these in the paragraphs below.

### *Discretion*

Individuals must also prove they have this quality in order to be eligible. Unfortunately, qualities such as these can only really be asserted through repeated interactions or through longer-term direct observation. Thus, the employee needs to try to convince the employer as quickly as possible that he is discreet. Employees, however, do not directly mention this factor as often as employers. When asked directly, they seemed to be more comfortable defining it as protection, or simply referring to it as the process of 'gaining their confidence' (WNV2, cleaning staff, 50s, female). Related to this process, WNV1 said:

> I take care of the house when they leave ... the other guys [other workers in other households] come and say to me 'let's go party' and I say just: have a good time! I stay here, when they [the employers] phone I am always here.

This driver's notion of trustworthiness is a good example of how it is constructed by employees in general. They are aware that they cannot prove themselves immediately and so use medium-term behaviours that prove to the employer that they are to be trusted. These behaviours may be ingrained in them through socialization since their childhood and therefore more a sign than a signal (Gambetta 2009), but they may also be conscious actions taken with the purpose of keeping the job.

Beyond the obvious 'not talking to anyone about the bosses', at least in the boss's presence (WNV3, cook, 70s, female and WNV4, cook, 50s, female), there are other mechanisms that transmit commitment to the job and to the demand for discretion. One of these mechanisms is related to how employees manage their time and how much of it they commit to the job. Employees sacrifice large amounts of their own time to prove their commitment to their employer. They are always available and ready to work. They give up birthdays and weekends to take care of the employer's homes and cater to their needs. This is not a short and easy process; it involves sacrifice and, in the case of WNV1 (driver, male, 30s), many weekends on his own. WNV2 (cleaner, 50s, female) spoke along the same lines:

> Yes well, taking care of their house, and, especially when they leave because they travel a lot, always take good care of their home; not because they are not here we are going to go away or not show up! They notice, they know when they leave they can call and they always find us here.

In this way, employees signal to their employers that they have their best interests at heart and, more importantly, that they are concerned about the security of their home. In a way, it is an act of selflessness that may seem somewhat backwards and reminiscent of a master–servant relationship, but that in effect signals a preoccupation that is at the core of employers' decision-making processes. Being available most of the time is perceived by employees to be part and parcel of their work activities, and all interviewees pointed in that direction in one way or another. It also means that they must strike a balance between letting their employers know they are taking care of their interests and keeping them from being abused.

The risk for the employee here is that his new employer will abuse this situation and exploit the employee. Most interviewees who were happy at work reported a form of reciprocity in exchange for their time and resources. Interviewee WNV7 (driver, 44, male) had been working for the same family for eight years and felt that he received a good deal, even though he worked many odd hours driving for an elderly person, especially on weekends. He echoed a statement heard many times over that his employers 'took care of him' in matters of loans, vacations, and even participation in family events. Of course, this status was not achieved overnight and the driver in question had to invest a significant amount of time to reach that position. It was clear to me that he had his employer's full trust. When asked how he gained it, the reply was: 'through time and doing my job well, treating [my employer] well and his family'. The result of this may ultimately be that bad employees or mimics realize that it is not cost-effective to pretend to be good for so long in order to gain the confidence of the employer. This is a subtler example, one that is reminiscent of Robert H. Frank's case of Mormon nannies in New York City (1988: 111).

Frank writes of how affluent couples in that city began advertising for nannies in Salt Lake City newspapers, having decided that local governesses could not really be trusted and that a Mormon upbringing signalled honesty and goodwill—necessary qualities for child care. Frank argues that a mimic or impostor would find it very difficult to fake being a Mormon. This very high cost would make hiring someone with that faith a safe bet. Mormonism in this case would be very nearly a perfect sorting signal.[7] Thus, in the case that concerns us here, a reputation for discretion acquired through one's network is strengthened and reinforced through sacrificing time to take care of an employer's goods, as well as by very visually not divulging sensitive information.

### *Honesty and disclosure*

Honesty and disclosure came up in all interviews as a way in which employees prove their trustworthiness. An intangible property by definition, honesty is highly valued by employees (and expected by employers). I call this property honesty/disclosure because in the field these qualities always seemed to go hand in hand and it is therefore useful to analyse them as such. To be honest in this case is to reveal the facts about one's life and situations. The working signal that transmits this is basically disclosing to the employer verbally and in documents whatever situation may affect the work of the employee. The other side of the coin would be to lie or conceal information and risk being caught, or at least make the employer think the employee is hiding something that would put his job at risk. The market for drivers is competitive as there is a significant supply of drivers, but very good ones (i.e. with a significant amount of experience, glowing recommendations, etc.) are rare. Therefore, the incentive for exceptionally good drivers, given that employers have a limited amount of information about

[7] A criminally inclined person could potentially come up with ways to dupe New York couples. A New York local could respond to a Salt Lake City advert (if it is online, for example) posing as a Mormon and, depending on the employer's security checks, could potentially pass off as one if she had the racial attributes typical to Mormons and could mimic a Utah accent. A Salt Lake City criminal could also tap into this. Difficult and costly perhaps, but not impossible.

them, is to give out as much information as possible to distinguish themselves from other less desirable ones.

This is consistent with some of the findings of To and Harbaugh (2007) in their study of university professors' disclosure of their credentials. As an example, during the hiring process, most drivers with a very good CV will try to disclose it. This information may include names of people they have worked with or high-profile jobs they might have had. One interviewee (WNV6, driver, 46, male) was very keen on disclosing that he had worked in the security detail of one of Mexico's richest men (he left due to an internal policy that prevented anyone in the detail remaining for more than three years, lest they get too familiar with other employees) and he could provide names and documentation to prove it. This clearly gave him an advantage over others who may not have such impressive credentials and also would force those other drivers to disclose their own information or risk being thought of as being less competent than they actually were. In another case (WV1, driver, 35, male), a driver working for a kidnapping victim did his best to disclose the fact that he had worked for a widely recognized Mexican corporation where he was sometimes in charge of transporting the payroll to different branches across the City. He described his professional progression from driving a taxi and, through luck (as he put it), developing an informal contract to drive an executive who worked in the firm and lived near his taxi base, to driving for the owners of the firm. This high-responsibility job, he believed, gave him an edge over other drivers who did not have that experience and he was keen to make it public; indeed, he claimed that the firm's owners would choose him to do personal tasks (like drive their children) over the firm's other drivers. Signaling honesty and credentials in this way is cheap for those who have them, but, in general, prohibitively costly for those who don't.

These examples follow the logic of the *full disclosure principle* (Board 2009; Frank 1988; Harbaugh and To 2007; Lewis 2010). The full disclosure principle basically states that (parentheses mine): 'lack of evidence that something resides in a favoured category [good employees] will often suggest that it belongs to a less favoured one' (Frank 1988). Employees in this market have an incentive to disclose information about themselves not only during the hiring process, but also throughout the course of their employment, because employees who do not openly disclose their situations and skills are usually thought to be suspicious or unskilled, even if they are nothing of the sort. As expected, proof of the facts disclosed is necessary to give the information any value. It is of no use to say that one has worked with Z if one has no way of proving it. Information is only as good as the evidence provided. Letters and the contact details of people are used regularly for this purpose and the employer will then use his own mechanisms to verify this.

Once the employee has been hired, the trend continues. Disclosure of any issues and problems that the employee may have are thought by them to be conducive to proving their trustworthiness to the employer and to strengthening the relationship. This mechanism can be visualized as one of constant disclosure. The logic is that the more informed the employer is, the better it will be for the employee. This proves his or her honesty, as well as a propensity to avoid lies and deceptive behaviour. It also helps build and reinforce the reputation of the family of employees or the individual employee. Interviewee WNV2 (cleaner, 50s, female) spoke about this concept in the following way (parentheses are my own):

> For example, if I have to do something, a family problem that might take time, in this way, it would be talking to them: you know, I have this problem and it will take me two, three months, four let's suppose ... if you wait for me [and keep my job secure], we go ahead, if not, well, we look for a way to solve it.

Most successful employees adhered to this policy. This, they believed, generates in the employer a sense of trust and confidence that if something goes wrong, they will find out about it. Over time, this may develop into a solid, long-term, trusting relationship.

A good example of the long-term benefits of establishing a trust-based relationship with an employer is access to medical care. In many cases (almost all the employees I interviewed), the employee will need access to money during their employment on at least a few occasions. Because employees do not make a substantial amount of money, savings are rare.[8] They also generally have no access to bank loans and, in many cases, their relatives are in the same situation. The social safety net in Mexico

[8] The low savings rate in Mexico generates a host of issues, such as those discussed by Ortega (2008).

is also notoriously weak, with its public health system being (in) famous for its variable quality and accessibility. This makes many Mexicans (28 per cent of insured people) prefer to pay for private services; worse still, up to 48 million people (almost 50 per cent of the total population) have no insurance at all, being forced to buy medical care (of very variable quality) in the private market (Barraza-Lloréns et al. 2002). In this context, a serious illness in the family of an employee may well be a catastrophic event that could potentially bankrupt the family. Even a small expenditure for an ambulatory procedure may prove too expensive. In these scenarios, the employee may ask his employer for a loan or some form of help. If the relationship is a good one, the employer may help at no cost or give the employee more freedom to repay. Some interviewees did describe a situation where their employer will help by buying medicines or paying doctor bills, without asking the employee to pay it back. During fieldwork, I observed these dynamics many times. Employees consider this a good trade-off for the services they give. Employers ENV2 (businesswoman, 60s) and ENV3 (housewife, 50s) were candid about this topic. They generally received this kind of help from their employers during illness, but interestingly they also received support from their employers for other situations which may not necessarily be life-or-death situations. These included special family occasions like baptisms, birthdays, and weddings. It is perhaps a stretch, but it seems at times that this reciprocal relationship is more an exchange of security (for the employer) for a safety net (for the employee). Curiously, these are two ideally public goods which the Mexican government is notoriously unable to provide.

### *Efficiency*

This property is understood as the ability to carry out a task in a reasonable amount of time with minimum possible use of resources. In practical terms, this means that a driver will carry out tasks in a way that does not interfere with other household activities, doing his job quickly, with a minimum amount of fuss for the employer. As with any other job, this is an important part of a successful work relationship. Having said this, efficiency is not very costly to signal and because of this it is not a property that carries much weight in itself. The tasks assigned to a driver, especially in the beginning, are rarely very complex and should therefore be relatively easy to perform by almost anyone. Of course, there will be very inept drivers who will not be able to perform properly even at this stage and they are usually not employed for very long. Efficiency, however, is a necessary characteristic to have when other more complicated tasks are given. Employee WNV1 (driver, 30s, male) was a poster boy for efficiency. He has a family of four (with a wife and two school-age girls) and he regularly worked between ten and eighteen hours a day, some weekends included. He not only drove for his employer—taking her children to school, doing errands, etc.—he also drove for his employer's company as a courier. At the time she was learning to drive, he also gave his employer's teenage daughter driving lessons. He believed that, having dropped out of school, he needed to work extra hard:

> ... if you don't take advantage of it [work], since, now, due to one's bad decisions ... one did not finish university ... then you get married and all that ... the situation is not easy to be [wasting opportunities].

As if to prove this hard-working philosophy, he also worked some nights, with the blessing of his main employer, driving a famous artist around to her dinners, shows, and other functions. This meant that he had to sleep in his car in the company's parking lot (he always carried a spare suit in his trunk), under the watchful eye of the security guards. While this may seem—and likely is—exploitative, he did not see it that way, viewing it simply as taking advantage of the fact that he had a good reputation and had access to large amounts of work.

It is important to further develop the issue of exploitation. In contexts where work is better regulated, the kind of work schedule like the one described above would probably be considered extreme, or illegal. Of course, there is a level of exploitation in employing someone who works for 14 hours a day. Informality and a weak rule of law allows for this to happen. However, it is important when studying contexts such as these to avoid what Siddiqi (2009: 1) refers to as the 'culture of global moralism',[9]

[9] Siddiqi applies this to feminist notions in the context of female sweatshop workers in Bangladesh. While this may seem a distant case from a driver in Mexico, I believe her framework can be effectively utilized in the context of informal employment. In both cases, workers are faced with potentially exploitative and dangerous situations and fall within the large numbers of people worldwide whose work conditions do not fit the Western ideal, and are also part of a capitalist structure subject to contestation.

which sees developing world workers, in Siddiqi's case female garment industry workers in Bangladesh, as helpless captives of exploitative relations. The reality is much more complex than this description would entail and calls for a balance between the global rights discourse and the realities of life on the ground, which includes and respects 'critical differences, [and] workers' own experiences and desires' (Siddiqi 2009: 171), while at the same time recognizing that their work conditions need substantial improvement.

Men working in this profession tend to self-select. Because of the demands and risks of the job, employers will normally demand men who are bigger and taller than average. These are the first categories for self-selection. Rarely did I find a small, very thin, male driving for a wealthy Mexican.[10] Thus, most drivers entering the market will have these physical characteristics. The case for largeness is similar; one can only alter one's muscular composition by hard work at the gym or by eating a lot, and both are time-consuming activities. Signaling these attributes is costless for those who carry the properties, but the converse is true for those who do not. However, physical traits are tricky as a basis for hiring. Criminals, one can expect, will also tend towards a certain physical description very similar to the one mentioned above. Also, because most drivers in the market will have these attributes anyway due to self-selection, they tend to have diminished value as signals, or barely fulfil the cost condition. This is where the second dimension of presence comes in. Employees know that, in order to be hired, being large helps, but does not provide any guarantees, and so they will also try to alter and mould their appearance.

Being hired as a driver—especially working for very wealthy people—is in some ways a route to acquiring status, especially compared to other household jobs. I have argued that drivers are hired to *protect* as well as to drive, and this is confirmed by the perceptions of drivers themselves. The act of supplying protection affords them a new status vis-à-vis other employees. It places drivers at a higher level in the hierarchy of employees. In fact, one of them (WNV6, driver, 46, male) usually referred to himself as

[10] Surely, perceptions of height and strength are relative. A tall man in Mexico may be considered average or even short in other contexts. Thus, I refer to these measures only within the Mexican context. Tall would refer to someone taller than around 1.75 metres.

an *escolta* or bodyguard, preferring this to being known as just a driver.

Drivers mimicking bodyguards notwithstanding, security concerns have placed new demands on drivers and forced them to professionalize and adopt a perhaps more corporate look. As the market for drivers became more demanding in terms of the risks involved, potential drivers incorporated new attitudes and strategies to attract employers, by looking more like bodyguards, for example. Before the times of high crime rates, not only were drivers less common, but those who were around were also drivers in the simpler sense of the word. They needed to keep information safe, but the notion of protection itself was not as important. Drivers know that nowadays this is not sufficient. All of them recognize that their job is a dangerous one. Respondent WNV6 (driver, 46, male) noted that he was regularly out at night, since he worked for a family with teenagers who visited clubs and went to parties often. He said he 'needed to keep well awake ... when driving [his employer] around, when she goes to a party or something like that'. At the very least, drivers must now look like somewhat dangerous persons, convey the possibility of violence, and even have a certain ingrained belligerence. They must not be afraid to risk their personal integrity, or at least they should signal this convincingly. Apparent physical strength is a good way of signaling this, but drivers also use body language and threatening behaviour towards others to do so.

An example of this practice is the following story I was told by a driver (WNV9, driver, 30s, male). While driving his employer home one day, and only a few hundred metres from the house, he was very aggressively overtaken by a group of men in a truck, causing his boss to yell out and him to almost crash. At that moment, he thought they were being attacked or that it was an attempted kidnapping. Swerving violently, he avoided the truck and sped away. Obscenities were exchanged between them and he drove his boss home. Upset about the incident, he and another driver working at the household quickly left to look for the men in the truck. This was something they did out of their own initiative, as the employer did not know about this until later. They found the truck parked nearby, the group of men eating at a food stand. One of the drivers pulled out a gun he carried and both of them confronted the men who happened to be carrying machetes (a tool used at work by many Mexicans).

The drivers threatened the men in the truck (some four of them, according to the driver) to 'be careful and watch out who you are messing with'. According to what he recalled, he said to them: 'because if not, you or I, someone is going to die'; the men in the truck eventually backed down and left. The drivers returned home and told their boss about this. This deeply angered the employer, and he made sure they knew this, but in a sense, it also reassured him regarding the loyalty of his employees. What the driver was signaling to his employer by telling him this story was that he had the potential to use violence when necessary in the employer's defence, even if it meant compromising his own safety. The motivations behind such an action may have an emotional component to them and may be all about signaling. The driver may just have a temper or have poor impulse control. In any case, this can still be constructed into an efficient signal (if an extreme one) of what drivers ultimately want to portray to their employers—that they are able to protect them and their families against external threats.

Not surprisingly, considering that hiring is a process that has been repeated many times over a long period, we see a certain degree of harmony between what the employees now display and what the employers want to see. This is evidence of a cognitive process that has developed over time on both sides of the relationship and evidences the micro-level strategies people use to navigate risk.

## When the Relationship Breaks Down

The focus of this chapter has been on the hiring process for drivers and how they and their employers solve the problems of trust through signaling mechanisms. The times when these relationships break down, while not central to the analysis of these last two chapters, are of interest, as it seems likely that kidnapping may be a heightened possibility at this point in time. Kidnapping may occur under two specific sets of circumstances: (1) when a mimic successfully fools an employer and is hired to work in the household; and (2) when good employees themselves fall prey to criminals who pressure them into divulging information. In the first scenario, we know what happens: the mimic gets the information needed to carry out the kidnapping, transmits such information to his peers and colleagues, and the crime takes place. In the second scenario, an honest driver (or any other employee) is threatened by criminals into disclosing information through different mechanisms. I described cases such as this one in Chapter 3. However, beyond these two situations, there are times when the relationship becomes unsustainable and breaks down. It is not common that, once into the relationship, the break-up will come from the employee's side, especially if other members of his or her family work in the household. Reasons for the breakdown may be labelled as external to the people involved in the relationship itself. Much like in any other work agreement, circumstances may change and even preferences and opinions. Mr X, whose story begins this book, admits to hiring bodyguards and then realizing he no longer wants to employ them. An employer's economic circumstances may change as well, and this will have an effect on their hiring practices. Employees may also decide to move, or choose a different career path. What is of special interest for our purposes is when the reasons for the breakdown are internal to the people involved.

These relationships break down when there is a perception from the employer that the employee is no longer trustworthy, evidenced, for example, by excessive absenteeism or perceived carelessness. When the employee stops displaying some of the necessary signals, employers become suspicious. If employees become less cooperative or their appearance deteriorates, it is sometimes taken to be a sign that something is amiss. Changing employees may be a security consideration. This is the case of the wealthy gated compound described in earlier chapters. In this case, an internal practice existed to change security companies every three or four years. This was allegedly so the employees would not have access to too much information. A driver interviewed later (2013) also recounted how he used to work for one of Mexico's richest men. He said this person—or his security managers—had a very strict policy not employ a driver/bodyguard for more than three years, no matter how good they were. The reason behind this was to avoid employees getting 'too comfortable'. One could question the logic behind this, since short-term employment would arguably increase the pay-off for betrayal. But good employees would receive upon finalizing their tenure a very good recommendation from a renowned employer, one which would certainly secure further good jobs.[11] This would certainly rebalance the pay-offs for defaulting in favour of cooperation.

The job market in Mexico is beset with legal uncertainty. A relations-based economy (Dixit 2004) means that contracts are verbal and rarely enforced by law. At the best of times, this type of market is risky as defaults can go unpunished, their rewards high. Over time, people in Mexico have devised mechanisms through which they can overcome issues of trust, in this case in the job market for household employees. Insecurity and the risk of kidnapping have made decisions based on trust especially important, as individuals seek to protect their families, property, and businesses as much as possible. The last two chapters have explored how, at the micro level, people have been able to solve problems of trust and thus protect themselves from crime better. It has allowed us to understand how relationships are entered into and sustained in an environment of insecurity, where the stakes are higher than just monetary loss.

[11] Having worked for this particular individual is certainly a strong status symbol for whoever can display it.

# Conclusion

The study of crime is by necessity multidimensional. Its causes, consequences, and histories are fluid. Kidnapping offers itself as a manifestation of national narratives which go beyond the fact of the crime itself. When looked at closely and examined, kidnapping offers a window into the very social fabric and structure of a society, its pitfalls and flaws, but also its virtues and potentials. It is an almost physical manifestation of the political economy of the country in question. It brings to the fore structural problems, but at the same time it is a micro-level individual conundrum. These statements became evident as research for this book progressed. Over time, it became clear that kidnapping is a very sui generis crime—one that requires a certain set of factors to be present in order to thrive and is also a very visible symptom of severe structural and institutional problems.

In the first instance, this book has sought to contribute to our understanding of kidnapping. On the one hand, it enters into a dialogue with the existing literature on crime in Mexico and Latin America, its causes, and its consequences. This particular body of literature is extensive, reflecting the violent histories of the region and its particular issues with the rule of law, corruption, and criminal activity (Morris 2009; O'Donnell 1998, 2004; Rubio 2003; Wiarda and Guajardo 1989, inter alia). The processes of liberalization and democratization which occurred in Mexico (and most of Latin America) over the last forty years had the unintended consequence of also 'liberalizing' crime. As authoritarian systems of governance collapsed, a long-standing equilibrium between criminals and the state was broken. The government ran out of resources to control crime and, in turn, criminals broke free of the shackles imposed by an all-powerful state. The Mexico City police forces are a perfect example of this. During Mexico's authoritarian era (1920s to the early 1990s), the forces were the 'biggest gang

Intimate Crimes: Kidnapping, Gangs and Trust in Mexico City. First Edition. Rolando Ochoa © Rolando Ochoa 2019. Published in 2019 by Oxford University Press

in town' controlling, especially throughout the tenure of Arturo Durazo as Chief of the City's police, most if not all of the criminal markets in the City, and indeed the country. Durazo's forces *professionalized* crime, using the police's traditional militaristic structure to their advantage. Police corporations are ideally situated to transit into criminal enterprises. They are disciplined and their members are well versed in the use of violence and arms. These skills transfer very well to the criminal realm. Democracy brought about the demise of Durazo and his ilk, but also opened up the criminal market to entrepreneurs willing to exploit new market opportunities. As Morselli and Giguere, elaborating on the organizing crime principle (2006: 187), put it: '(Organized) crime is directed by processes emerging from legitimate society.' As part of this political-economic process, inequality increased and after successive economic crises became one of the most entrenched characteristics of Mexican society. Thus, we were able to further establish the undeniable links between the political economy and crime.

In this context, the next objective of the book became clear: to discover the historical nuts and bolts of kidnapping, a crime that has captured the minds and imaginations of citizens, politicians, academics, and even artists in the region. Through providing a methodologically sound account of the evolution of this crime, we are in a better position to understand how criminals, their victims and the state interact in this milieu, as well as the structural, social, economic, and institutional factors that make kidnapping such a prevalent event in Mexico. But why kidnapping? What makes this crime special? Furthermore, why is it that it only happens (to a large extent) in some countries and not in others? What makes Mexico so ideal for kidnappers?

Kidnapping does not take place in all countries; indeed, it is the bane of a minority of nations around the globe, such as Mexico, Brazil, Venezuela, South Africa, and Nigeria. Some countries may have high crime rates, but lack a significant kidnapping problem. Countries may be poor, but lack a serious kidnapping problem. Kidnapping in the case of Mexico is the result of structural factors such as very high inequality, which creates the conditions for high crime rates (Blau and Blau 1982; Fajnzylber et al. 1998). The other countries mentioned above also happen to be among the most unequal countries in the world. Kidnapping is also the result of a very weak rule of law. It is a risky crime which may take place over long periods of time, making it a high-cost affair. Impunity allows for this crime to thrive as it reduces the risk associated with it. This issue has been thoroughly documented in the Latin American region (Mendez at al. 1999), and is further reinforced by the findings in this book. Mexico has a very weak rule of law. Crimes are rarely reported and even more rarely punished, prisons are full of petty criminals, and the criminal justice system has little capacity (or sometimes willingness) to respond to serious crimes. Tyler (2003) argues that cooperation with authorities is deeply linked to the perceptions of fairness of the process on behalf of the populace. Trust in government institutions, particularly the police and the courts, is very low in Mexico. Citizens do not trust the criminal justice system. This is not an irrational lack of trust: it is rooted deeply in the criminal justice system's well-known biases, corruption, and inefficacy. This issue is central to the crime problems faced by Mexico as pay-offs for most crimes are high, especially if criminals have the capacity to corrupt law enforcement. Crime pays in Mexico and this has allowed kidnapping gangs—whether professional or opportunistic—to thrive.

Another factor which is found here to influence the behaviour of kidnapping is a repressive or at least an authoritarian past. In Mexico, during the authoritarian period, criminal structures became ingrained in the social structure and many of these survive—in one form or another—today. Forces of order in authoritarian contexts are created as a tool of social control (of dissent or of competing criminal organizations), as opposed to being a vehicle for the delivery of public goods. These types of forces, as we see in the case of Mexico, have an easier time transiting from enforcing a social order to full-time criminal activities. It is no coincidence that some of the most notorious kidnappers in Mexico were trained under Durazo's police forces. Based on the evidence found, I can conclude that *kidnapping becomes an issue as a result of a process of liberalization, a high concentration of wealth in a few hands, an authoritarian past, and a very weak rule of law*. Of course, one can question the generalizability of these findings. Perhaps this is only found in the case of Mexico. Further research would be needed to establish this fully.

On a more detailed level, this book has sought to explain the changes in the nature of kidnapping over the years. Intuitively, kidnapping would be a crime which affected only wealthy people, as the pay-off would therefore be higher. This was in fact the case over the 1990s and early 2000s. However, evidence presented in this book shows that, during the first years of the twenty-first century, kidnapping saw a very curious change. Wealthy people, the ideal kidnapping victims, were no longer targeted as much. It was this change which became the original puzzle behind this research. Nowadays, kidnappers are victimizing mostly working- and middle-class people in Mexico City. This particular change was a significant driver of the desire to investigate the historical evolution of kidnapping in Mexico. This book presented an account of the evolution of this crime based on extensive primary- and secondary-source research. Thus, the evolution of kidnapping can be mapped into three different eras. First, a political era, when kidnapping was used mostly by left-wing urban and rural guerrilla groups as a way to raise funds or highlight their objectives. The second era of the early to late 1990s belonged to a handful of highly organized gangs, most with a past in the police forces, which kidnapped very wealthy individuals. Under pressure from wealthy sectors of society, the government successfully dismantled these organizations by the early 2000s. At the same time, wealthy elites were implementing new and better strategies to avoid being kidnapped. These strategies have been perfected over the last fifteen years or so. During this time, the government was struggling in its attempts to establish a strong rule of law. This situation persists to this day. Many examples are presented in this book of just how dire the situation is in the criminal justice system. Crimes are not reported, corruption abounds, and technical capacity is lacking. This brings us to the third era of kidnapping, which continues to this day. Almost immediately after the demise of the original, highly organized gangs, an increase in kidnapping in poorer areas of the City became evident as poorly organized younger gangs entered the kidnapping market that was once controlled by bigger, better organized gangs. This resulted in an overall increase in kidnappings and in the number of homicides related to them. Three factors are found to have determined this very suboptimal result. First, wealthy individuals enacted very successful protection strategies at the community level by using their money and political clout, which meant they simply became too difficult to kidnap. Second, the government was successful in eradicating highly organized and trained gangs which victimized the wealthy; this opened this particular criminal market to new, younger, less experienced gangs who saw an opportunity to supplant the old gangs. And, third, the state failed to create a strong rule of law as Mexico transited to a liberalized democracy. This was translated into very high levels of impunity and corruption, which allowed for crime, including kidnapping, to grow with little hope of being controlled.

While these three factors are presented separately here, they are meant to be understood as concurrent, dynamic processes. This aims to explain why this particular crime became so widespread, and why its victim type changed despite the best efforts of the government to stop it altogether. This points to another main conclusion: *the failure of the government to establish a strong rule of law and working justice system institutions overshadows and undermines any short-term success in crime-fighting policy.* Indeed, an unintended consequence of such successes within a weak institutional framework is more violence and higher crime rates in this case. By responding politically to crime (through pressure from the elites), the Mexican government unwittingly created the conditions for a rise in kidnapping rates.

Moving onto the micro level, the book explored the ways in which communities and individuals navigate the risk of being kidnapped. The uncovering of elite survival strategies allows us to understand how community- and individual-level decisions are made in this environment and also how non-state actors can have a large impact on how crime develops and on how the state responds to it. The literature on social mechanisms (Hedström and Bearman 2009) offers a valuable tool to frame and understand social processes found in the field. This relates in particular to the use of theories of trust (Gambetta 1988, 2009; Gambetta and Hamill 2005). I wanted to uncover how individuals can solve problems of trust in a context where the state offers little protection and where the stakes are high (in this case, the potential to be kidnapped). Therefore, this book has provided an empirically rich, qualitative implementation of trust and signaling theories in response to a context of high crime rates and high levels of informality. It has shed light on how potential victims to a most horrible crime negotiate the risks of being victimized with the need for certain types of employees, and has illustrated the processes behind decision-making in this informal context. It has also made sense of decisions (such as hiring a driver) that would at first glance seem risky and to some eyes even irrational.

In terms of the job market for household employees, employers and employees seek to make the hiring process secure through different mechanisms, which can be approached through signaling as a way to solve both problems of trust, as described by Bacharach and Gambetta (1997), among others. Employers can acquire the extra benefit of protection for their family and themselves by solving these issues. The process of hiring points to a strategic interaction between employer and employee through which both actors will try to signal the possession of certain properties deemed to be trust-warranting. This process has been perfected over time through repeated iterations of the hiring game. Signaling in this case has allowed us to understand how trust problems are solved in household employment processes, and how employers and employees use signals to reduce risk and secure, on the one hand, gainful employment and, on the other, a good driver/protector. The stress on social networks as a source of security is one of the main findings of this work. In an environment of informality and low state protection, a tight network becomes a vital tool for many tasks, such as reducing the risk of hiring a dishonest driver (through mechanisms of reputation and self-policing) and efficiently and cheaply transmitting information that is verifiable and trusted. Both employers and employees have, over time, closed in on their networks in order to make their relationships and transactions more secure. Vertical integration (Williamson 2005b) also serves as a way to understand the ability of wealthier people to protect themselves from kidnapping and other crimes which are based on access to information about the victim.

## The Centrality of Trust

Individuals are able to find solutions to problems of trust even in the most hostile environments, when a poor decision may be the difference between life and death. This not only reinforces the notion that trust can and is established in instances of informality as described by, among others, Greif (1993), but that it is indeed the glue that helps societies function. These results can also alter our interpretation of what happens to trust when crime rates are high. In Mexico, survey work has shown that levels of interpersonal trust have declined in recent times. However, this research shows that perhaps the story is more complex. Networks of trust exist in Mexico City, but they have become more compact and closed to the outside world. One can picture them as small, tight networks of trust which have been established over time. They are 'clusters of social structure' where trust is granted and taken, but which are isolated from other clusters. This points us to a certain atomization of society, but perhaps not along the lines which those claiming the death of trust had assumed. This has clear class implications. It deserves attention that, in the case of the groups studied here, social classes which are seemingly very separate (the wealthy and the working classes) come to rely on each other for security and the economic stability that governments will not provide, be it through a social safety net or the provision of security. This is not to say that classism does not exist or that these divisions are not pernicious and damaging in the long term. However, this kind of inter-class cooperation deserves attention, if only to discover how an unequal social structure survives and how best to disturb it. Focusing on micro-mechanisms allows for a wealth of detail to come to the surface, allowing us to explain actions and outcomes that may not be self-evident.

## Future Directions, New Questions

Sometimes, in the course of research, one is left with some answers and many more questions than when one started. Fascinating questions arise at every turn when the social world is observed. There are some interesting questions posed by this research that could possibly be explored in the future. The first one that arises is related to the patterns followed by kidnapping in the last few years. It will be interesting to explore and confirm whether or not the shift in kidnapping I pointed towards in this book can be confirmed over a longer period of time and with better data. The Mexican government has begun to collect and disseminate better data on kidnapping. New evidence seems to suggest that the trends explored in this book are indeed sustained and kidnapping has become a very widespread crime which affects mostly working-class people. A recent news report described how a steel worker was kidnapped for US $500. Extensive and resource-intensive research will be needed to explore the dynamics of this in the future, as well as its implications for issues of security and trust. Most importantly, hard data that is consistent over time would be ideal to answer these questions. Promisingly, the government of Mexico City is now publishing crime information at the district level, although this may stop being done at any point, as has happened in the past. This is, therefore, a call for better data collection and gathering. This is the ideal information to pick up on trends and correlations which can point towards new research directions.

Comparative exercises are also interesting ways of developing the findings presented. An ideal scenario would be to make a comparison between two neighbourhoods among which there is some variation. Another wealthy neighbourhood could potentially have different outcomes. More interestingly, an analysis of the survival strategies of communities in other social classes could also be carried out. By the same token, it would be very useful to carry out studies such as this one in other Latin American countries to see whether or not the dynamics are similar. Brazil is a case in point. Cities like Sao Paulo have many similar socioeconomic circumstances to Mexico City. They are both mega cities of over 20 million people in the greater city area, central to the development of their respective countries, and command a good percentage of each country's GDP. They also have important inequalities between rich and poor, high crime rates, and are both in large Latin American countries. These similarities would make a solid case for comparisons. Do these structural similarities between cities mean that the micro-mechanisms of survival strategies will be similar? Not necessarily, as this does not 'imply that two collectivities with an identical macro-level property will necessarily have identical micro-level properties' (Hedström and Bearman 2009: 10). On another continent, South Africa would be an ideal site for comparative work. Cities like Johannesburg have very high kidnapping rates. Once again, it would be interesting to see if those structural similarities are reflected at the micro-social level. Both Brazil and South Africa have important racial elements that Mexico does not have to the same extent—perhaps this could produce different outcomes. It would be very interesting to see if this crime and indeed society's response to it has evolved in a similar manner or if important differences exist. Studies in other areas of the developing world will surely yield important and interesting results.

The all-important social networks used to have access to employees and jobs also warrant future attention. As a mechanism for guaranteeing a certain quality and reputation, they seem to operate in similar ways to older networks of trade (Greif 1993).

The inner workings of these networks would make a fascinating study topic for the future. Reputation once again seems to be a key ingredient in the success of the hiring process. The mechanisms by which it operates and also how it is enforced in the network deserve more attention than I could apply here. Reputation as a central element in the establishment of relationships also cuts across class barriers: this deserves more attention. The importance of family networks (or strong ties) is also worthy of more research, as it may illustrate well what individuals do in a context of lawlessness (Dixit 2004) and high levels of informality so as to have access to high quality services.

The narrative of kidnapping addressed in Chapter 2 also raises some interesting questions. More research is needed in the area of kidnapping gangs, as some essential questions about their composition and operation remain unanswered. It is argued by Vilalta and Fondevila (2014: li) that a significant percentage of the gangs engaged in kidnapping are now family (42.4 per cent) or friendship-based (47.5 per cent). The first question that comes to mind, therefore, is when do families decide to enter into the kidnapping business? How do they recruit other members of the family or other people in their social circle? How are these groups structured? How do they plan their attacks? A family would in some cases make a very good kidnapping gang, with loyalty issues somewhat already resolved by kinship relations and family allegiance. Yet, families can sometimes be conflictive and one only needs to look at family feuds in the news to get an idea of how badly things can go within families when money is involved. There is a saying in Mexico that loosely translates into: 'clear accounts, long friendships', but this may not necessarily be the case for family-based gangs. In any case, these hypotheses lend support to the argument made in this book that there has been a sort of de-professionalization of kidnapping gangs in recent times. Thus, the role of the family-based gang (not to be confused with the family-based mafia, a very different phenomenon) remains a topic to be explored and analysed in depth. Right now, we know much more about the old kidnapping gangs than we do about the newer generation of kidnappers, and these questions could be addressed in further research.

This story, however, cannot be reduced only to kidnapping. This crime does not occur in a vacuum, and this is why it is important to understand the political and economic contexts in which it happens. The opening chapters of this book aim to do just that: situate kidnapping in the wider context of social and economic change in Mexico. Crime is, more so today, part of Mexico's social structure. It is related to organized crime, to Mexico's long history of corruption, impunity, and poor government performance. It is true that this is not a product of recent times and it is also true that reform will face many resistances; the challenges of integrating human rights to police and prosecutorial work is a good example of this.

Crime is very damaging to society. It is also, fundamentally, a series of problems in need of a solution. With regard to security policy, Mexico is certainly mired in a 'security trap' (Bailey 2014), where structural, political, and institutional factors converge to form the actual reality. Bailey argues that this 'trap' describes a situation where pervasive corruption (including tax evasion, bribery, etc.), crime, and violence consistently undermine efforts to improve the country's governance structures. Thus, Mexico is in a seemingly endless cycle of failed reforms. The country is in need of decisive policy ideas to break these inertias. The case of kidnapping illustrates very well how in a context of weak rule of law, no amount of success in the policy arena will suffice. The government, for the reasons exposed in this book, was very successful in dealing with the older, more sophisticated kidnapping gangs which operated in the City. However, because of the government's inability to guarantee law abidance and deal with corruption and impunity, the success was short-lived. Today, kidnapping rates are rising once more and victims are middle- and lower-class individuals, who have fewer elements to defend themselves from it. This emanates from the fundamental unfairness that pervades governance in Mexico. Ideally, rich and poor should have the same level of access to justice and state protection. However, this is not the case: the wealthy have been able to buy protection in an open market (both privately and from the government) and have succeeded in protecting themselves better, essentially buying the services the government will not provide (ironically, sometimes from the government itself). The government, on its part, plays the role of a private provider, at the service of those who can afford the cost of what should be a public good. This is incredibly detrimental to the quality of democracy in Mexico. Institutional change takes a very long time, generations even. Today, many in public office see their employment as a way to acquire private gains. In fact, there seems to be a pervasive misinterpretation of the public as a private good, for the benefit of those in office. The endless catalogue of corruption and conflict of interests (some of them described in this book) in which the government is involved is proof of this phenomenon. This will take enormous drive from society to change.

To compound this, the current War on Drugs being carried out by the government and which began in 2006 has left the country scarred, with hundreds of thousands dead and missing, and families torn apart. On the one hand, Mexico now deals with crime and drug-trafficking-related violence and, on the other, it deals with a government that does not, through lack of will or lack of ideas, deliver what is the most prized public good for Mexicans today: legal certainty, safety, and security. This is a major issue and it needs to be dealt with. Unfortunately, the institutional foundation through which security is delivered, such as the police, courts, and the entirety of the Mexican governance structures, has severe deficiencies. Due to its historical development, the political system in Mexico is more akin to a self-serving corporation than to a series of actors delivering public goods to the entire population. This is why the passing of new laws, or the creation of new police forces, seems to solve little; the country must take a further step backwards to the foundational aspects of what constitutes a working democracy. Unfortunately, there is no silver bullet to remedy this, nor can the country 'start form zero' once again. Therefore, the question remains: what next?

First of all, the government must signal that it is taking the population's demands for security and safety seriously. These demands must be recognized and assumed as part of the democratic process. Even today, most politicians are happy to assure the population that, if elected, they will fix the security problem. These promises have tended to stay at the campaign level. Recent events in Mexico, such as the political crisis surrounding the disappearance of forty-three students in the southern state of Guerrero in 2014, are a clear signal that the general population is no longer willing to maintain a system of governance which only benefits those in power. The massive protests that occurred all over the country (and in many other countries) were triggered by the students' case, but were also about much more. They were fundamentally also against the pervasive corruption in which Mexico is mired. The government can no longer hide its corrupt practices behind discourse and pork-barrel politics.

As a starting point, the current (and future) government must recognize the fact that it has not responded in an appropriate manner to the security issue. It needs to address this fact directly with the population and make it clear that the government is aware of the fact that it has not acted in ways that would be appropriate in a democracy. Only then can it regain the legitimacy necessary to move forward on the policy agenda. Therefore, there needs to be a national dialogue on what direction the country needs to take. It is quite clear that after twenty-five years of liberalization this alone will not solve the structural issues suffered by Mexico and that the provision of safety must be recognized as a cornerstone of democracy. This dialogue must be inclusive, and while it may not be able to answer all demands from all people, they need to be listened to. There needs to be a signal of absolute commitment from the government at all levels that security and openness is a priority. This is difficult to accomplish when, as we have seen, the highest echelons of government may be involved in, at the very least, serious conflict of interest and cronyism.

Some policies have already been put into place, but need new impetus. This is the case of the 2008 reform of the courts. This project, which later became law, seeks to change the justice system in Mexico from a purely accusatory, paper-based, system into one of oral trials, which would make the judicial process much more transparent. This reform has slowly been adopted, but it is only in place in a minority of courts. It would be beneficial to push the adoption of this reform further, alongside other policy programmes.

On top of deep institutional change, which can take a very long time to materialize (Williamson 2000), other policies have yet to be implemented and need to be implemented as a part of a holistic policy programme to reform the justice system. Some of these may be as outlined below.

*Change the country's approach to drugs.* It is no secret that the current policy on drugs has failed. Since its launch during the Nixon administration in the United States, the cost of the drug war has been immense and the results poor. The results of these policies in Mexico have been devastating in terms of lost lives, infrastructure, and national income, not to mention other social impacts in terms of community ties, social capital, etc. Every year, an increasing number of voices are added to those calling for a new way to interpret and deal with drugs. The Global Commission on Drug Policy, launched by a number of former Latin American presidents—among them Ernest Zedillo of Mexico—has been instrumental in changing the discourse on drugs in the region and in standing up to those promoting the older policies. Recently, there is a growing call for decriminalization of certain drugs, and of switching the view on them from a criminal/repressive perspective to a public health/harm reduction strategy. For example, Canada legalized recreational cannabis in 2018. This approach would still target large-scale traffickers as well as the networks of corruption and finance that allow them to exist, but would cease to criminalize personal users, instead providing the necessary health resources to deal with problematic drug use. The tide is changing in the War on Drugs—not because it is being won, but because more decision-makers as well as society in general are recognizing its failures and the possibility of other approaches. One key aspect of this is the need to demilitarize security in Mexico. Using the military for the purposes of providing security undermines the quality of democracy and produces adverse outcomes in terms of human rights and lethality.

*Professionalization of the entire justice system is another path towards reform.* This is a key issue and one that is brought up time and time again in Mexico. Without a professional justice system, there can be little in the way of advances in the fight against crime. This must include at the very least the introduction of human rights programmes and initiatives to fully integrate the notion of due process and the rights themselves in the police and prosecution institutions, including all practitioners and other actors in those institutions. Another key issue is building technical capacity, this includes forensics, crime investigation, and all other aspects related to the effective investigation of crimes.

In order to signal their intentions, the government could create an independent commission against corruption. These have worked in other contexts, even those where corruption is rife. An institution such as this would need to be fully independent and have prosecutorial powers. It would also need to have the capacity to prosecute individuals at all levels of government, and this would include the presidency. The president's 'white house' case and the subsequent inaction of the Ministry of Public Function made it very clear that the arrangements in place today are not much more than a political tool and that the higher levels of politics are still untouchable.

These initiatives and any others along the same lines should be underpinned by a broad agenda to strengthen the rule of law, which must include other areas besides the justice system. These are, of course, just ideas which emanate from the research carried herein. There may be other options we do not know about at this present time. Strong leadership is needed to make these, and indeed any, reforms work. The political and economic elite must be willing not only to give up power, but also to run the risk of losing unfair privileges which they have amassed in decades of corruption and ignored conflicts of interest. This will not be done easily and will require deep changes in the people in politics. Mexican society is, by and large, no longer willing to play its part in maintaining the status quo, and recent events point to a deep structural change in the way in which society perceives its government and what it expects of it. In many ways, the demands of the population have outrun the willingness of the political elite to change. It is time for those who represent society to listen.

# Methodological Appendix

Here, the reader can find descriptive analyses of the data used throughout this book. This section includes a comprehensive list of the interviews and codes for them, as well as a breakdown of information about the interviewees across different categories such as class, gender, and age. It also includes a description of the KNRD, as well as the coding framework for the data used.

For security reasons, as mentioned in the Introduction chapter, and at the behest of many of the interviewees, I decided on providing anonymity to all people interviewed. I coded each interview according to a set of parameters per group, as follows:

- *employers* who had been victims of kidnapping were coded as 'EV', followed by the interview number (e.g. EV1, EV5);
- *employers* who had *not* been victims of kidnapping were coded as 'ENV', followed by the interview number (e.g. ENV3, ENV22);
- *employees* of non-victims[1] were coded as 'WNV', followed by the interview number (e.g. WNV3);
- *employees* of victims were coded as 'WV', followed by the interview number (e.g. WV1);
- *law enforcement* interviews were coded as 'LE', followed by the interview number (e.g. LE3, LE16); and
- *other* interviews not belonging to the groups described above but also used were coded as 'O', followed by gender 'M' or 'F', followed by the interview number (e.g. OM3, OF4).

Tables 1 to 4 present detailed information about the interviewees. The district of Miguel Hidalgo has been shortened to 'MH' in the 'location' column in Tables 1 and 2.

Table 5 presents the coding framework of the interviews. Although the table seems to separate the coding process clearly, in practice it is a fluid, ongoing process, especially with regard to the relationship between open and axial codes. Selective codes imply the most micro level

[1] It is important to note that I did not interview all the employers of the drivers I spoke to. Nor did I interview all the drivers of the employers I talked to. I was able to do so in a number of cases (4), but those interviews did not show any important variation *vis a vis* the rest, which is why I only report this in a footnote.

**Table 1 Employer Interviews**

| Code | Occupation | Age | Gender | Location | Taped |
|---|---|---|---|---|---|
| ENV1 | Home | 64 | F | MH | N |
| ENV2 | Imports | 60s | F | MH | Y |
| ENV3 | Home | 50s | F | MH | Y |
| ENV4 | Retired | 60s | F | MH | Y |
| ENV5 | Business | 60s | M | MH | Y |
| ENV6 | Business | 70s | M | MH | Y |
| ENV7 | Real Estate | 60s | F | MH | Y |
| ENV8 | Marketing | 60s | F | MH | Y |
| ENV9 | Home | 70s | F | MH | Y |
| ENV10 | Accountant | 47 | F | MH | Y |
| ENV11 | Manufacturing | 45 | F | MH | Y |
| ENV12 | Academic | 62 | F | MH | Y |
| ENV13 | Dentist | 40 | M | MH | Y |
| ENV14 | Student | 60 | M | MH | Y |
| ENV15 | Pollster | 64 | F | MH | Y |
| ENV16 | Business | 55 | F | MH | N |
| ENV17 | Artist | 27 | M | MH | N |
| ENV18 | Academic | 44 | F | MH | N |
| ENV19 | Actor | 50s | M | MH | N |
| ENV20 | Advertising exec. | 50s | F | MH | N |
| ENV21 | Software design | 20s | M | MH | N |
| ENV22 | Researcher | 30s | M | MH | N |
| ENV23 | Professor | 35 | M | MH | N |
| ENV24 | Business | 60s | F | MH | Y |
| EV1 | Architect | 35 | F | MH | Y |
| EV2 | Home/business | 37 | F | MH | Y |
| EV3 | Finance/activist | 55 | M | MH | Y |
| EV5 | Art curator | 34 | F | MH | Y |
| EV6 | Student | 20s | M | MH | N |

of analysis, where mechanisms become clear. Table 6 presents the coding for the News Reports Database.

Tables 5 and 6 are based on Strauss and Corbin (1990) and Bailey et al. (1999).

**Table 2 Employee Interviews**

| Code | Occupation | Age | Gender | Location | Taped |
|---|---|---|---|---|---|
| WNV1 | Driver/handyman | 30s | M | MH | Y |
| WNV2 | Cleaning | 50s | F | MH | Y |
| WNV3 | Cook | 70s | F | MH | Y |
| WNV4 | Cook | 50s | F | MH | Y |
| WNV5 | Driver | 29 | M | MH | N |
| WNV6 | Driver | 46 | M | MH | N |
| WNV7 | Driver | 44 | M | MH | N |
| WNV8 | Cook | 39 | F | MH | N |
| WNV9 | Driver | 30s | F | MH | N |
| WNV10 | Driver | 30s | M | MH | Y |
| WNV11 | Cleaning | 50s | F | MH | N |
| WNV12 | Driver/taxi | 40s | M | MH | N |
| WNV13 | Driver | 35 | M | MH | N |
| WV1 | Driver | 35 | M | MH | Y |
| WV2 | Driver | 30s | M | MH | N |

**Table 3 Law Enforcement Interviews**

| Code | Occupation | Age | Gender | Location |
|---|---|---|---|---|
| LE1 | District Prosecutor | 46 | M | Mexico City |
| LE2 | District Official | 36 | M | Mexico City |
| LE3 | State Prosecutor | 47 | M | Mexico City |
| LE4 | Prosecutor | 30s | M | Mexico City |
| LE5 | Prosecutor | 30s | M | Mexico City |
| LE6 | Junior Prosecutor 1 | 27 | F | Mexico City |
| LE7 | Junior Prosecutor 2 | 29 | F | Mexico City |
| LE8 | Junior Prosecutor 3 | 33 | M | Mexico City |
| LE9 | Policeman 1 | 25 | M | Mexico City |
| LE10 | Policeman 2 | 20s | M | Mexico City |
| LE11 | Admission Clerk | 40s | F | Mexico City |
| LE12 | Investigative Police Shift Commander | 44 | M | Mexico City |
| LE13 | Inv. Police 1 | 30s | M | Mexico City |

*(continued)*

**Table 3** (*Continued*)

| Code | Occupation | Age | Gender | Location |
|---|---|---|---|---|
| LE14 | Inv. Police 2 | 30s | M | Mexico City |
| LE15 | Inv. Police 3 | 30s | M | Mexico City |
| LE16 | Homicide Prosecutor City | 50s | M | Mexico City |
| LE17 | Homicide Jr Prosec. City 1 | 40s | M | Mexico City |
| LE18 | Homicide Jr. Prosec. City 2 | 40s | M | Mexico City |
| LE19 | Homicide Jr Prosec. City 3 | 30s | M | Mexico City |
| LE20 | Junior Prosecutor 4 | 30s | M | Mexico City |
| LE21 | File Manager | 40s | F | Mexico City |
| LE22 | State Prosecutor | 50s | M | Mexico State |
| LE23 | State Kidnapping Prosecutor | 60s | M | Mexico State |
| LE24 | Junior State Prosecutor | 30s | F | Mexico State |
| LE25 | Crime Victim 1 | 25 | M | Mexico City |
| LE26 | Crime Victim 2 | 20s | M | Mexico City |
| LE27 | Crime Victim 3 | 30s | F | Mexico City |

Note: None of these interviews was taped. Notes were taken throughout.

**Table 4 Other Interviews**

| Code | Occupation | Age | Gender | Location |
|---|---|---|---|---|
| OM1 | Building admin. | 46 | M | Mexico City |
| OM2 | Mechanic shop owner | 60 | M | Mexico City |
| OF3 | Food vendor | 55 | F | Mexico City |
| OM4 | District employee | 36 | M | Mexico City |
| OM5 | Federal government employee | 36 | M | Mexico City |
| OF6 | Graduate student | 30 | F | Mexico City |
| OF7 | Academic | 37 | F | Mexico City |
| OF8 | Activist | 32 | F | Mexico City |

**Table 5 General Coding Framework of Interviews**

| Open codes | Axial codes | Selective codes |
|---|---|---|
| Socioeconomic Information | Class self-perception<br>Income<br>Family<br>Status<br>Professions | Upper-middle<br>No one is upper class<br>High income<br>Married/single etc.<br>Business/art/home etc. |
| Crime | Fear of crime<br>Kidnapping<br>Out of control<br>Corruption<br>Impunity | Permanent fear<br>No law<br>Criminals rule<br>Criminal politicians<br>Fear of kidnapping<br>We all know someone<br>Police always involved<br>No use denouncing<br>The Earchopper etc. |
| Trust | In government<br>In others<br>In society<br>Definition<br>Signs of<br>Indentifying<br>'The sixth sense'/ cognitive process | Zero trust in government<br>Declining trust in others<br>No community<br>No one helps<br>Paranoia<br>No one can define trust<br>No one trusts except me etc. |
| Employee relations | Like family<br>Social distance<br>Inequality<br>Deep relation | Keeping distance is safe<br>Becoming family is safe<br>etc. |
| Hiring process | Social networks<br>Assessment<br>First impression<br>Vertical integration at the family level<br>Signaling<br>Employee's version | Recommendations only<br>Test period<br>Body language<br>Looks<br>Papers easy to fake<br>From the interior/less evil<br>Family networks (vert. integr.)<br>Age<br>Gender<br>Threat etc. |
| Survival strategies | Lifestyle change<br>Buying protection<br>Radical measures<br>Cynicism<br>Government relations | Leaving country<br>Arms<br>I no longer care/no change<br>Government carrot<br>Government stick etc. |

**Table 6 General Coding Structure of KNRD**

| Open Codes | Axial Codes | Selective Codes |
|---|---|---|
| Kidnapping | Evolution<br>History<br>Federal crime<br>Local crime<br>Mexico City<br>Gangs<br>Policy<br>New gangs<br>Victims/profiles | Political-economic<br>Authoritarian past<br>Laws<br>'Caletri Gang'<br>'El Coronel Gang'<br>'El Mochaorejas Gang'<br>Spanish community<br>Jewish community<br>Lebanese community<br>Working-class victims |
| Police/ government | Corruption<br>Police involvement<br>Policy<br>Federal strategy<br>Local police<br>Official discourse | Change to local police<br>Santiago Vasconcelos<br>Police protection<br>Police<br>Success/failure |
| Trust | In government<br>In others<br>In society<br>Definition<br>Signs of<br>Indentifying<br>'The sixth sense'/ cognitive process | No trust in government<br>Declining trust in others<br>No community<br>No one helps<br>Paranoia<br>No one can define trust<br>No one trusts except me etc. |
| Employee relations | Like family<br>Social distance<br>Inequality<br>Deep relation | Keeping distance is safe<br>Becoming family is safe<br>etc. |
| Hiring process | Social networks<br>Assessment<br>First impression<br>Vertical integration at the family level<br>Signaling<br>Employee's version | Recommendations only<br>Test period<br>Body language<br>Looks<br>Papers easy to fake<br>From the interior/less evil<br>Family networks (vert. integr.)<br>Age<br>Gender<br>Threat etc. |
| Survival strategies | Lifestyle change<br>Buying protection<br>Radical measures<br>Cynicism<br>Government relations | Leaving country<br>Arms<br>I no longer care/no change<br>Government carrot/mobilization<br>Government stick etc./protest |

**Table 7 KNRD, 1999–2008**

| Year | News reports |
|---|---|
| 1999 | 33 |
| 2000 | 99 |
| 2001 | 156 |
| 2002 | 175 |
| 2003 | 96 |
| 2004 | 266 |
| 2005 | 219 |
| 2006 | 163 |
| 2007 | 100 |
| 2008 | 467 |

Source: Author's work with data from *El Universal* and *La Jornada* dailies.

## News Reports Database

In this section, I present basic descriptive statistics for the KNRD. As mentioned above, the database contains 1,774 news reports from two national newspapers. The newspapers were chosen on a number of factors, including: (1) their coverage of kidnapping; (2) their accessibility (due to the limited fieldwork time, this was an important factor to consider—both newspapers have accessible web pages and databases searchable by topic); and (3) both papers have a different reporting style, which means that news reports are less likely to be repeated in each newspaper. All efforts were made to ensure the database was clean, with no repetition or double reporting; however, given the limited time frame, I cannot guarantee this with 100 per cent certainty. This weakness is addressed during coding as it is in that process when double reporting is also easily identifiable and dealt with. The quantitative use of the database proved problematic for a number of reasons. The data collection process proved very difficult. Newspapers do not report homogenously across time and this leads to the regular occurrence of missing information. The quality of data available is not only inconsistent, but also of general poor quality. I have spoken to local experts (academics working on crime and with experience in data gathering) and was repeatedly told that great care needed to be taken when using the data available, as it was notoriously unreliable. Survey and census data, as well as the data gathered on KNRD, would be risky to use quantitatively as its solidity could be put into question. I have used as much quantitative evidence as

I can gather at this time from the database and such information is well spread throughout the book.

As is visible, there is a steady increase in the reports from 1999 to 2002, an unexplained lull in 2003, and then the numbers jump again to 266 reports in 2004. This year saw an important rise in overall crime rates and a number of high-profile kidnappings, which may have made the media more aware of the topic. The reporting then goes back to early 2000s levels until 2008, when there is a massive increase to 467 reports in the database. This is due to one factor. In that year, the teenage son of a very prominent businessman, Fernando Marti (the owner of a very large chain of sports clothing stores), was kidnapped and murdered over a ransom of close to 6 million pesos (around US$150,000). The boy's father made the case extremely public and this caused a massive public outcry, mass protests, and the involvement of political actors, including the President of Mexico, who made a point of attending the boy's funeral and proposing a series of reforms to tackle crimes like these. The fact that a Federal Policewoman was involved in the kidnapping made the matter even more outrageous in the public's eyes. The National Council for Public Security, involving all levels of government, was created after this incident as a response to Mr Marti's harsh criticisms of everyone in government. His phrase, declared in front of the president, 'if you can't do it [solve the crime problem] … quit!' has since become a war cry for anti-crime activists.

# References


Abadinsky, H. (2012). *Organized Crime*. Cengage Learning. California, United States.

Ablanedo, I., Layton, M., and Moreno, A. (2008). 'Encuesta Nacional sobre Filantropía y Sociedad Civil (ENAFI): Capital Social en México'. CEPI Working Paper 17, Mexico.

Acosta, M. (2011). 'Superar la impunidad: hacia una estrategia para asegurar el acceso a la justicia en México' México, Distrito Federal, CIDE. http://es. scribd. com/doc/64415702/Superar-la-impunidad-haciauna-estrategia-para-asegurar-elacceso-a-la-justiciaen-Mexico-Mariclaire-Acosta-coordinadora. Accessed June 2012.

Aranda, J. (2011). *En la lucha de Calderón contra el narco, Sedena y Semar duplicaron su presupuesto*. La Jornada, 6 September 2011. Mexico.

Arias, E. D. (2006). *Drugs and Democracy in Rio de Janeiro: Trafficking, Social Networks, and Public Security*. Chapel Hill, NC: University of North Carolina.

Arrow, K. (1969) . 'The Organization of Economic Activity: Issues Pertinent to the Choice of Market versus Nonmarket Allocation'. Joint Economic Committee of Congress. Washington, DC, US.

Aviña, A. (2014). *Specters of Revolution: Peasant Guerrillas in the Cold War Mexican Countryside*. Oxford University Press, UK.

Axelrod, R. (1984). *The Evolution of Cooperation*. New York: Basic Books.

Azaola, E. (2006). *Imagen y Autoimagen de la Policía de la Ciuidad de México*. Book Manuscript Draft Copy. Mexico City.

Bacharach, M. and Gambetta, D. (2001). 'Trust in Signs' in K. Cook (ed.), *Trust in Society*. New York: Sage, pp. 148–84.

Bagley, B. (2013). 'The Evolution of Drug Trafficking and Organized Crime in Latin America' (71) *Sociologia, Problemas e Práticas* 99–123.

Bailey, J. (2014). *The Politics of Crime in Mexico: Democratic Governance in a Security Trap*. Boulder, CO: Lynne Rienner.

Bailey, C., White, C., and Pain, R. (1999). 'Evaluating Qualitative Research, Dealing with the Tension between "Science" and "Creativity"' 31(2) *Area* 169–83.

Banfield, E. C. (1967). *The Moral Basis of a Backward Society*. Free Press, New York.

Barkbu, B., Eichengreen, B., and Mody, A. (2011). 'International Financial Crises and the Multilateral Response: What the Historical Record Shows'. NBER Working Paper 17361. https://www.nber.org/papers/w17361 Accessed July 2019.

Barraza-Lloréns, M., Bertozzi, S., González-Pier, E., and Gutierrez, J. (2002). 'Addressing Inequity in Health and Health Care in Mexico' 21(3) *Health Affairs* 47–56.

Bellingeri, M. (1993). 'La Imposibilidad del Odio: La Guerrilla y el Movimiento Estudiantil en México, 1960–1974' in E. Semo (ed.), *La Transición Interrumpida: México 1968–1988*. Mexico: Universidad Iberoamericana, pp. 49–75.

Benton, A. L. (2012). 'Bottom-Up Challenges to National Democracy: Mexico's (Legal) Subnational Authoritarian Enclaves' 44(3) *Comparative Politics* 253–71.

Bergman, M., Azaola, E., and Magaloni, A. (2002). 'Encuesta a la Población en Reclusión en el Distrito Federal, Morelos y Estado de México—2002'. Centro de Investigación y Docencia Económicas (México); Programa de Estudios para la Seguridad Pública y Estado de Derecho, México.

Bergman, M., Azaola, E., and Magaloni, A. (2005a). 'Delincuencia, Marginalidad y Desempeño Institucional'. Working Paper. Division de Estudios Jurídicos, Centro de Investigacón y Docencia Economicas, Mexico.

Bergman, M., Azaola, E., and Magaloni, A. (2005b). 'Encuesta a la Población en Reclusión en el Distrito Federal y Estado de México—2005'. Centro de Investigación y Docencia Económicas (México); Programa de Estudios para la Seguridad Pública y Estado de Derecho, México.

Bergman, M. Azaola, E., Magaloni, A., and Negrete, L. (2009). 'Encuesta a la Población en Reclusión en el Distrito Federal y Estado de México—2009'. Centro de Investigación y Docencia Económicas (México); Programa de Estudios para la Seguridad Pública y Estado de Derecho, México.

Bethell, L. (ed.) (1995). *Cambridge History of Latin America*. Cambridge: Cambridge University Press.

Blau, J. R. and Blau, P. M. (1982). 'The Cost of Inequality: Metropolitan Structure and Violent Crime' 1 February *American Sociological Review* 114–29.

Board, O. (2009). 'Competition and Disclosure' 57(1) *Journal of Industrial Economics* 197–213.

Booth, T. and Booth, W. (1994). 'The Use of Depth Interviewing with Vulnerable Subjects: Lessons from a Research Study of Parents with Learning Difficulties' 39(3) *Social Science & Medicine* 415–24.

Brambila, J. and Cazzavillan, G. (2008). 'The Dynamics of Parallel Economies: Measuring the Informal Sector in Mexico'. Working Paper. Venice: Department of Economics, University of Venice.

Briggs, R. (2002). 'Hostage Inc.' 131 *Foreign Policy* 28–9.

Buffie, E. and Krause, A. S. (1989). 'Mexico 1958–86: From Stabilizing Development to the Debt Crisis' in Sachs, J. (Ed.) *Developing Country Debt and the World Economy*. University of Chicago Press, pp. 141–68.
Buffington, R. (2001). *The Social Construction of Crime in Mexico*. Chapel Hill, NC: University of Notre Dame Press.
Caldeira, T. (1997). 'Seguranca pública e sequestros no Rio de Janeiro: 1995–1996' Vol 9. No. 1 *Revista Brasileira de Ciencias Criminais*. 115–153.
Caldeira, T. (2000). *City of Walls, Crime, Segregation and Citizenship in São Paulo*. Berkeley, CA: Berkeley University of California Press.
Calvo, G. A. and Mendoza, E. G. (1996). 'Petty Crime and Cruel Punishment: Lessons from the Mexican Debacle'86(2) *The American Economic Review* 170–5.
Campbell, H. (2009). *Drug War Zone: Frontline Dispatches from the Streets of El Paso and Juárez*. Austin, TX: University of Texas Press.
Carpizo, J. (1978 [2008]). *El Presidencialismo Mexicano*. Mexico City.: SXXI publishers.
Castellanos, L. (2008). *México Armado 1943–1981*, Mexico City: Era.
Castillo, C. (1999). 'El Secuestro Como Distincion'. *El Universal*, 25 September 1999.
Chambre Franco-Mexicaine de Commerce et d'Industrie (2004). *Encuesta*. Mexico City: CFMCI.
Clarke, R. V. and Weisburd, D. (1994). 'Diffusion of Crime Control Benefits: Observations on the Reverse of Displacement' 2 *Crime Prevention Studies* 165–84.
Coase, R. H. (1937). 'The Nature of the Firm' 4(16) *Economica* 386–405.
Comité Eureka (2007). *2007 Report*. Mexico City: Comité Eureka.
Conklin, J. (1989). *Criminology*. New York: Macmillan.
Consejo Pro Defensa del Migrante/American Friends Service Committee (CPDM/AFSC). (2016). Vidas en la incertidumbre: Migracion forzada Mexicana hacia la frontera norte de Mexico. ¿y nuestra solidaridad?. Mexico.
Consejo Nacional de Evaluación de la Política de Desarrollo Socia (CONEVAL). (2012). 'Pobreza y Población Indigena'. Mexico City.
Consejo Nacional de Evaluación de la Politica de Desarrollo Social (CONEVAL). (2014a). 'Pobreza'. Accessed 10 December 2014. http://www.coneval.gob.mx/Medicion/Paginas/Medici%C3%B3n/Pobreza%202012/Pobreza-2012.aspx.
Consejo Nacional de Evaluación de la Politica de Desarrollo Social (CONEVAL). (2014b). 'Evolucion de las Dimensiones de la Pobreza'. Accessed 10 December 2014. http://www.coneval.gob.mx/Medicion/Paginas/Evolucion-de-las-dimensiones-de-la-pobreza-1990-2010-.aspx.
Cook, K. (ed.) (2001). *Trust in Society*. Russell Sage Foundation. New York.

Cook, K. and Gerbasi, A. (2009). 'Trust' in P. Hedström and P. Bearman (eds), *The Oxford Handbook of Analytical Sociology*. Oxford, UK: Oxford University Press, 218–45.

Córdova, A.([1972] 2001). *La formación del poder político en México*, vol. 15. Ediciones Era. Mexico City.

Cotte Poveda, A. (2011). 'Socio-Economic Development and Violence: An Empirical Application for Seven Metropolitan Areas in Colombia' 17(1) *Peace Economics, Peace Science and Public Policy* 1–21.

Davis, D. (1994). *Urban Leviathan: Mexico City in the Twentieth Century*. Philadelphia, PA: Temple University Press.

Davis, D. (2006a). 'The Age of Insecurity, Violence and Social Disorder in Latin America' 41(1) *Latin American Research Review* 178–97.

Davis, D. (2006b). 'Undermining the Rule of Law, Democratization and the Dark Side of Police Reform in Mexico' 48(1) *Latin American Politics and Society* 55–86.

Densley, J. (2013). *How Gangs Work*. New York, NY: Palgrave Macmillan.

Detotto, C., McCannon, B. C., and Vannini, M. (2015). 'Evidence of Marginal Deterrence: Kidnapping and Murder in Italy' 41 *International Review of Law and Economics* 63–7.

De Vos, S. (1987). 'Latin Anerican Households in Comparative Perspective' 41(3) *Population Studies* 501–17.

Diaz-Cayeros, A., Magaloni, B., and Weingast, B. (2003). 'Democratization and the Economy in Mexico: Equilibrium (PRI) Hegemony and Its Demise'. Typescript, Stanford University.

Dixit, A. (2004). *Lawlessness and Economics*. Princeton, NJ: Princeton University Press.

Edwards, S. (1998). 'The Mexican Peso Crisis: How Much Did We Know? When Did We Know It?' 21(1) *The World Economy* 1–30.

Elster, J. (1998). 'A Plea for Mechanisms' in Hedström, P., and Swedberg, R., (Eds.) *Social Mechanisms: An Analytical Approach to Social Theory*. Cambridge University Press, New York. p. 49.

Elster, J. (2004). 'Emotions and Rationality' in Mastead, A., Frijda, N., and Fischer, A. (Eds.) *Feelings and Emotions*. Cambridge University Press, New York. pp. 30–48.

Enamorado, T., López-Calva, L. F., Rodríguez-Castelán, C., and Winkler, H. (2016). 'Income Inequality and Violent Crime: Evidence from Mexico's Drug War' 120 *Journal of Development Economics* 128–43.

Encuesta Mitofski (2005). *Delincuencia en México*. Mitofski, Mexico City: Ecuesta Mitofski.

Escobar, A. (2018). *The Making of Social Movements in Latin America: Identity, Strategy, and Democracy*. Routledge. UK.

Fajnzylber, P., Lederman, D., and Loayza, N. (1998). *Determinants for Crime Rates in Latin America and the World: An Empirical Assessment*. Washington, DC: The World Bank.

Fearon, J. and Laitin, D. (1996). 'Explaining Inter-Ethnic Cooperation' 90(4) *The American Political Science Review* 715–35.
Frank, R. (1988). *Passions within Reason: The Strategic Role of the Emotions*. New York: Norton
Frühling, H. H., Tulchin, J. S., and Golding, H. (eds) (2003). *Crime and Violence in Latin America: Citizen Security, Democracy, and the State*. Woodrow Wilson Center Press. Washington DC.
Gabbert, W. (2004). 'Of Friends and Foes: The Caste War and Ethnicity in Yucatan' 9(1) *Journal of Latin American Anthropology* 90–118.
Gambetta, D. (1988). 'Can We Trust Trust?' in D. Gambetta (ed.), *Trust: Making and Breaking Cooperative Relations*. Oxford: Basil Blackwell, pp. 213–39.
Gambetta, D. (1996). *The Sicilian Mafia: The Business of Private Protection*. Boston, MA: Harvard University Press.
Gambetta, D. (2000). 'Can we Trust Trust' in Gambetta, D. *Trust: Making and Breaking Cooperative Relations*, pp. 213–37. B. Blackwell. New York.
Gambetta, D. (2009). 'Signaling' in P. Hedström and P. Bearman (eds), *The Oxford Handbook of Analytical Sociology*. Oxford: Oxford University Press, pp. 168–95.
Gambetta, D. and Hamill, H. (2005). *Streetwise: How Taxi Drivers Establish their Customer's Trustworthiness*. New York: Rusell Sage.
Garland, D. (1996). 'The Limits of the Sovereign State: Strategies of Crime Control in Contemporary Society' 36(4) *The British Journal of Criminology* 445–71.
Garrido, L. J. (1991). *El Partido de la Revolución Institucionalizada. Medio siglo de poder político en México: La formación del nuevo estado (1928–1945)*. Mexico City: Siglo XXI Publishers.
Goldthorpe, J., Llewellyn, C., and Payne, C. (1980). *Social Mobility and Class Structure in Modern Britain*. Oxford: Clarendon Press.
Gonzales, G. (1983). *Lo Negro del Negro Durazo*. Mexico City: Posada.
Good, D. (2000). 'Individuals, Interpersonal Relations and Trust' in D. Gambetta (ed.), *Trust: Making and Breaking Cooperative Relations*. Oxford: Basil Blackwell, pp. 31–49.
Granovetter, M. (1973). 'The Strength of Weak Ties' 78(6) *American Journal of Sociology* 1360–80.
Granovetter, M. (1983). 'The Strength of Weak Ties: A Network Theory Revisited' 1(1) *Sociological Theory* 201–33.
Greif, A. (1993). 'Contract Enforceability and Economic Institutions in Early Trade: The Maghribi Traders' Coalition' 83(3) *American Economic Review* 525–48.
Guerette, R. T. and Bowers, K. J. (2009). 'Assessing the Extent of Crime Displacement and Diffusion of Benefits: A Review of Situational Crime Prevention Evaluations' 47(4) *Criminology* 1331–68.

Guerrien, M. (2006). 'Arquitectura de la Inseguridad, Percepción del Crimen y Fragmentación del Espacio Urbano en la Zona Metropolitana del Valle de México' in P. Bonastra, Q. Rodríguez, G. Arella, and C. Fraile (eds), *Paisaje Ciudadano, Delito y Percepción de la Inseguridad*. Madrid: Dykinson, pp. 24–47.

Guerrero-Gutiérrez, E. (October 2011). 'Security, Drugs, and Violence in Mexico: A Survey'. 7th North American Forum, Washington DC.

Harbaugh, R. and To, T. (2007). 'False Modesty: When Disclosing Good News Looks Bad'. July. Accessed 23 May 2019. Available at SSRN: http://ssrn.com/abstract=777924.

Hardin, R. (2006). 'The Street Level Epistemology of Trust' in R. Kramer (ed.), *Organizational Trust*. Oxford, Oxford University Press, pp. 21–48.

Hedström, P. and Bearman, P. (2009). *The Oxford Handbook of Analytical Sociology*. Oxford: Oxford University Press.

Hedström, P. and Swedberg, R. (1998). 'Social Mechanisms: An Introductory Essay' in Hedström, P. and Swedberg, R. (Eds.) *Social Mechanisms: An Analytical Approach to Social Theory*. pp. 1–31.

Hinton, M. (2006). *The State on the Streets: Police and Politics in Argentina and Brazil*. Boulder, CO: Lynne Rienner.

Hiskey, J. (2012). 'The Return of "The Local" to Mexican Politics' in Camp, R. *The Oxford Handbook of Mexican Politics*. Oxford University Press. P. 545–571.

Holston, J. (2007). *Insurgent Citizenship: Disjunctions of Democracy and Modernity in Brazil*. Princeton: Princeton University Press.

Instituto Ciudadano de Estudios Sobre Inseguridad (ICESI) (2003). *Segunda Encuesta Nacional Sobre la Inseguridad en las Entidades Federativas*. Mexico City: ICESI.

Instituto Ciudadano de Estudios Sobre Inseguridad (ICESI) (2003). *Tercera Encuesta Nacional Sobre Inseguridad*. Mexico City: ICESI.

Instituto Ciudadano de Estudios Sobre Inseguridad (ICESI) (2005). *Encuesta Nacional Sobre Inseguridad Urbana*. Survey. Mexico City: ICESI.

Instituto Ciudadano de Estudios Sobre Inseguridad (ICESI) (2005a). *Secuestro Total y por cada 100,000 Habitantes*. Mexico City: ICESI.

Instituto Ciudadano de Estudios Sobre Inseguridad (ICESI) (2005b). *Tercera Encuesta Sobre la Inseguridad 2005*. Mexico City: ICESI.

Instituto Ciudadano de Estudios Sobre Inseguridad (ICESI) (2007). *Encuesta Nacional Sobre Inseguridad 5*. Mexico City: ICESI.

Instituto Ciudadano de Estudios Sobre Inseguridad (ICESI) (2008). *Secuestro Total y Por Cada 100,000 Habitantes*. Mexico City: ICESI.

Instituto Ciudadano de Estudios Sobre Inseguridad (ICESI) (2011). *Ecuesta: Ciudadania y Violencia*. Mexico City: ICESI.

Instituto Nacional de Estadística Geografíae Informática (INEGI) (2005). 'II Conteo de Población y Vivienda 2005'. Accessed 2 December 2009. http://www.inegi.gob.mx.

Instituto Nacional de Estadística, Geografía e Informática (INEGI) (2008). *Producto Interno Bruto Estatal 2006*. Statistical Report. Mexico City: INEGI.

Instituto Nacional de Estadística, Geografía e Informática (INEGI) (2013). *Estadisticas a Proposito del Dia Internacional de la Eliminacion de la Violencia Contra la Mujer* [Statistics Pertaining to the International Day against Violence against Women]. Mexico City: INEGI.

Instituto Nacional de Estadística, Geografía e Informática (INEGI) (2015). Boletin de Prensa 395/15 [press release 395/15]. Aguascalientes, Mexico.

Instituto Nacional de Estadística, Geografía e Informática (INEGI) (2017). Encuesta Nacional de Victimizacion y Sobre Percepcion de Seguridad Publica. Mexico.

Instituto Nacional de Estadística, Geografía e Informática (INEGI) (2019). Principales causas de mortalidad por residencia habitual, grupos de edad y sexo del fallecido. Mexico. Accessed 22 July 2019.

Jiménez Ornelas, R. (2000). 'La Cifra Negra de la Delincuencia en México: Sistema de Encuestas Sobre Victimización'. Working Paper. Instituto de Investigaciónes Sociales de la UNAM (UNAM).

Jimenez Ornelas, R. and Islas de Gonzalez Mariscal, O. (2002). *El secuestroproblemas sociales y juridicos* (No. 343.43 345.72052). e-libro, Corp.

Jung, C. (2003). 'The Politics of Indigenous Identity: Neoliberalism, Cultural Rights, and the Mexican Zapatistas' 70(2) *Social Research: An International Quarterly* 433–61.

Jütting, J. and de Laiglesia, J. R. (2009). 'Employment, Poverty Reduction and Development' OECD Development Centre, OECD, Paris.

Kellogg, S. (2005). *Weaving the Past: A History of Latin America's Indigenous Women from the Prehispanic Period to the Present*. Oxford University Press. New York.

Kelly, M. (2000). 'Inequality and Crime' 82(4) *Review of Economics and Statistics* 530–9.

Kidnapping News Reports Database (KNRD) (2009). Mexico.

Knight, A. (1985). 'The Mexican Revolution: Bourgeois? Nationalist? Or Just a "Great Rebellion"?' 4(2) *Bulletin of Latin American Research* 1–37.

Knight, A. (1990a). 'Racism, Revolution, and Indigenismo: Mexico, 1910–1940' in R. Graham, T. E. Skidmore, A. Helg, and A. Knight (eds), *The Idea of Race in Latin America, 1870–1940*. Austin, TX: University of Texas Press, pp. 71–113.

Knight, A. (1990b). *The Mexican Revolution: Counter-Revolution and Reconstruction*, vol. 2. Lincoln, NE: University of Nebraska Press.

Krebs, V. (2002). 'Mapping Networks of Terrorist Cells' 24(3) *Connections* 43–52.

Kreps, D. and Wilson, R. (1982). 'Reputation and Imperfect Information' 27(2) *Journal of Economic Theory* 253–79.

Kroll, L., Miller, M., and Serafin, T. 'The World's Billionaires'. Forbes.com. Accessed 23 July 2010. http://www.forbes.com/2009/03/11/worlds-richest-people-billionaires-2009-billionaires_land.html.

Lagrange, H. (2003). 'Crime and Socio-Economic Context' 44 (supplement: An Annual English Selection) *Revue française de sociologie* 29–48.

Latinobarómetro (2011). *Informe 2009*. Santiago: Latinobarómetro.

Lee, R. (1993). *Doing Research on Sensitive Topics*. London: Sage.

Lee, R. and Renzetti, C. (1990). 'The Problems of Researching Sensitive Topics: An Overview and Introduction' 33(5) *American Behavioral Scientist* 510–28.

Levitt, S. and Rubio, M. (2005). 'Understanding Crime in Colombia and What Can Be Done about It' in A. Alesina (ed.), *Institutional Reforms: The Case of Colombia*. P. 131–173. Cambridge, MA: MIT Press.

Lewis, G. (2010). 'Asymmetric Information, Adverse Selection and Online Disclosure: The Case of eBay Motors'. 12 January. Accessed 23 May 2019. Available at SSRN: http://ssrn.com/abstract=1358341.

Ley Federal Contra la Delincuencia Organizada (LFCDO) (2017). Mexico City, Mexico.

Lin, S. A. (ed.) (2014). *Theory and Measurement of Economic Externalities*. Academic Press. New York.

Loader, I. (1999). 'Consumer Culture and the Commodification of Policing and Security' 33(2) *Sociology* 373–92.

Looney, R. E. (1985). *Economic Policy Making in Mexico: Factors Underlying the 1982 Crisis*. Durham, NC: Duke University Press.

Lustig, N. (1995). *The Mexican Peso Crisis: The Foreseeable and the Surprise*. Washington, DC: Bookings Institution.

Lustig, N. (2001). 'Life Is Not Easy: Mexico's Quest for Stability and Growth' 15(1) *Journal of Economic Perspectives* 85–106.

Macaulay, S. (1963). 'Non-contractual Relations in Business: A Preliminary Study' Vol 28 No. 1. *American Sociological Review* 55–67.

Machamer, P., Darden, L., and Craver, C. F. (2000). 'Thinking about Mechanisms' 67(1) *Philosophy of Science* 1–25.

Magaloni, A. and Zepeda, G. (2004). 'Democratization and the Rule of Law' in K. Middlebrook (ed.), *Dilemmas of Political Change in Mexico*. San Diego, CA: Trans-Border Institute, pp. 168–97.

Mendez, J., O'Donnell, G., and Pinheiro, P. (1999). *The (Un)Rule of Law and the Underprivileged in Latin America*. Notre Dame University, US: Helen Kellogg Institute for International Studies.

Mexico Federal Government (2008). 'Ley Federal Contra la Delincuancia Organizada'. Federal Law. Mexico City.
Meyer, L. and Aguilar Camin, H. (1993). *In the Shadow of the Mexican Revolution: Contemporary Mexican History 1910 1989*. Austin, TX: University of Texas Press.
Migdal, J. (2001). *State in Society, Studying How States and Societies Transform and Constitute One Another*. Cambridge: Cambridge University Press.
Milenio, D. (2008). 'Accidentes Automoviliísticos' 31 August 2008.
Morfin, C., Elizarraras, R., Ezquivel, P. (2016). 'Indice Delictivo Metropolitano'. ON Partners. Mexico.
Morris, S. D. (2009). *Political Corruption in Mexico: The Impact of Democratization*. Boulder, CO: Lynne Rienner.
Morselli, C. and Giguere, C. (2006). 'Legitimate Strengths in Criminal Networks' 45(3) *Crime, Law and Social Change* 185–200.
Müller, M. M. (2010). 'Private Security and the State in Latin America: The Case of Mexico City' 5(SE) *Brazilian Political Science Review* [online].
Naim, M. (2000). 'Washington Consensus or Washington Confusion?' (No. 118, Spring) *Foreign Policy* 87–103.
Nieto, F. (2013). 'En Tres Decadas se Duplico el NUmero de Militares'. *El Universal*, 27 December 2013.
Ochoa, R. (2006). 'Bridging the Class Divide? A Study on Community Reactions to Violence in Mexico City'. Unpublished thesis, MPhil in Latin American Studies. Oxford: University of Oxford.
Ochoa, R. (2012). 'Not Just the Rich: New Tendencies in Kidnapping in Mexico City' 13(1) *Global Crime* 1–21.
Ochoa, R. and Graycar, A. (2016). 'Tackling Conflicts of Interest: Policy Instruments in Different Settings' 18(1) *Public Integrity* 83–100.
O'Donnell, G. (1998). 'Polyarchies and the (Un)Rule of Law in Latin America'. Presented at the Meeting of the Latin American Studies Association, Chicago.
O'Donnell, G. (2004). 'Why the Rule of Law Matters' 15(4) *Journal of Democracy* 32–46.
O'Neil, S. (2009). 'The Real War in Mexico' 88(4) *Foreign Affairs* 63–77.
Ortega, J. A. (2008). *El Secuestro en México*. Mexico City: Grijalbo.
Padilla, T. (2008). *Rural Resistance in the Land of Zapata: The Jaramillista Movement and the Myth of the Pax-Priísta, 1940–1962*. Durham, NC: Duke University Press.
Parés Hipolito, A. (2007). *El Fenómeno del Secuestro en México*. Mexico City: Porrua/UNAM.
Parsley, J. (2001). 'Basic Examination of the Correlation Between Crime Rates and Income Inequality'. Research Paper, vol. 19. Regional Research Institute at West Virginia University.

Pensado, J. M. (2013). *Rebel Mexico: Student Unrest and Authoritarian Political Culture during the Long Sixties*. Stanford University Press. California.

Pérez Correa, C., Azaola, E., Salgado Ibarra, J., Perez, G., Bergman, M., Vilalta Perdomo, C. J., Meneses, R., Quintana Navarrete, M., and Silva, K. (2012). 'Primera Encuesta a Población Interna en Centros Federales de Readaptación Social—2012'. Centro de Investigación y Docencia Económicas, México.

Pires, S. F., Guerette, R. T., and Stubbert, C. H. (2014). 'The Crime Triangle of Kidnapping for Ransom Incidents in Colombia, South America: A "Litmus" Test for Situational Crime Prevention' 54(5) *British Journal of Criminology* 784–808.

Prado Veiras, J. (2016). 'México cumple una década de duelo por el fracaso de la Guerra contra el Narco'. *New York Times*, 7 September 2016.

Procuraduria general de Justicia del Distrito Federal (2007). *Presenta PGJDF Resultados en Materia de Secuestros*. Mexico City: PGJDF.

Propiedades.com. (2017) Reporte de Mercado – Polanco. Mexico. http://propiedades.com/blog/informacion-inmobiliaria/polanco-condesa-las-colonias-mas-buscadas-2017. Accessed July 2019.

Purcell, S. K. (1981). 'Business-Government Relations in Mexico: The Case of the Sugar Industry' 13(2) *Comparative Politics* 211–33.

Raub, W. and Weesie, W. (1990). 'Reputation and Efficiency in Social Interactions: An Example of Network Effects' 96(3) *American Journal of Sociology* 626–54.

Reuter, P. (1983). *Disorganized Crime: The Economics of the Visible Hand*. Cambridge, MA: MIT Press.

Reuter, P. (1985). 'Organization of Illegal Markets: An Economic Analysis'. Research Report, National Institute of Justice Research Report, Washington, DC.

Rios Contreras, V. (2013). 'How Government Structure Encourages Criminal Violence: The Causes of Mexico's Drug War'. Doctoral dissertation. Harvard University.

Rubio, M. (2003). 'Del Rapto a la Pesca Milagrosa: Breve Historia del Secuestro en Colombia'. Working Papers. Universidad de los Andes, Bogotá.

Ruiz Harrel, R. (1996). 'El Saldo de la Impunidad' 1(2) *Revista Mexicana de Procuración de Justicia* 15–30.

Ruiz Harrel, R. (1998). *Criminalidad y Mal Gobierno*. Mexico City: Sansores y Aljure.

Sánchez-Reaza, J. and Rodríguez-Pose, A. (2002). 'The Impact of Trade Liberalization on Regional Disparities in Mexico' 33(1) *Growth and Change* 72–90.

Sachs, J., Tornell, A., and Velasco, A. (1996). 'The Collapse of the Mexican Peso: What Have we Learned?' 11(22) *Economic Policy* 13–63.

Sanderson, T. (2004). 'Transnational Terror and Organized Crime: Blurring the Lines' 24(1) *SAIS Review* 49–61.

Schelling, T. C. (1958). 'The Strategy of Conflict. Prospectus for a Reorientation of Game Theory' 2(3) *Journal of Conflict Resolution* 203–64.

Secretaria de Desarrollo Social (2006). *La Violencia en Mexico*. Mexico City: SEDESOL.

Secretaria de Seguridad Pública del Distrito Federal (2009). 'Estadisticas sobre Seguridad Privada'. Accessed 8 August 2009.

Secretaria de Seguridad y Proteccion Ciudadana (SSP) (2019). 'Informe de víctimas de homicidio, secuestro y extorsión 2017'. Mexico City, Mexico.

SeguriLatam (2016). 'Sólo la mitad de las empresas mexicanas de seguridad privada está regularizada'. Mexico. Accessed 22 July 2019. http://www.segurilatam.com/buscador/search?SearchText=mexico+seguridad+privada&nodo=0&fDesde=01%2F01%2F2016&fHasta=31%2F12%2F2016.

Seligman, A. B. (1997). *The Problem of Trust*. Princeton: Princeton University Press.

Shelley, L. (2001). 'Corruption and Organized Crime in Mexico in the Post-PRI Transition' 17(3) *Journal of Contemporary Criminal Justice* 213–31.

Siddiqi, D. M. (2009). 'Do Bangladeshi Factory Workers Need saving? Sisterhood in the Post-Sweatshop Era' 91(1) *Feminist Review* 154–74.

Silva Forné, C., Pérez Correa, C., and Gutiérrez Rivas, R. (2012). 'Uso de la fuerza letal: Muertos, heridos y detenidos en enfrentamientos de las fuerzas federales con presuntos miembros de la delincuencia organizada' (40) *Desacatos* 47–64.

Skaperdas, S. and Konrad K. (2004). 'What Order Out of Anarchy? Self-Governance, Autocracy and Predatory Competition'. Paper WP2004'2. Institute of Governmental Studies, University of California, Berkeley, CA.

Skaperdas, S. (2001). 'The Political Economy of Organized Crime: Providing Protection when the State Does Not' 2(3) *Economics of Governance* 173–202.

Soares, R. (2004). 'Development, Crime and Punishment: Accounting for the International Differences in Crime Rates' 73(1) *Journal of Development Economics* 155–84.

Spence, M. (1974). *Market Signaling: Informational Transfer in Hiring and Related Screening Processes*. Massachusetts, MA: Harvard University Press.

Stinchcombe, A. L. (1991). 'The Conditions of Fruitfulness of Theorizing about Mechanisms in Social Science' 21(3) *Philosophy of the Social Sciences* 367–88.

Strauss, A. and Corbin, J. (1990). *Basics of Qualitative Research: Grounded Theory Procedures and Techniques*. Newbury: Sage Publications.

Sztompka, P. (ed.) (1999). *Trust: A Sociological Theory*. Cambridge: Cambridge University Press.

Trebilcock, A. (2005). 'Decent Work and the Informal Economy'. WIDER Discussion Papers No. 2005/04. World Institute for Development Economics (UNU-WIDER).

Trejo, G. (2012). *Indigenous Insurgency: The Breakdown of Religious and Political Monopolies and the Rise of Ethnic Mobilization in Mexico*. Cambridge: Cambridge University Press.

Turbiville, G. H. (1997). *Mexico's Other Insurgents*. Foreign Military Studies Office, pp. 1–21.

Tyler, T. R. (2003). 'Procedural Justice, Legitimacy, and the Effective Rule of Law' 30(30) *Crime and Justice* 283–357.

Varese, F. (2000). 'Pervasive Corruption' in A. Kurkchiyan and M. Ledeneva (eds), *Economic Crime in Russia*. London: Kluwer Law International.

Varese, F. (2001). *The Russian Mafia, Private Protection in a New Market*. Oxford: Oxford University Press.

Vilalta, C. and Fondevila, G. (2014). *Perfiles criminales I: frecuencias y descriptivos*, vol. 2. Mexico City: CIDE.

Weisburd, D., Wyckoff, L. A., Ready, J., Eck, J. E., Hinkle, J. C. and Gajewski, F. (2006). 'Does Crime Just Move around the Corner? A Controlled Study of Spatial Displacement and Diffusion of Crime control Benefits' 44(3) *Criminology* 549–92.

Weldon, J. (1997). 'Political Sources of Presidencialismo in Mexico' in S. Mainwaring and M. Soberg (eds), *Presidentialism and Democracy in Latin America*. Cambridge: Cambridge University Press.

Wiarda, H. and Guajardo, C. (1989). 'Mexico: The Unravelling of a Corporatist Regime?' 30(4) *Journal of InterAmerican Studies and World Affairs* 1–28.

Wilkie, J. (1989). 'La Problemática Mexicana: Retrospectiva y Prospectiva' 51(2) *Revista Mexicana de Sociología* 481–506.

Williamson, O. E. (2000). 'The New Institutional Economics: Taking Stock, Looking Ahead' 38(3), *Journal of Economic Literature*, 595–613.

Williamson, O. E. (2005a). 'The Economics of Governance' 95(2) *American Economic Review* 1–18.

Williamson, O. E. (2005b). 'Transaction Cost Economics' in C. Menard and M. Shirley (eds), *Handbook of New Institutional Economics*. Dordrecht: Springer.

Wilson, R. (1985). 'Reputations in Games and Markets', in Roth, Al., E. (Ed.) *Game-Theoretic Models of Bargaining*, 27–62.

Zahavi, A. (1975). 'Mate Selection: A Selection for a Handicap' 53(1) *Journal of Theoretical Biology* 205–14.

Zepeda, G. (2004). *Crimen Sin Castigo, Procuración de Justicia Penal y Ministerio Público en México*. Mexico City: FCE.

# Index

Note: *For the benefit of digital users, indexed terms that span two pages (e.g., 52–53) may, on occasion, appear on only one of those pages.*

Tables and figures are indicated by *t* and *f* following the page number


all-in payoffs *see* pay-offs
analytical sociology 23
  mechanisms-based approach 23, 24
  micro-macro links, based on 24
  nature of 23
  usefulness of 23

bribery 96–97

Calderón, President Felipe 50–52, 53, 57–58, 64
conclusions 167–80
  centrality of trust 172
  changes in nature of kidnapping 169–71
  communities navigating risk of kidnap 171–72
  future direction, new questions 173
  policy proposals 178–80
corruption 67–68, 94
  combating corruption at checkpoints 146n2
  ethos of 51–52, 55–56
  impact of 51–52
  police and law enforcement 3, 4–5, 51–52, 53, 78–79, 82
    Mexico City 79–82, 167–68
    kidnapping, involvement in 79–82
    protection selling 4–5, 51–52, 79–80
  structural existence, as part of 94
  War on Drugs, and 51–52
  weak rule of law allowing corruption to thrive 55–56, 94, 168–69
costly-to-fake-principle 30
courts
  civil courts not policing military 67
  contracts enforced outside 7, 9–10, 27, 34–35, 148–49, 166
  federal offences 98
  low trust in 169
  reform to implement oral trials 52, 178
  special courts 77
crime
  affecting significant amount of population 41
  bribery 96–97
  drug-related crime *see* drug cartels; drug gangs; drug trafficking; organized crime
  homicides *see* homicides
  kidnapping *see* kidnapping
  kidnapping and liberalization, and *see* crime, kidnapping and liberalization (1994–2015)
  largely unpunished 94–95
  limited state protection from 8, 11–12
  low conviction rates for serious crimes 42, 95–96, 168–69
  most salient social phenomena, as 6–7
  non-reporting of 55–56, 71n1, 168–69
  organized crime *see* organized crime
  petty crime, high conviction rates for 55–56, 94–95, 168–69
  rates of crime
    economic crisis increasing crime rates 16–17, 42, 46, 82
    Fox administration, crime increasing under 48, 49
    high crime rates in Mexico 37, 40, 168–69
    increasing 65
    loss of control over underworld contributing to 42, 48
    rising in 1990s 19
  reasons for 6–7

crime (*cont.*)
small percentage of crimes investigated/effectively investigated 52–53, 95–96
trust and signaling, and *see* crime, trust and signaling
crime, kidnapping and liberalization (1994–2015) 41–68
crime in an open market 46
democratization 47–48
economic crisis increasing crime rates 46
Fox administration, crime increasing under 48, 49
kidnapping increasing as economic activity 46
PRI party, organized crime controlling 46–48
current situation of crisis in Mexico 55
distrust of police and government 55–56, 168–69
insecurity, perceptions of 57
malpractice in criminal justice system 56
non-reporting of crimes 55–56, 71n1
weak rule of law allowing corruption to thrive 55–56, 94, 168–69
market economy, transition to 42
economy until 1980s 42–43
EZLN uprising 44–45, 46
financial and debt crises 43–44, 45
GATT and free market, joining 43–44
ISI as model of development 43–44
NAFTA membership 44, 45
natural resources 42–43
oil price collapse 43
Peso crisis 45, 46
regional inequalities exacerbated 42–43
Tequila crisis 45
military, new role of 66
neo-liberal economic model, impact of 41–42
new PRI/Peña Nieto's government 57
criticisms of 62
disappearance of 43 students, failure to deal with 59–62, 65
economic reforms 57–58
financial scandal relating to 'White House' 62–63
gender-based violence, increase in 65–66
progression towards liberalization/free market economy 58
reliance on force, continuation of 57–58
safety and security, not addressing 57–59
security situation in Mexico deteriorating 65
street protests and violent police response to 61–62
ten-point plan for dealing with crime and insecurity 63–65
profound changes in Mexico's social composition/demography 41
street protests 61–62
War on Drugs 50, 57
Calderón's use of army to restore security/combat violence 50–51
cartels/criminal gangs moving into other illicit activity 54
corruption, impact of 51–52
deaths and disappearances resulting from 53
homicides and crime rates, increases in 54
law enforcement institutions, problems in 52–53
migration and displacement resulting from 53
widespread security concerns 50
crime, trust and signaling 21–36
changing schedules and activities as a result of crime concerns 22–23
insecurity as routine part of life 21–22
interpersonal trust, reduction in 22–23
normalising scenes of criminality/violence 21–22
security as integral part of life in Mexico 21–22

value of mechanisms in understanding social world 23
analytical sociology 23–25
signaling, trust and risk 25
violence, ever-increasing 22
criminal justice system *see* criminal justice system

democracy
democratization 5–6, 41–42, 47–48
pro-democracy movements
Mexico City earthquake, after 60
social mobilizations leading to student massacre in 1968 73–74
'dirty war' 77
drivers, hiring of
age and other factors 136, 142
age costly to mimic 142
ideal type of driver 142–43
dangerous nature of driving work 133, 146–47, 163
discretion, and 133
age, and 136
difficult to screen for 133–34
existing employees in screening process, use of 137
geographical origins 138–39
importance of 130
non-signals and signals 134–36, 139
protracted observation, need for 136
recommendation process, screening in 134, 142–43
vertical integration, advantages of 137–38
employee's perspective *see* employee's perspective
helpfulness and initiative, and 139
hiring, test period after 130
factors determining length 132–33
hiring process
certain characteristics not easily observable 129–30
common properties employers screen for 130, 131*t*
discretion, importance of 130, 133
filtering through employer's networks 126–29
implicit acceptance of risk 133, 163
secondary screening stage 129
importance of 122–23
increased numbers of 10–11
part-time drivers in middle class families 122–23
presence 140
intangible 140–42
physical 140–42, 162
self-enforcing relationships 125
nature of pay-offs governing driver 125, 126
sensitive information, protecting 122, 123–24
importance of 124–25
technical capacity 28
trust and signaling, and 122
establishing whether employer can trust prospective employee 125–26
hiring as a problem of trust 11–12
risks of employing 123–24
when relationship breaks down 164
widely employed by wealthy families 122–23
drug cartels 6–7, 39
Calderón government combating 50–51
conflict between 49, 65
Fox's policy to destroy, impact of 48
government, collusion with 117
*Los Zetas* 51
moving into other illicit activity 54
new cartels forming 48
PRI party, and 46–48
staffed by former security personnel 39, 51
use of military and navy against 66–67
*see also* War on Drugs
drug gangs
feuds between drug gangs 4, 50–51
kidnapping, and 3, 39
drug trafficking
drug traffickers/dealers embedded in society 22
fights for drug trafficking routes 50–51
related violence, increase in 49
War on Drugs increasing cost of 54

Durazo, Arturo 'El Negro' 79–82, 167–68, 169

economy of Mexico
economy until 1980s 42–43
financial and debt crises 43–44, 45, 46
GATT and free market, joining 43–44
ISI as model of development 43–44
NAFTA membership 44, 45
natural resources 42–43
oil price collapse 43
Peso crisis 45, 46
Tequila crisis 45
transition to market economy 42
employee's perspective 145–66
accessing work by giving correct signals 8, 11–12, 25–26
competition for driving jobs high 147
dangerous nature of driving work 133, 146–47, 163
discretion 155
being available/ready for work 146–56
commitment to the job, demonstrating 155–56
employees proving this quality for eligibility 155
exploitation, risk of 156
medium-term behaviours proving trustworthiness 155
drivers' jobs valued 147
efficiency 160
meaning of 160–61
environment of uncertainty 146
exploitation 161
realities of life on the ground 161–62
risk of 156
work schedule not regulated 161–62
honesty and disclosure 157
continuing disclosure 159
demonstrating credentials 157–58
family occasions, employer attending 159–60
full disclosure principle 158–59
medical care as trade-off, access to 159–60
trustworthiness, proving 157–58
household employees *see* household employees
networks and vertical integration 147
deeper, personal relationships, formation of 151–52
effects of betrayal 152–53
family connections, use of 147–49
gaining employment through personal network 147–48
membership of a family of good employees 149
reputation 149–51
self-regulating and self-policing 152–54
vertical integration, effect of 151, 152–53
physical size 162, 163
presence 162
protection role
affording status 162–63
bodyguards, resembling 163
physical size/presence 162, 163
risks, awareness of 163
threatening behaviour, use of 163–64
self-selection 162
signaling trustworthiness 154
discretion 155
gender and age 154–55
police record, diving licence and geographical origins 154–55
taxi drivers 145
well paid nature of driving jobs 147
when relationship breaks down 164
express kidnappings 38–39, 145
extortive kidnappings in Mexico City 38–39
smaller gangs focusing on poor/middle-class sectors 39
sophisticated, hierarchical gangs, origins as 39
EZLN uprising 44–45, 46, 66, 75–76

field research *see* methodology and field research
Fox, Vincente 48, 50–51
crime increasing under 48, 49
policy to destroy drug cartels, impact of 48
*Fuenteovejuna* (de Vega) 2–3

gangs
actors in kidnapping, as 89
drug gangs
feuds between drug gangs 4, 50–51
kidnapping, and 3, 39
moving into other illicit activity 54
extortive kidnappings in Mexico City 38–39
fights between gangs 1–2
kidnapping gangs 89
beginning with careers in police 51
combating 89–90, 91–93, 98
fighting kidnapping gangs as government priority 54
former officers joining 39, 51, 89
less well-organized gangs kidnapping for profit 73, 82, 88
organized criminal gangs in Tepito 4
smaller gangs focusing on poor/middle-class sectors 39
sophisticated, hierarchical gangs, origins as 39
government *see* state/government

hiring process
certain characteristics not easily observable 129–30
common properties screened for 130, 131*t*
age and other factors 136, 142
discretion 130, 133
helpfulness and initiative 139
presence 140
trustworthiness/loyalty 8, 33, 34*t*
drivers *see* drivers, hiring of
employee's perspective *see* employee's perspective
filtering through employer's networks 126–29
implicit acceptance of risk 133, 163
importance of 7, 9
informal nature/context of relationships with household employees 13, 37, 161–62
oral nature of contracts 9–10, 37, 166
protracted observation, need for 136
recommendation process, screening in 134, 142–43
risks of employing 123–24
secondary screening stage 129
self-enforcing relationships, advantages of 125
sensitive information, protecting 122, 123–24
importance of 124–25
signaling, trust and risk 25, 122
communication problems 29
cooperative relationships, establishing 27
costly-to-fake-principle 30
distinguishing mimics from non-mimics 30, 31–33, 164–65
employee generating best impression 25–26
filtering stage 32–33
honesty and integrity, importance of 28
imperfect/asymmetrical information 25, 28–29
lottery, hiring as 25–26
minimizing risk of victimization 31
non-signals and signals 134–36, 139
past experience, employer's use of 25–26
pay-offs 28–29
private information, protection of 28, 31
qualities, signs and screening strategies 8, 33, 34*t*
signals, searching for 25–26
sorting, pooling and semi-sorting equilibrium 31–32
trust, decisions based on 40
trust, meaning of 27
trust, uncertainty about behaviour as key component 28
trust warranting properties, establishing 11–12, 29–30, 31–33, 125–26
test period after hiring 130
trust decision, as 11–12
vertical integration 33, 122–23

hiring process (*cont.*)
advantages of vertically integrating employees 35–36, 137–38, 149
continued cooperation, importance and value of 35, 36–37
externalities, definition of 34–35
hiring process becoming more efficient 149
household employees, vertically integrating 13, 35–37
in-group policing equilibria 36
meaning of 33–34
middle class families not able to achieve 36–37
resources required for 36–37
transaction cost economics 33–34
homicides 22
increase in 46, 49*f*, 65
War on Drugs, after 54
most feared crime, as 6n3
organized crime, and 22
reduction in 46, 48, 54
household employees 9
accessing work by giving correct signals 8, 11–12
*see also* hiring process
cash payments 9–10, 37
cooks/cleaners 10–11, 122
drivers *see* drivers, hiring of
employment contracts not enforced by courts 7, 9–10, 27, 34–35, 148–49, 166
continued cooperation, importance of 35
cooperative relationships, establishing 27
frequently employed in range of important roles 9
government, limited role of 7, 9–10, 15, 26–27, 37–38
high percentage involved in kidnapping 2, 9–10
hiring process *see* hiring process
importance of 7, 9
informal nature/context of relationships with household employees 13, 37
household work traditionally of informal nature 37–38
members of same family, hiring of 13
oral nature of contracts 9–10, 26–27, 166
part-time employees 10–11
private/sensitive information
employees protecting 28, 122
need to protect 11–12, 122
protecting as key component in hiring 31
risks of employees' access to 11–12
relationships based on trust 9, 11–12, 26–27
trustworthiness of employee, establishing 11–12
*see also* hiring process
treason phenomenon 6–7, 122
high cost of betrayal 28
weak rule of law *see* weak rule of law
when relationship breaks down 164
human rights 179
accused persons, rights of 56, 61–62
'dirty war' 77
human rights failings/abuses
military 67, 178–79
police 61, 175–76
prosecutors 53, 61, 175–76
proposals to improve 64

inequality 6–7, 40, 42, 45–46, 101
capturing/shaping the state 108–10
high levels of 67–68, 168–69
regional inequalities 42–43
segregation, self-protection, and 104, 119–20
unequal access to justice and redress 37, 101–2
insecurity *see* security and insecurity

justice system 94
bribery 96–97
crimes largely unpunished in Mexico 94–95
human rights 179
accused persons, rights of 56, 61–62
human rights failings/abuses 53, 61, 67, 175–76, 178–79

malpractice in criminal justice system 56
political dimension, cases with 96
problems with 94
prosecutors' offices, problems in 52–53
reform proposals to deal with organized crime 57–58
reform to implement oral trials 52, 178
small percentage of crimes investigated/effectively investigated 52–53, 95–96
unequal access to justice and redress 37, 101–2
*see also* courts; crime

kidnapping 69–100
actors in kidnapping 89
gangs 89
law 97
state 94
avoiding *see* strategies to avoid kidnapping
context and class of kidnapping in Mexico 37
crime, kidnapping and liberalization *see* crime, kidnapping and liberalization (1994–2015)
data on kidnapping, problems of verification and inconsistency of 43–44
district level, kidnapping at 86, 87*t*
drug-related 3
earlier research on 38–39
economic/extortive kidnappings in Mexico City 38–39
smaller gangs focusing on poor/middle-class sectors 39
sophisticated, hierarchical gangs, origins as 39
express kidnappings 38–39, 145
fear generated by 6–7, 6n3, 70–71, 72
fighting kidnapping gangs as government priority 54
heightened risk of when employment relationship breaks down 164–65
household employees, and *see* household employees
impact of 5
income stream, as 69
increases in 2, 6–7, 54, 54*f*, 65, 82–84, 83*t*
Mexico having one of highest kidnapping rates 39–40
key issue, as 67–68
kidnapping gangs beginning with careers in police 51
kidnapping statistics 6–7
lawlessness favourable to kidnapping 38–39
media reporting 6n3, 8, 19, 71–72
creation of kidnapping paranoia 71–72
Mexico City, in 84
district level, kidnapping at 86, 87*t*
increases in 84–85, 86
kidnapping rates as percentage of population 88, 88*t*
kidnappings reported to authorities 85*t*
ransom amounts decreasing 88–89
shift in kidnapping 86
statistics 6–7, 84–85, 88*t*
middle and working classes kidnapped 39, 69, 86–89, 119–20
ransom amounts decreasing 88–89
modern history of kidnapping *see* kidnapping, modern history of
motivated by money 5
nature of kidnapping as an offence 97–99
non-reporting of kidnappings 55–56, 71n1
parents pressuring government into acting 2, 4, 5
pinnacle of evil, as 5, 70–71
Polanco, kidnappings in 14–15
police combating 89–90, 91–93, 98
police involvement in 4–5, 73, 78
political tool, as 69, 73
ransoms 88–89, 93
rare occurrence after revolutionary period 72
revenge kidnappings 5, 38–39
shift in kidnapping 86

kidnapping (*cont.*)
states with most kidnapping 82–84, 84*t*
survival strategies *see* strategies to avoid kidnapping
treason phenomenon *see* treason phenomenon
victim's inner circle facilitating 6–7
wealthy families 1–3, 5, 6–7
hiring household employees *see* household employees
strategies to avoid kidnapping *see* strategies to avoid kidnapping
kidnapping, modern history of 73–82
1995 onwards 82
kidnapping gangs 89
less well-organized gangs kidnapping for profit 73, 82, 88
police as criminals/kidnappers 73, 78
Durazo's involvement in crime/ kidnapping 79–82
police forces keeping political order 78–79
political phase 73
Clandestine Armed Groups kidnapping for funds/political protest 74–76
'dirty war' 77
'extermination policy', implementation of 76–77
left-wing groups seeking to depose government 73–74
policy of payment and negotiation 76

law 97
law enforcement *see* police and law enforcement
legal structures in Mexico City 97–98
weak rule of law *see* weak rule of law
Lopez Obrador, Andres Manuel 65
Lucas X 1
investigating daughter's kidnapping murder 1–3
justice reform, involvement in 3
murder of daughter 1–2
macro properties 24
market economy, transition to 42
mechanisms-based approach 23, 24
definition of a mechanism 24
nature of 24
media
crime and kidnapping, extensive reporting on 6n3, 8, 19, 71–72
creation of kidnapping paranoia 71–72
kidnapping news report database (1999–2010) 19, 70
police, scrutinizing 17–18
weak rule of law, reporting on 37
methodology and field research 13
field research, nature of 13–15
fieldwork, description of 17–18
interviews 15, 16–17, 17*t*
consent, importance of 18
informal conversations/ interviews 18
law-enforcement officials with 15, 17–18
rapport and trust with interviewee 18–19
kidnapping news report database (1999–2010) 19
nature of Miguel Hidalgo research district 13–14
Polanco neighbourhood, reasons for choice of 14–15
sensitive nature of research 15
definition of sensitive topic 16
interviews by groups 15, 16–17, 17*t*
network-based recommendations/ snowballing methods 16–17
types of groups sampled 16–17
Mexico
authoritarian past 41–42, 47, 60, 61–62, 73–74, 77, 78–79, 138–39, 167–68, 169
changes in social composition and demography 41
corruption ethos 51–52, 55–56
crime *see* crime
crime, trust and signaling *see* crime, trust and signaling
current situation of crisis in 55
distrust of police and government 55–56, 168–69

insecurity, perceptions of 57
malpractice in criminal justice system 56
non-reporting of crimes 55–56, 71n1
weak rule of law allowing corruption to thrive 55–56, 94, 168–69
democratization 5–6, 41–42, 47–48
economy *see* economy of Mexico
government *see* state/government
indigenous Mexicans 41–42, 44–45, 139
inequality *see* inequality
kidnapping *see* kidnapping
lawlessness, situation of 8, 35, 37, 38–39
liberalization, in *see* crime, kidnapping and liberalization (1994–2015)
market economy, transition to 42
poverty *see* poverty in Mexico
President, extreme powers of 73n3, 78–79
relation-based economy, as 9–10, 166
security as integral part of life in Mexico 21–22
states, role of 98
violence in Mexico *see* violence in Mexico
Mexico City
characteristics 13
crime increasing in 65
earthquakes, government and civil society response to 60, 60n6
insecurity, perceptions of 57
kidnapping 84
district level, kidnapping at 86, 87*t*
increases in 84–85, 86
kidnapping rates as percentage of population 88, 88*t*
kidnappings reported to authorities 85*t*
ransom amounts decreasing 88–89
shift in kidnapping 86
statistics 6–7, 84–85, 88*t*
legal structures 97–98
massacre of students in 1968 58, 66, 73–74
Miguel Hidalgo Polanco district 13–14
nightlife/*afters* 3, 118–19
*Heaven*, disappearance of young people from *see* youth, interrupted
organized crime in 65
Polanco neighbourhood 13–14
kidnapping in 14–15
nature of 14–15
wealthy communities 14–15
police *see* police and law enforcement
reputation as an 'armoured city' 4
social classes and income
income of wealthy people 39–40
upper-middle class incomes 40
Tepito neighbourhood 4
micro-level entities 24
military and navy 66
drug cartels, use of military and navy against 66–67
'extermination policy' against kidnappers, involvement in 76–77
EZLN uprising 44–45, 46, 66
formal legal framework in providing public security, and 67–68
human rights abuses 67, 178–79
important role in security 66
increase in numbers and budget 66–67
policing activities, military role in 66–67
effects of 67
political control, use for 66
social mobilization, suppressing 77
War on Drugs, armed forces in 66
modern-day avenger 1, 5

NAFTA 44, 45
navy *see* military and navy

Obama, President Barack 58
organized crime
definition 98
drug cartels *see* drug cartels
*gendarmerie* proposed to combat organized crime 57–58
government, and 46–48, 51–52

organized crime (*cont.*)
homicides, and 22
increase in 22
infiltrating police/law enforcement institutions 59
kidnapping *see* kidnapping
Mexico City, in 65
targeting civilians 50–51, 59
violence, and 67–68

PAN party 48, 50
dissatisfaction with 57
pay-offs
all-in-one 28–29, 125, 126
high pay-offs for crime 168–69
raw 28–29, 125, 126
self-enforcing relationships 125
transforming from raw to all-in-one 29–30
Peña Nieto, President Enrique 57–58, 62, 65–66, 67–68
Polanco 13–14
kidnapping in 14–15
nature of 14–15
wealthy communities 14–15
police and law enforcement
bribery 96–97
civilians targeted by police 59
constant scrutiny, under 17–18
corruption 3, 4–5, 51–52, 53, 78–79, 82
kidnapping, involvement in 79–82
Mexico City 79–82, 167–68
protection selling 4–5, 51–52, 79–80
difficulties in reforming law enforcement 52
former officers joining gangs 39, 51, 89
*gendarmerie*, proposal for 57–58
human rights 53, 61, 175–76
incompetence 2, 3
involvement in kidnappings and murder 4–5, 73, 78
kidnapping gangs, combating 89–90, 91–93, 98
lack of training in law enforcement institutions 52
lacking capacity to investigate crimes 52, 61
little or no trust in police 55–56, 116–17, 168–69
*Madrinas* 79–80
malpractice in criminal justice system 56
media scrutinizing police 17–18
military role in policing activities *see under* military and navy
Ministerial Police 95–96
petty crime, high conviction rates for 55–56, 94–95
political control, as means of 51–52, 78–79
private protection, providing 109–10
prosecutors' offices, problems in 52–53
reform proposals to deal with organized crime 57–58
slow response to kidnapping 4
small percentage of crimes investigated/effectively investigated 52–53, 95–96
violent response to street protests 61–62
poverty in Mexico 67–68, 99
economic recovery not fully reducing 45–46
high levels of 6–7, 37
indigenous Mexicans 44–45
statistics 46
PRI party 42, 47–48, 49, 50
creation 78–79
defeat in 2018 elections 58, 65, 78–79
Peña Nieto, Enrique 57–58, 62, 65–66, 67–68
private security companies 105–7
gated communities, securing 106–7
illegal/informal security companies 106
size of private security industry 105
value of private security industry 105–6
wealthy communities hiring 106

raw pay-offs *see* pay-offs
relation-based economic system 9–10, 26–27, 166
research *see* methodology and field research

rule of law *see* weak rule of law
rules-based economic system 26–27

security and insecurity
  insecurity as routine part of life 21–22
  military
    important role in security 66
    role formal legal framework in providing public security 67–68
  perceptions of 57
  police *see* police and law enforcement
  PRI/Peña Nieto's government
    not addressing security and safety 57–59
    ten-point plan for dealing with crime and insecurity 63–65
  security as integral part of life in Mexico 21–22
  security situation in Mexico deteriorating 65
  use of army to restore security 50–51
  widespread security concerns 50
security companies *see* private security companies
signaling
  crime, signaling and *see* crime, trust and signaling
  equilibrium
    pooling 31
    semi-sorting 31–32
    sorting 31
  evolutionary biology, origins in 25
  nature of 12–13
  signals and signs, compared 12–13
  signaling theory 8, 12–13, 25
    nature of 26
  signaling theory, cost condition in 30–31, 40
    definition of cost condition 30–31
    sorting, pooling and semi-sorting equilibrium 31–32
  trust problems, and
    signaling theory explaining trust problems 12–13, 25
    *see also* hiring process
  trust, risk, and 25
social world, understanding *see under* crime, trust and signaling
state/government
  Calderón, Felipe 50–52, 53, 57–58, 64
  capturing/shaping the state 108
  cooperation/confrontation with 7–8
  drug traffickers/dealer, contact with 22
  Fox, Vincente 48, 50–51
  household employees, and 7, 9–10, 15, 26–27, 37–38
  justice system *see* justice system
  law 97
  limited state protection from crime 8, 11–12, 15, 35
  little or no trust in government 55–56
  Lopez Obrador, Andres Manuel 65
  PAN party 48, 50
    dissatisfaction with 57
  Peña Nieto 57–58, 62, 65–66, 67–68
  police *see* police and law enforcement
  President, extreme powers of 73n3, 78–79
  PRI party 42, 47–48, 49, 50
    creation 78–79
    defeat in 2018 elections 58, 65, 78–79
    Peña Nieto 57–58, 62, 65–66, 67–68
  role of 15
  slow response by authorities to kidnapping 4
  states, role of 98
  weak rule of law *see* weak rule of law
strategies to avoid kidnapping 6–7, 101–20
  capturing/shaping the state 108
    obtaining extra services 109–10, 111–12
    police protection rackets 109–10
    self-defence groups 110–11, 112
  cooperation/confrontation with the state 7–8
    demanding extra protection 101–2

strategies to avoid kidnapping (*cont.*)
 family-based protection 112
  ad hoc strategies of protection 113–14
  awareness of surroundings/dangers 118
  bullet-proof vehicles and guns 116–17
  not going out 113–14, 118–19
  stopping sharing information 114–16
  taking precautions 117–19
 improved hiring strategies 7–8
 private security companies 105–7
  exemplary punishments, policy of 107
  gated communities, securing 103–4, 106–7
  self-segregation, and 103–4
  spillover effects 107–8
  street closures 104
  wealthy communities hiring 106
 professional bodyguards 7–8, 101–2, 103
 providing social benefits in return for police patrols 7–8, 107–8
 safety as way of life in the City 104–5
 threats of divestment and loss of political support 7–8

Tepito neighbourhood
 discrimination against residents 4
 organized criminal gangs in 4
transaction–cost economics 13
treason phenomenon 6–7, 93–94
 *see also* household employees
trust/problems of trust
 centrality of trust 172
 crime, signaling and trust *see* crime, trust and signaling
 hiring process, and *see under* hiring process
 interpersonal trust, reduction in 22–23
 police/government, little or no trust in 55–56, 116–17, 168–69
 primary and secondary problems of trust, employers facing 11–12
 signaling and risk, and 25
 signaling theory, and 12–13, 25–26, *see* hiring process; signaling
 trust as central to most activities 40
 trust game 11–12
  basic trust game 29
 trust, meaning of 27, 121–22
 trust, uncertainty about behaviour as key component 28
 trustworthiness of employee, establishing 11–12

Vega, Lope de 2–3
vertical integration 33, 40
 advantages of vertically integrating employees 35–36, 137–38
 continued cooperation, importance and value of 35, 36–37
 externalities, definition of 34–35
 hiring process becoming more efficient 149
 household employees, vertically integrating 13, 35–37
 in-group policing equilibria 36
 meaning of 13, 33–34
 middle class families not able to achieve 36–37
 networks and vertical integration 147
  deeper, personal relationships, formation of 151–52
  effects of betrayal 152–53
  family connections, use of 147–49
  gaining employment through personal network 147–48
  membership of a family of good employees 149
  reputation 149–51
  self-regulating and self-policing 152–54
  vertical integration, effect of 151, 152–53
violence
 Calderón's use of army to combat violence 50–51
 crime *see* crime
 'dirty war' 77
 drug trafficking, and 49
 gender-based violence, increase in 65–66
 increasing 22, 65, 117
  increasing since War on Drugs 22, 39

kidnapping *see* kidnapping
lawlessness, situation of 8, 35
massacre of students in 1968 58, 66, 73–74
Mexican chapter of War on Drugs *see* War on Drugs
normalising scenes of criminality/violence 21–22
organized crime, and 67–68
recent years, violence in 57, 65

War on Drugs 37, 50, 57, 66, 177
Calderón's use of army to restore security/combat violence 50–51
cartels/criminal gangs moving into other illicit activity 54
corruption, impact of 51–52
crime statistics 39
deaths and disappearances resulting from 53
exacerbating fear and distrust of police/authorities 117
homicides and crime rates, increases in 54
increasing violence since launch of 22, 39
law enforcement institutions, problems in 52–53
migration and displacement resulting from 53
unpopularity of 57
widespread security concerns 50
weak rule of law 6–7, 11–12, 13, 14–15, 26–27, 37, 40, 54, 67–68, 94, 101, 119–20, 168–69
allowing corruption to thrive 55–56, 94, 168–69
crimes largely unpunished 94–95
due process disregarded 61
institutional vacuum 37
limited state protection from crime 8, 11–12
low conviction rates for serious crimes 42, 95–96, 168–69
malpractice in criminal justice system 56
media reporting on 37
non-reporting of crimes 55–56, 71n1, 168–69
offending and 7, 55–56, 94–95, 168–69
petty crime, high conviction rates for 55–56, 94–95, 168–69
police/government, little or no trust in 55–56, 116–17, 168–69
small percentage of crimes investigated/effectively investigated 52–53, 95–96
state not enforcing contracts 7, 9–10, 27, 34–35, 37, 40, 148–49, 166
unequal access to justice and redress 37, 101–2

X, Lucas *see* Lucas X

youth interrupted 3
disappearance and murder of young people from *Heaven* nightclub 3–5
kidnapped youths from Tepito 4
slow response by authorities 4

Zapatista movement/uprising 44–45, 46, 51, 66, 75–76

The manufacturer's authorised representative in the EU for product safety is Oxford University Press España S.A. of el Parque Empresarial San Fernando de Henares, Avenida de Castilla, 2 – 28830 Madrid (www.oup.es/en or product.safety@oup.com). OUP España S.A. also acts as importer into Spain of products made by the manufacturer.

www.ingramcontent.com/pod-product-compliance
Lightning Source LLC
LaVergne TN
LVHW011512200926
848484LV00001B/19
*9780198798460*